MIGRATION LETTERS

ISSN: 1741-8984
e-ISSN: 1741-8992

Abbreviated title: Migrat. Lett.

Migration Letters seeks to advance knowledge of human migrations and mobility by providing a forum for discussion of research, policies, and practices.

Migration Letters is indexed and abstracted in:

- Cabell's Directory of Educational Curriculum & Methods
- Cabell's Directory of Psychology & Psychiatry
- CEEOL
- China Academic Journals Database (CNKI Scholar)
- ERIH PLUS

- ESCI (Emerging Science Citation Index, Web of Science)
- International Bibliography of the Social Sciences (IBSS)
- Norwegian Register
- Research Papers in Economics (RePEc)
- SCOPUS

Migration Letters is published six times a year in January, March, May, July, September and November.

Migration Letters is published by Transnational Press London, UK.

Addresses:
URL: www.MigrationLetters.com
Email: editor@migrationletters.com

MIGRATION LETTERS | ISSN: 1741-8984 e-ISSN: 1741-8992

MIGRATION LETTERS
An International Journal of Migration Studies

Volume 17
Number 5
September 2020

MIGRATION LETTERS | ISSN: 1741-8984 e-ISSN: 1741-8992

September 2020
Volume: 17, **No**: 5, pp. 563 – 567
ISSN: 1741-8984
e-ISSN: 1741-8992
www.migrationletters.com

MIGRATION
LETTERS

First Received: 9 September 2020
DOI: https://doi.org/10.33182/ml.v17i5.1153

Editorial: Foreign seasonal migrants in agriculture and COVID-19

Elli Heikkilä[1]

Abstract

Foreign seasonal migrants fill labour shortages in host countries if employers do not or cannot find available short-term labour from among the country's own labour reserves. In reality, it is difficult to find seasonal workers from among the native population ready to work in the primary sector, making the sector highly dependent on a foreign workforce. Migration Letters as an international journal addresses the diversity of human migration and mobility, which includes a wide range of dynamic aspects affecting the modern world. The current fifth issue of volume 17 of the journal includes multi-sided content on the topic from papers around the world. It includes papers dealing with refugees, asylum seekers, displaced populations, migrant workers, job-education mismatch, the language proficiency of migrants, their personal networks and sex traffickers.

Keywords: *migration; seasonal migrants; COVID-19; collective insecurity.*

Introduction

A large number of migrants move for work-related reasons on a temporary basis. Seasonal migration is one increasing form of temporary human migration, which can occur both within the country as well as internationally. The common feature is that work is available for part of the year and there is a certain high season when temporary labour in heavily needed. Well-known examples of seasonal migrants include seasonal employees engaged in primary production, i.e. in agriculture and forestry, including berry picking on farms, and in other economic sectors covering wild berry picking in the forests, and tourism.

Foreign seasonal migrants fill labour shortages in host countries if employers do not or cannot find available short-term labour from among the country's own labour reserves. In reality, it is difficult to find seasonal workers from among the native population ready to work in the primary sector, making the sector highly dependent on a foreign workforce.

When looking at development trends in Finland, the professional cultivation of berries began in the 1960s. Still in the 1980s, Finnish youngsters were hired to pick berries during their summer holidays. "Going to work for the summer in the strawberry fields of Suonenjoki", a city in central Finland famous of its strawberries, was a popular saying at the time. In the 1990s, foreign seasonal labour started to arrive in Finland: first they came from Estonia, then from Russia, and nowadays mainly from Ukraine and Belorussia (see Konttinen, 2020). According to Kavén (2020), the farms had to start searching for cheaper labour because of the price level of the products. When berries and vegetables started to be imported at a low price from abroad, the prices of domestic products had to be lowered, too. This in turn reduced the payroll capacity of farmers.

---

[1] Elli Heikkilä, Research Director, Migration Institute of Finland, and Adjunct Professor of the Universities of Oulu and Turku, Finland. E-mail: elli.heikkila@utu.fi.

Foreign seasonal workers from Ukraine point out that one of the main pull factors to come to Finland is, however, the higher salary level. They say that the rate of 9 euros per hour is many times higher than the salary for a similar job in Ukraine. According to the World Bank (2020), Ukraine's per capita GDP was US$3,659 in 2019. Seasonal workers can invest in their origin country: for instance, they can buy an apartment or a house or renovate a dwelling, buy a car or invest in their children's education. For Ukraine, remittances constitute an essential input for the national economy. The National Bank of Ukraine estimates that, based on preliminary data, 2019 remittances from Ukrainians working abroad amounted to US$12 billion, some 7.8 per cent of the country's entire GDP (Current time, 2020). Many Ukrainians are quite familiar with and skilled in agricultural work. Agricultural products and food industry products accounted for nearly 48 per cent of the total export of Ukrainian goods between January 2019 and January 2020 (Ukrinform, 2020).

Seasonal farm work requires professionalism, and those engaged in it are not so-called unskilled workers. Klocker et al. (2019) conceptualise this idea with four points. First, "manual" work is not unskilled, even when it seems to be occurring instinctively or unconsciously. Second, skilled work involves withing one's hands, materials, tools and machines and is not just "manual" work; it is also knowledge work because skill is more than "the mere application of mechanical force", as it involves "care, judgement and dexterity". Third, hands-on work occurs through ongoing dialogue with materials and environment, in ways that always exceed instructions, plans or designs, i.e. workers are constantly reasoning and adapting their practice to fit the circumstances. Fourth, narrow definitions of knowledge demean certain workers, setting a framework for their exploitation.

Many seasonal migrants can be classified as circular migrants, which refers to repeated migration experiences between a point of origin and destination involving more than one migration and return migration. They bring back enhanced skills and new ideas to the home community and can help develop networks with destination countries (Hugo, 2013). Seasonal and circular migrants can return to the host country, even to the same farm, to do the same work as in previous years. In this case, employers do not have to expend so much effort or resources in training and guiding the workers.

Farmers themselves had to learn human resource management: ensuring that once a worker had been hired, that person would return the next year. Countries also compete for the same workers: it is important to ensure that foreign seasonal workers feel themselves welcome and also consider the host country attractive in the future. They bring their personal views to the home country. In the best case, a positive recommendation in the sphere of their social network can lead to chain seasonal migration to the same destination country and even to the same farm.

Effects of COVID-19

Spread of the COVID-19 Pandemic and human mobility have been linked in an earlier study published in Migration Letters (Sirkeci and Yucesahin, 2020) and yet further impact of the pandemic on human mobility is slowly unfolding. In Europe, at the height of the coronavirus crisis in March 2020, the German government closed the country's borders and capped the number of seasonal workers allowed to enter the country at 80,000. In June, Germany eased entry restrictions for these workers. From 16 June until the end of the year 2020, seasonal workers from the European Union and the passport-free Schengen zone are once again allowed to freely enter Germany to help harvest crops. German farms usually require some 300,000 foreign harvest workers a year, mainly from Poland and Romania (Euractive.com, 2020).

When looking at the Nordic countries during COVID-19, the Federation of Swedish Farmers said in mid-May of 2020 that around 8,000 seasonal workers were needed in the forestry and gardening sectors. Later on Sweden's farms and forestry industry have not suffered a feared labour shortage due to the coronavirus because workers from other countries came to Sweden after restrictions were lifted for seasonal agricultural workers. Seasonal migration for work has continued, including labour from outside the EU, after exemptions were granted by the Swedish government and the European Union. They decided that seasonal agricultural workers would be excluded from the travel bans (Dammberg, 2020). The Norwegian Agrarian Association stated that 20,000 to 30,000 seasonal workers are needed in Norway (Östling, 2020).

In Finland, during a so-called normal year 16,000 seasonal workers from abroad are engaged in agricultural work. The Finnish government (Ministry of Agriculture and Forestry, 2020) decided at the end of May 2020 that in addition to the entry of 4,500 seasonal workers, on which a decision had been made earlier, a further 4,500 seasonal workers from third countries could come to Finland beginning 1 June to meet the needs in primary production. The majority of seasonal workers' permits are processed by the Finnish Immigration Service, which also makes the decisions on the permits. The final decision on entry into the country is made by the Border Guard. People arriving in Finland are still recommended to stay in quarantine-like conditions for 14 days.

In the early spring of 2020, Ukraine did not let its citizens travel to Finland or other foreign countries for seasonal work in order to avoid spread of the virus pandemic. In early May, Ukraine finally permitted seasonal workers to travel abroad. Ukraine insisted that there should be a work contract for at least three months, that the salary level had to be decent and also that good living conditions, healthcare and necessary insurance would be provided (Uber, 2020).

Access to a seasonal migrant labour force is critical during COVID-19 to guarantee a continuous supply of farm products to the shops and consumers. The demand for domestic berries and vegetables is constantly increasing. To secure the successful recruitment of foreign workers in Finland, interested parties have turned to social media campaigns, creating a new Work from Finland (Töitä Suomesta, 2020) web service and To the Farms (Maatilalle.fi, 2020) web service in the agricultural sector for employers to inform foreign workers searching for a job about open vacancies. Also, the campaigns have looked for seasonal workers from domestic labour pools, like students and immigrant-background persons. The legislation on the right of asylum seekers to work has been temporarily amended as of 29 June 2020. The act will remain in force until 31 October 2020. The amendment will temporarily extend the right to work to asylum seekers in fields that offer seasonal work, i.e. in agriculture, forestry, horticulture or fisheries (Finnish Immigration Service, 2020).

Migration flows are nowadays more diverse and complex, and patterns are multi-layered (Heikkilä, 2020). There is a need for more research on temporary migration, including seasonal and circular migration, as their numbers are increasing year by year. The national statistics rarely provide information on these forms of human migration. To better understand the global dimensions of temporary migration, surveys and panel data are needed that can provide information on these phenomena across time and space (Zimmermann, 2014).

New issue of Migration Letters

Migration Letters as an international journal addresses the diversity of human migration and mobility, which includes a wide range of dynamic aspects affecting the modern world. The current fifth issue of volume 17 of the journal includes multi-sided content on the topic from papers around the world. It includes papers dealing with refugees, asylum seekers, displaced populations, migrant workers, job-education mismatch, the language proficiency of migrants, COVID-19 impact, Hukou system in China, migrants' personal networks and sex traffickers.

Teodorowski explores how micro-level activities, such as education in local schools, lifelong learning and community activities delivered within the council area, influence the integration of refugees. It is based on a case study of one Scottish council, which decided to welcome Syrian refugees in 2015 and had no prior experience with refugee relocation. Refugees are also dealt with in **Kayaoglu Yılmaz's** paper, which looks at the informal textile sector in a rather homogenous urban neighbourhood in Istanbul, where the main competition for jobs are between Kurds and Syrians. The paper shows that employment rates for natives declined in that specific field due to other factors unrelated to the Syrians, beginning before the Syrians had arrived, not after. **García-Juan's** paper focuses on integration measures within the reformed Common European Asylum System (CEAS) and the unsolved limbo of asylum seekers.

Xie investigates the hukou system, i.e. horizontal, vertical and full job-education mismatch and wage progression among the floating college population in Beijing, China. **Ganjour, Widmer, Viry, Gauthier, Kaufmann** and **Drevon** examine how residential trajectories influence the spatiality and composition of personal networks in Switzerland. Three mechanisms are considered: the addition of spatially close network members, the selection of spatially distant network members and the substitution of spatially distant network members with spatially close ones.

Angulo's research focus is on knowing the variables that make it possible to predict the spending level for displaced victims that returned to La Palma, Cundinamarca, Colombia. Migrant workers are analysed in **Sabban's** paper, which examines the historical and contemporary evolution of migrant domestic work in the United Arab Emirates (UAE) and the Gulf Cooperation Council (GCC) region. This fifth issue also presents **Izcara Palacios's** research, which analyses the strategies used by sex traffickers to recruit women from Mexico and Central America to satisfy the demands of the illegal US sex industry.

Diekmann and **Fröhlich** conduct detailed quantitative analyses of how various language variables influence migrants' social position in Germany, by which they mean the International Socio-Economic Index of Occupational Status (ISEI). The ISEI is mainly based on occupation, but also on education and income. What Money Can't Buy: Educational Aspirations and International Migration in Ecuador is an intriguing study by **Arias-Medina** and **Rivera** drawing on a multilevel survey and structured interviews.

Bhagat and colleagues are offering an early insight into the COVID-19 plight in India and its impact on human mobility in the sub-continent. **Lumayag** and colleagues are reflecting on human insecurity and the Pandemic in Malaysia as they argue that the collective experience of insecurity among migrant workers can be framed at both individual and structural levels.

Maniruzzaman Al Masud, Binti Hamzah and **Ahmad's** case study highlights the role and contribution of imported labour to the Malaysian economy. Most of the migrant workers are low-skilled or uneducated, and much public debate is taking place regarding their outcome, whether it is substantial or not. Final paper in this issue is a report by **Huxter** as on 9-10th September 2019 academics from universities around the UK met at Loughborough University to discuss working with children and young people, particularly those with a migrant/diasporic background.

References

Current time (2020). Despite COVID-19 Restrictions, Ukraine's Seasonal Workers Set Their Sights On EU Farms. https://en.currenttime.tv/a/30605748.html

Dammberg, Henrik (2020). No shortage of seasonal workers in farming industry. Radio Sweden 22.6.2020.

Euractive.com (2020). Germany relaxes restrictions on seasonal workers. https://www.euractiv.com/section/economy-jobs/news/germany-relaxes-restrictions-on-seasonal-workers/

Finnish Immigration Service (2020). Asylum seeker's right to work in seasonal work. https://migri.fi/en/asylum-seeker-s-right-to-work-in-seasonal-work

Heikkilä, E. (2020). Migration Statistics – A Need for More Information in the World. Siirtolaisuus-Migration 1/2020, 62. https://siirtolaisuusinstituutti.fi/wp-content/uploads/2020/03/sm1_2020-1.pdf

Hugo, G. (2013). What we know about circular migration and enhanced mobility. Migration Policy Institute, Policy Brief 7/2013.

Kavén, H. (2020). Maatiloilla avoimia työpaikkoja. Turun Sanomat 5.4.2020, 2.

Klocker, N., O. Dun, L. Head and A. Gopal (2019). Exploring migrants' knowledge and skill on seasonal farm work: more than laboring bodies. Agriculture and Human Values (2020) 37, 463–478.

Konttinen, J. (2020). Apu saapuu Ukrainasta. Helsingin Sanomat viikko 22/2020, A15–A19.

Maatilalle.fi (2020). https://www.maatilalle.fi/

Ministry of Agriculture and Forestry (2020). Maximum number of seasonal workers from non-EU countries increases by 4,500. Press release 29.5.2020.

Östling, B. (2020). Labour shortage for Nordic agriculture and forestry. Nordic Labour Journal 15.5.2020. http://www.nordiclabourjournal.org/nyheter/news-2020/article.2020-04-29.3257059422

Sirkeci, I., & Yucesahin, M. M. (2020). Coronavirus and Migration: Analysis of Human Mobility and the Spread of Covid-19. Migration Letters, 17(2), 379-398. https://doi.org/10.33182/ml.v17i2.935

The World Bank (2020). GDP per capita (current US$) – Ukraine. https://data.worldbank.org/indicator/NY.GDP.PCAP.CD?locations=UA

Töitä Suomesta (2020). https://www.töitäsuomesta.fi/

Uber, M. (2020). Ukrainalaisten työpanos pelastaa monen tilan kesän. Turun Sanomat 10.5.2020, 8.

Ukrinform (2020). Ukraine increases export of agricultural products by over 14%. https://www.ukrinform.net/rubric-economy/2884429-ukraine-increases-export-of-agricultural-products-by-over-14-mylovanov.html

Zimmermann, K. F. (2014). Circular migration. Why restricting labour mobility can be counterproductive. IZA World of Labour 2014 (1), 1–10.

September 2020
Volume: 17, **No:** 5, pp. 569 – 581
ISSN: 1741-8984
e-ISSN: 1741-8992
www.migrationletters.com

MIGRATION
LETTERS

First Submitted: 30 July 2019 Accepted: 17 January 2020
DOI: https://doi.org/10.33182/ml.v17i5.830

Micro-level Initiatives to Facilitate the Integration of Resettled Refugees

Piotr Teodorowski [1]

Abstract

Integration, a two-way process involving refugees and the host population, is a politically contentious issue. Successful integration of newcomers in a receiving community is required to create a cohesive society. Yet, there is still little understanding of how integration strategies are employed at a community level. This paper explores how micro-level activities such as education in local schools, lifelong learning and community activities delivered within the council area influence integration of refugees. It is based on a case study of one of the Scottish councils which decided to welcome Syrian refugees in 2015 and had no prior experience of refugees' relocation. The findings showed the role of micro-level initiatives in the successful integration and proved that even a council with no prior experience of relocating refugees could build a cohesive community upon their arrival.

Keywords: *refugees; Scotland; integration; schools; education.*

Introduction

European states have received millions of refugees since 2015 what required communities which previously did not have an experience of resettling refugees to welcome them. This created challenges to how newcomers could be integrated. The paper presents the single case study discussing how integration is applied at a community level. Firstly, the theoretical framework of integration and micro-level interventions are discussed. Secondly, the reader is introduced to the background of the refugee situation in Scotland. Methodology, findings and discussion sections follow.

The term 'integration' remains unclear in the literature and policy (Castles et al., 2002; Spencer, 2011). Robinson (as quoted by Castles, et al., 2002, p.123) called the term 'chaotic', However, integration assumes that newcomers settle permanently in the new environment (Favell, 2001). This paper understands integration as a two-way process of change and adaptation by both refugees and the host population (Ager & Strang, 2004; Berry, 1997). The theory of acculturation (Berry, 1997, 2006) separates integration from other concepts: separation, assimilation and marginalisation. Only integration allows both groups to retain their ethnic and cultural identity and actively interact between each other (Berry, 2006).

What constitutes successful integration is still debated (Crisp, 2004). It requires 'durable solutions' (Crisp, 2004, p. 1) and change in both refugees and the host population to become a cohesive community (Ager & Strang, 2008). The United Kingdom (UK) has a long-term experience of integrating refugees, and thus over the years practitioners and academics developed a framework which acts as a middle-range theory to analyse integration (Ager & Strang, 2004; Ager & Strang,

[1] Piotr Teodorowski, School of Nursing and Midwifery, Robert Gordon University, Garthdee Road, Aberdeen, AB10 7QG, Scotland, UK. E-mail: p.teodorowski@rgu.ac.uk.

2008; Ndofor-Tah et al., 2019). The shaping of the framework was robust- it included four components: literature and documentary analysis, fieldwork, secondary analysis of cross-sectional survey data and verification of findings with stakeholders such as policymakers (Ager & Strang, 2008).   Academics from seven different institutions have developed a recent version of the framework (Ndofor-Tah et al., 2019). It specifies four different principles of successful integration. Firstly, it is multi-directional as it requires the cooperation of newcomers, host population and service providers. Secondly, no aspect of the framework is more important than others. Thirdly, the success is the responsibility of all actors such as local authority, central government and employers. Lastly, it is context-specific- no golden rule exists to define the success of integration. Instead, this success should be measured by progressive development over time.

The integration framework (Ndofor-Tah et al., 2019) is structured around fourteen domains which are grouped in four headings: markers and means, social connections, facilitators, and foundation. Markers and means assist in exploring the context of integration. Only if refugees are employed, they can fully be independent and integrated (Ager & Strang, 2008). Good housing conditions are essential, but the quality of neighbourhoods is more relevant to newcomers (ibid). However, without secured housing refugees do not get involved in other domains of integration (Mulvey, 2015; Phillimore & Goodson, 2008). Formal education such as schools are the most important place to support refugees, especially adolescents who can improve their language skills and mix with local peers (Ager & Strang, 2008).

Table 1. Integration framework by Ndofor-Tah et al., 2019

Headings	**Domains**				
Markers and means	Work	Housing	Education	Health and Social Care	Leisure
Social connections	Bonds	Bridges		Links	
Facilitators	Language and Communication	Culture	Digital Skills	Safety	Stability
Foundation	Rights and Responsibilities				

The domain of health explores the overall experience with health and social care services (ibid). In the last version of the framework, the domain 'leisure' was added to cover activities which allow newcomers to develop knowledge about the host community and thus build rapport (Ndofor-Tah et al., 2019). Social connections focus on relations with people sharing similar cultural and religious background (bonds), individuals from other cultural groups, (bridges) and institutions (links) developed through settling in the new environment (ibid). Facilitators are factors which remove barriers during the integration process (Ager & Strang, 2008). Understanding the language and culture of the host culture is necessary to build links with the local population (Ndofor-Tah et al., 2019). Better language skills result in more trust and better access to additional sources of support (Kearns & Whitley, 2015). Safety covers issues around trust with the police and if there are any incidents of prejudice or hate crime towards refugees (Ndofor-Tah et al., 2019). Length of residence in the area is a factor in successful integration (Kearns & Whitley, 2015). Stability of newcomers' lives ensures that they can enjoy the fruits of other domains without a regular change of their surroundings (Ager & Strang, 2008). Digital skills are a new domain. In the digitalised world, refugees need to understand and access all ways of communication (Ndofor-Tah et al., 2019). Lastly, only rights and responsibilities are placed within the foundation which explores how refugees exercise their privileges and duties (ibid). Without understanding what their rights are, refugees cannot enjoy other domains of integration. Successful integration in any of these headings depends on cooperation between refugees, the host population and local stakeholders.

Previous research utilised and evaluated the integration framework (Phillimore, 2012; Phillimore & Goodson, 2008; Platts-Fowler & Robinson, 2015). It has some limitations. Platts-Fowler and Robinson (2015) criticised it for oversimplifying the concept of integration. Phillimore (2012) found it too poor to analyse and theorise how different domains are interrelated. Despite its drawbacks, the framework captures through its domains main concepts around the integration of refugees (Platts-Fowler & Robinson, 2015). As data for this paper was collected in the UK, the framework would also take into consideration the British context.

This paper perceives local interventions to support integration as micro-level initiatives. These can be introduced by the local authority, charities, schools, police and other stakeholders. Academics have been discussing them for a long time. Schools play a vital role in pro-refugee advocacy (Taylor & Sidhu, 2012) and have a function of explaining 'rules of the game', how one should behave, and what the consequences of breaking generally accepted principles are (Heyneman, 2002). When schools offer language groups for refugee pupils, it may limit their opportunity to mix with other children (Ager & Strang, 2008). Education has to be provided in an organised and right manner to speed up the integration of newcomers in society (Matthews, 2008). When there is a small number of children refugees, it may be difficult for schools to justify dedicating limited resources to a small group of pupils (Block et al., 2014a). However, Pagani (2014) argues that cohesive groups of young people are built through dialogue and acknowledgement of diversity. School-led activities include actions to welcome refugees, peer-support schemes and assisting local pupils in understanding refugees' experiences (McBride et al., 2018). Acquiring new knowledge does not stop when one leaves formal education, but continues throughout adult life. Lifelong learning is voluntary and includes informal learning, which shapes attitudes and behaviours (Scottish Government, 2003). English language café assist newcomers in learning the language (Sorgen, 2015). Sport offers a distraction from everyday worries and thinking about the situation in their home country and gives a sense of belonging through a game (Stone, 2018). Media coverage impacts the views of host population toward refugees, for example, tabloids often run negative campaigns towards newcomers, framing them as 'others' and encourage hostile reactions (Matthews & Brown, 2012). For micro-initiatives it would be the coverage of local newspapers which would focus on refugees living in the area. Volunteers have an important role in delivering some of the micro-initiatives (Jones, 2014). Despite all these studies, there is still little understanding of what can be done on a micro level to support the integration of refugees (Bowes et al., 2009). This paper moves away from looking only at one initiative but shall analyse the collective impact of them on the integration of refugees within one area.

Since its beginning, the Syrian Civil War forced over five million people to seek refuge in neighbouring countries (OCHA, 2019). In response to the humanitarian emergency, the UK government responded by promising to resettle up to 20,000 Syrians from Middle East camps in Jordan, Lebanon, Iraq, Egypt and Turkey within five years (Home Office, 2017). Local councils would volunteer to host refugees. Relocated refugees were identified jointly by the Home Office and the United Nations Refugee Agency. A local government had to consider whether they had the infrastructure and support network to provide the appropriate assistance for refugees, as there was the limited backing offered by the central government (Home Office, 2017). Scotland was assigned 10% of the UK's total share and reached its target of receiving Syrian refugees or as they are called in Scotland 'New Scots' three years before the deadline (COSLA, 2017).

It is still not clear how relevant the local context is in the integration experience (Platts-Fowler & Robinson, 2015). Thus, this paper draws on a single case study design as it allows to conduct nuanced account of how micro-level initiatives improve integration within the local context and to analyse in-depth unique cases (Yin, 2014). Usually, researchers studied area with a high number of refugees such as Glasgow (Deuchar, 2011; Kearns & Whitley, 2015; Strang et al., 2018; Wren, 2007). Consequently, the second aim of this paper is to explore how a community, which had no prior experience of welcoming refugees, approach their integration. This is one of the first papers which has utilised the updated integration framework (Ndofor-Tah et al., 2019).

Research methods and participants

A qualitative descriptive single case study approach (Yin, 2014) was utilised to provide an empirically-reached understanding of the integration process within a Scottish council area. The local authority decided to take around one hundred refugees. The area had not been traditionally a destination for refugees or asylum seekers, but it is multicultural. The council decided to approach the integration process through a partnership group involving key local stakeholders to ensure everyone's voices were heard. The Syrian refugee population included both families with children and single adults. They were of mixed ages, had varying employment experiences (coming from both labour and professional backgrounds), and their knowledge of English was limited. Refugees came from different parts of Syria and religious groups- thus, they supported opposing sides of the conflict.

Data came from three sources. The Lexis Library database was searched for articles in local newspapers which included the word 'refugee*' and were published after the Council announced that it would invite refugees in the area. The initial search of newspapers identified 282 articles which were screened for relevance (a reference to refugees living in the area of the study) and 273 were excluded. A manual search of a community-led magazine added another article about refugees. In total, eight newspaper articles were included in the analysis. Secondly, the council website was searched for minutes of committee meetings discussing the integration process. Lastly, ten semi-structured qualitative interviews with community stakeholders recruited through snowball sampling were conducted. Each interviewee was assigned a random number. Table 2 shows interviewees' demographics. Interviews with elites such as policymakers can be challenging as they tend to exaggerate and misrepresent facts in their answers (Berry, 2002); thus, these interviews took place at the last stage of data collection. Participants needed to ensure that whatever they shared would not impact negatively on the refugees. When requested, interviewees could see their data, and on two occasions, alterations were made to ensure the confidentiality of refugees.

All interviews were recorded and transcribed or in-depth notes were taken. Interviews, media coverage and council papers were uploaded in NVivo, utilised to support the thematic analysis (Braun & Clarke, 2006). Data were coded deductively guided by the integration framework (Ndofor-Tah et al., 2019), which mapped the integration process in the studied area.

The results of this study have some limitations. As this is a single case study, the results from this research cannot be thought to adequately represent the integration strategies of all of 32 Scottish local authorities or other parts of the UK. Overall, Scotland is slightly more open to migration than

England but still faces challenges (Hunter & Meer, 2018; Trevena, 2018), so the discussed experience here may not be transferable to areas where the arrival of refugees is more contentious political issue. This research also focused only on one particular nationality of refugees, which may not necessarily be representative of the general refugee population.

Table 1. Demographics of interviewees

Participant number	Community role of interviewee	Ethnicity and language skills.
4	Councillor	Ethnic minority
1	Member of local planning board	British
3, 6, 8	Employee of local charity	Two British and one ethnic minority
7	Journalist and activist	Ethnic minority and speaks Arabic
2	Police officer	British
9, 10	School teacher	British
5	Interpreter	Ethnic minority and speaks Arabic

The Ethics Officer granted ethical approval for this study at the Politics and International Department, School of Social Science, University of Aberdeen. Additional ethical issues are present when researching vulnerable groups such as refugees to ensure that a researcher does no harm. (Block et al., 2014b; Jacobsen & Landau, 2003). This research took place during the first months of resettlement in the area and based on stakeholders' advice- it was decided not to interview refugees.

> '[To] protect their interest. There are for a start a vulnerable group and not everyone is particularly welcome. There is a lot of stigma of bad press' (Interviewee 6).

In the future, it may be worth returning to the area and exploring the perspectives and experiences of refugees on the events and their impacts discussed here.

Findings

All micro-level initiatives, identified in data, were mapped within the integration framework. Table 3 presents the results of these findings which will be discussed within the four headings: markers and means, social connections, facilitators and foundations. Participants themselves recognised that one intervention to improve integration is not enough but a holistic approach is required.

> 'Something that is being focused on very heavily throughout the city is reducing the number of those who are experiencing social isolation, and raising the awareness of the impact this can have on people's health and wellbeing. This isolation has been evidenced to be due to a number of factors such as certain disabilities and mobility challenges, access to and affordability of transport, or even the ways in which services and partners communicate. For example, to ensure that there are translation services and other formats for those who may not be familiar with the English language or even certain forms of language such as spoken or written.' (Interviewee 1)

Table 4. Micro-level initiatives to facilitate integration. Adopted from Ndofor-Tah et al., 2019

	Work	Housing	Education	Health and Social Care	Leisure
Markers and means	Unemployed but did volunteering.	Accommodation provided by the local authority in an affluent area of the city.	Children attended school and offered additional English classes.	Trauma and pre-relocation health issues present. Registered to and accessed health services.	Getting refugees involved in the local groups in small steps, e.g. attending a football match.
	Bonds	**Bridges**		**Links**	
Social connections	Building links with the local Muslim community. Regular city-wide events to celebrate multiculturalism. Positive media coverage.	Exhibition and theatre play to highlight the journey of refugees. Befriending with local volunteers. Football clubs for young people. Talking about refugees at school.		Local charities, religious organisations worked together with public bodies.	
	Language and Communication	**Culture**	**Digital skills**	**Safety**	**Stability**
Facilitators	English for Speakers of Other Languages (ESOL) classes.	Local events to celebrate diversity.	-	Training for civil servants, police officers and teachers.	-
Foundations	**Rights and responsibilities**				
	Information leaflets in Arabic Drop-in sessions 24/7 phone line in Arabic Provision of interpreters so refugees can access services				

Markers and means

When the fieldwork was conducted, none of the refugees had a job. When they were professionals, they could not prove their qualifications or their diplomas were not recognised in the UK. For others, the language barrier was a challenge in finding employment. However, the majority volunteered with local charities to have a sense of purpose and show gratitude to the community, which welcomed them. After data collection, refugees wanted to thank some of the charities which supported them during the initial relocation period, and they organised a charitable evening with Syrian food and music to raise money for these charities. Refugees were eligible for social benefits and received material support from local charities.

The council provided accommodation to refugees in an affluent area of the city to ensure that they have an adequate living standard and settle in the safe neighbourhood. Some of these houses were rented from private landlords, and all were equipped with essential household items. All refugees were registered to primary health providers. Some of them came with pre-relocation health issues such as trauma and these used specialised services.

Refugee children were enrolled in local schools – many of them had had an extended break from formal education due to a lack of schools at refugee camps. They also attended additional English classes. The support workers tried to arrange leisure activities for newcomers, such as a one-day trip to visit another part of Scotland. Activities within the local community were taken on a small step by step basis. Firstly, they took place within Syrians only, and then refugees could have invited their local friends. Some initiative took place thanks to the support of local organisations. For example, Syrian families received free tickets to attend a football match at the local stadium. They went there as a group and were accompanied by a bilingual support worker.

Social connections

Sport, next to music, is a universal language which can bring diverse communities together. A local football association offered a range of youth activities in the region. The additional group was set up after school and at school grounds for refugee children to play, with an instructor and an interpreter assisting with communication. Initially, it was a Syrian only group, but that soon changed.

> *'After a few sessions they brought their pals from school. At the start, locals and refugees were standing at the opposite sites, but as soon as the game started they mixed.'* (Interviewee 3)

As the research was conducted, local coaches were invited to attend equality courses to learn how to work with diverse communities, especially obstacles they may face when training refugees. It was intended for Syrians to join their local teams within their age groups so they could participate in local competitions.

In the neighbourhood areas, there were activities targeting the adult population. Media reported how a local charity organised an exhibition to highlight the journey of refugees on how and why they had to leave their homes. It included images capturing civil war to help the host population experience what newcomers went through. Furthermore, a play about the political situation in Syria and the lives of refugees was played at local festivals. Initiatives targeting the host population aimed to explain and show an identifiable story behind the arrival of refuges. Thus, this allowed the local population to connect with their new neighbours.

In the area, there was a limited number of Arab interpreters, so refugees kept seeing similar faces during appointments. Refugees mostly did not know each other (except their own family), so they felt isolated. Many interpreters and volunteers involved in the local Mosque came from the same region and shared similar experiences with refugees; thus, they started spending time together. This was easily facilitated as they shared the same mother tongue. These befrienders had been living in the area for a long time and were able to provide some useful tips from basic information about the neighbourhood to advice on public services.

> *"I walked with families around [area] and showed them streets and interesting places."* (Interviewee 7)

With time, there was also a growing number of volunteers and befrienders coming from non-ethnic minority group who engaged with and supported refugees.

Schools were used as first-line of influencing negative views and stereotypes towards Syrian refugees. Young people often have the same perspectives as their parents.

'Often the young people in class have the wrong impression of refugees and have the narrow-minded opinion that these people are "coming over here, stealing our jobs and claiming benefits". They have no idea of the terrible situation that is going on in their home country. They often get confused between refugees and migrant workers, thinking that they are all the same.' (Interviewee 10)

As the teaching curriculum was not specifically designed to assist teachers in discussing these refugees' relocation, additional training for teachers was offered. This was delivered by a local charity specialising in development courses for teachers and youth workers. Sessions were free of charge and open to anyone interested. Learning activities depended on the age groups teachers worked with, for example, primary or secondary school.

'As for an activity, as it is not a focus of the topic we generally have a class discussion where I highlight the differences between refugees and immigrants. I often remind the pupils that these people are escaping war and trying to keep their families safe and are nurses, doctors, teachers etc.' (Interviewee 10)

Participants spoke about how they used case studies from training, such as racial diversity in the US, to initiate a discussion with their pupils about Syrian refugees. These activities had an impact on pupils.

'The pupils are surprised to hear about the terrible conditions [which Syrian refugees endured]' (Interviewee 10)

Youth-led activities were supported by a local charity which delivered equality workshops to schools and encouraged young people to set up their own equality projects. These would be run within a school and results of projects (from research to artistic work) were shared with colleagues. Young people could present their work at the award ceremony organised by the charity. The aim of this event was to celebrate youth achievements.

Participants pointed out that no matter how much work was done at schools, these positive messages were undermined by some national media. However, local press ran very positive coverage around Syrian refugees resettling in the area. Newspapers focused on fundraising to support newcomers organised by local schools and churches, as well as the successful work of charities and volunteers who support refugees. Media also reported appeals from elected politicians to praise people who raise awareness of why Syrian refugees had to come to Scotland.

The engagement with refugees was coordinated by the partnership of local charities, religious organisations (not only Mosque but also churches were involved) and the public bodies. These shared experiences of engaging with the hard to reach groups and the good practice. Members of the community were consulted on regular basis, for example, when community events were organised. These good links with local Muslim community were key to ensure this event was successful as council employees asked for advice on how to arrange the evening.

"And then she went to speak to the refugees themselves and we realised that it wasn't so good idea to do it that time as it was in the middle of Ramadan... and it would be one of the longest days." (Interviewee 6)

However, this advice was not always appropriate. During the first event, which brought all newly arrived Syrians, there were two rooms arranged: one for women with children and second for men. Refugees found it unacceptable and decided to be together as one group.

Facilitators

Arabic is the first language spoken by Syrians, and their English skills were described as '*not fantastic*' (Interviewee 5) and '*very limited*' (Interviewee 2). To remedy this, the council arranged weekly, free of charge classes of English for Speakers of Other Languages (ESOL). There were separate groups for men and women to respect cultural differences.

Local charities organised yearly events to celebrate diversity through international food, music and dance. A similar idea was employed by the council as Syrians arrived. The event was on a smaller scale and by invitation only. It was mostly attended by people who would work and support refugees in the following months, for example, council employees and volunteers from the local mosque. Volunteers were invited to share their stories of their journey to a new home.

'Fascinating, as we spoke with one of the refugees at the table and he was talking about the situation in Syria, and we realised that we don't know a lot of... to understand their perspective... how they feel.' (Interviewee 8)

The evening included traditional Scottish and Arab dances. The former was taught by professional Scottish dancer and the latter by refugees themselves.

Arrival of refugees in the area for the first-time created new challenges for social workers, NHS staff and police officers who had no or limited knowledge of supporting refugees. Thus, civil servants attended internal and external courses. For example, police officers attended intensive diversity training on current equality and hate crime legislation. At a regional level, police designated an officer with in-depth knowledge who could be contacted for advice. External training was provided by a local charity which specialises in working with diverse ethnic and religious groups. The focus of the course was to provide practice examples of how to deal with challenging scenarios.

'We were given discrimination case studies (...) one of the cases was of female refugee, who complained to be discriminated by a receptionist because she didn't cover her face. It was interesting to see that discrimination can be wrongly perceived, as she wasn't discriminated. It told us equality and mutual understanding needs to work in both ways' (Interviewee 9)

This one-off training was perceived by participants as an opportunity to broaden their horizons. It also taught how to avoid cultural misunderstandings and build trust with refugees.

Foundations

Both according to interviewees and official documents, the language barrier was the main challenge for refugees, for example, to access services, thus the local authority provided them with qualified interpreters free of charge. Also, the majority of support workers, who were employed by the council, spoke Arabic. Upon arrival in the UK, leaflets providing basic information about life in the host country were distributed to refugees. A typical example would be '*Welcome to Scotland. A Guide to Scots Law*' jointly designed by Police Scotland, the Procurator Fiscal Office and New College Lanarkshire (2016). The translated booklet provided an overview of the Scottish legal system, from family and criminal law to where victims of crimes can look for support. However, participants mentioned that not all of the refugees were confident readers and writers in their mother tongue, so they were not convinced that this information was helpful for everyone.

Ongoing support for refugees was arranged through regular drop-in sessions, which were supported by a professional interpreter. Sessions offered the opportunity to not only bring Syrians and their support workers together, but also to raise and discuss challenges faced by newcomers. Syrians were encouraged to bring any materials such as letters or leaflets (including not translated materials) which they were not sure about. For example, some of the refugees brought a letter informing them that they are responsible for obtaining a TV license and should answer to the message or face legal consequences. The less official way of offering advice was set up in partnership with a local Mosque. Volunteers fluent in Arabic run 24/7 phone line for refugees who could call and ask any question on the topic of their choice. Some participants felt that Syrian refugees often trusted their peers more than council employees.

Discussion

These findings showed that micro-level initiatives assisted as a basis for a successful integration process. These could not have happened as a single initiative, but only together acted as the right approach to the successful integration when charities, community and public bodies worked together. This proved that the principle of shared responsibility was vital in achieving integration (Ndofor-Tah et al., 2019). However, this shared responsibility had to be set up and supported by the council officers – thus it would have not developed on its own. These findings presented the captured point of time in the integration process of Syrian refugees. With time, challenges around integration transform but do not cease to exist (Kearns & Whitley, 2015). Stakeholders have to continue these initiatives but also develop new interventions to continue the integration process.

The integration framework (Ndofor-Tah et al., 2019) was a useful tool to map the micro-level initiatives. It was designed for both practitioners and researchers (Ager & Strang, 2008). If more academics start to use this framework, the data around integration initiatives could be more comparable. However, mapping some of the activities was challenging as they overlapped within different domains. Consequently, assigning some of the interventions within the framework was subjective. For example, multicultural events were assigned to both bonds and culture. The latter factor looked at how these events celebrated diversity in the community, whereas the former brought people of similar cultures together. Similarly, receiving free tickets to the football match were assigned to leisure as it was a spare time activity but could have also been in social connections. When refugees watched and cheered on the local team, they built rapport with the host population.

Overall, the framework was appropriate for the analysis as it not only mapped the micro-level initiatives within this case study but also identified what local community failed to address. No interventions were identified within the domains of digital skills and stability. As these were first months since refugees relocated in the area, it was no possible to locate any initiatives within the stability of their integration. Interviewees did not mention how refugees improve their digital skills.

The reason behind could have been that language barrier, and literacy issues were seen for the support workers as priority before moving to modern technology.

The underperforming domain was work as none of the refugees managed to secure employment. Previous studies showed that refugees wanted to be active (Williams, 2006) but experienced lengthy returns to professions they practised in their home countries (Kum et al., 2010) and responded differently to these structural barriers (Piętka-Nykaza, 2015). In this case, local support managed to arrange volunteering opportunities. Thanks to volunteering, refugees found their own way to contribute to the community and thus became 'good citizens' (Yap et al., 2010). Successful integration requires not any employment but one which suits the skills of newcomers (Smyth & Kum, 2010). Longer Syrians will rely on social support, less independent and thus cannot fully integrate into the local community.

These findings confirmed some results from previous studies. Keeping links between refugees and social workers and holding regular consultation was essential for successful integration (Phillips, 2006). In contrast to other interventions, some mistakes were avoided. For example, refugees were not settled without prior preparations (Wren, 2007) neither were placed in low-income areas (Kearns & Whitley, 2015). The possible explanation behind avoiding these errors was that previous experiences and advice from national bodies were available (e.g. by the Scottish Refugee Council) to local civil servants who successfully utilised it.

Future research should focus on the comparison of approaches to integration in areas with small and large influxes of refugees. This comparison should utilise both qualitative and quantitative methods collected over long periods to register progress of integration. It should explore differences between male and female refugees as Cheung and Phillimore (2017) pointed out gender impacts the integration process. Literature utilising the integration framework needs to be reviewed to examine if academics always assign similar interventions to the same domain.

Conclusion

This paper showed that micro-level initiatives were an important factor in the integration process of new refugees in the local community. Local charities, culturally close communities, social workers were vital actors in delivering the initiatives. The strength of these interventions was particularly visible within the heading of social connections where the local community had the leading role. However, other dimensions could not have been successful within the right approach of the local community.

Even a modest number of newcomers required extensive actions taken by a local council to ensure their successful integration. The relocation of Syrian refugees in the area was a learning curve for local officers and policymakers. This case study proved that even a local council which did not have prior experience of welcoming refugees was capable of successfully integrating refugees. However, it required bringing multiple partners and community onboard. Without a proactive and successful strategy at the council level, refugees would not integrate successfully.

References

Ager, A., & Strang, A. (2004). *Indicators of Integration: final report.* Retrieved from https://webarchive.nationalarchives. gov.uk/20110218141321/http://rds.homeoffice.gov.uk/rds/pdfs04/dpr28.pdf

Ager, A., & Strang, A. (2008). Understanding Integration: A Conceptual Framework. *Journal of Refugee Studies, 21*(2), 166-191. doi:10.1093/jrs/fen016

Berry, J. M. (2002). Validity and Reliability Issues in Elite Interviewing. *PS: Political Science and Politics, 35*(4), 679-682.

Berry, J. W. (1997). Immigration, Acculturation, and Adaptation. *Applied Psychology: An International Review, 46*(1), 5-34. doi:10.1111/j.1464-0597.1997.tb01087.x

Berry, J. W. (2006). Contexts ofacculturation. In D. L. Sam & J. W. Berry (Eds.), *The Cambridge Handbook of Acculturation Psychology* (pp. 27-42). Cambridge: Cambridge University Press.

Block, K., Cross, S., Riggs, E., & Gibbs, L. (2014a). Supporting schools to create an inclusive environment for refugee students. *International Journal of Inclusive Education, 18*(12), 1337-1355. doi:10.1080/13603116.2014.899636

Block, K., Riggs, E., & Haslam, N. (2014b). *Values and vulnerabilities: The ethics of research with refugees and asylum seekers*. Toowong: Australian Academic Press.

Bowes, A., Ferguson, I., & Sim, D. (2009). Asylum policy and asylum experiences: interactions in a Scottish context. *Ethnic and Racial Studies, 32*(1), 23-43. doi:10.1080/01419870701722570

Braun, V., & Clarke, V. (2006). Using thematic analysis in psychology. *Qualitative Research in Psychology, 3*(2), 77-101. doi:10.1191/1478088706qp063oa

Castles, S., Korac, M., Vasta, E., & Vertovec , S. (2002). *Integration:Mapping the field*. Retrieved from Oxford:

Cheung, S. Y., & Phillimore, J. (2017). Gender and Refugee Integration: a Quantitative Analysis of Integration and Social Policy Outcomes. *Journal of Social Policy, 46*(2), 211-230. doi:10.1017/S0047279416000775

COSLA. (2017). Council praised for humanitarian efforts as Scotland welcomes 2000th Syrian Refugee.

Crisp, J. (2004). *The local integration and local settlement of refugees: a conceptual and historical analysis*. Retrieved from Geneva:

Deuchar, R. (2011). 'People Look at Us, the Way We Dress, and They Think We're Gangsters': Bonds, Bridges, Gangs and Refugees: A Qualitative Study of Inter-Cultural Social Capital in Glasgow. *Journal of Refugee Studies, 24*(4), 672-689. doi:10.1093/jrs/fer032

Favell, A. (2001). Integration policy and integration research in Europe: a review and critique. In A. T. Aleinikoff & D. e. Klusmeyer (Eds.), *Citizenship today: global perspectives and practices* (Vol. 349-399). Washington, DC: Brookings Institute/Carnegie Endowment for International Peace.

Heyneman, S. (2002). *Defining the influence of education on social cohesion* (Vol. 3).

Home Office. (2017). *Syrian Vulnerable Person Resettlement Scheme (VPRS) Guidance for local authorities and partners*. Retrieved from https://www.gov.uk/government/uploads/system/uploads/ attachment data/ file/ 472020/Syrian_Resettlement_Fact_Sheet_gov_uk.pdf

Hunter, A., & Meer, N. (2018). Is Scotland Different on Race and Migration? *Scottish Affairs, 27*(3), 382-387. doi:10.3366/scot.2018.0249

Jacobsen, K., & Landau, L. B. (2003). The Dual Imperative in Refugee Research: Some Methodological and Ethical Considerations in Social Science Research on Forced Migration. *Disasters, 27*(3), 185-206. doi:10.1111/1467-7717.00228

Jones, C. (2014). Volunteers working to support migrants in Glasgow: a qualitative study. *International Journal of Migration, Health and Social Care, 10*(4), 193-206. doi:10.1108/IJMHSC-10-2013-0034

Kearns, A., & Whitley, E. (2015). Getting There? The Effects of Functional Factors, Time and Place on the Social Integration of Migrants. *Journal of ethnic and migration studies, 41*(13), 2105-2129. doi:10.1080/1369183X.2015.1030374

Kum, H., Menter, I., & Smyth, G. (2010). Changing the face of the Scottish teaching profession? The experiences of refugee teachers. *Irish Educational Studies, 29*(3), 321-338. doi:10.1080/03323315.2010.498570

Matthews, J. (2008). Schooling and settlement: refugee education in Australia. *International Studies in Sociology of Education, 18*(1), 31-45. doi:10.1080/09620210802195947

Matthews, J., & Brown, A. R. (2012). Negatively shaping the asylum agenda? The representational strategy and impact of a tabloid news campaign. *Journalism, 13*(6), 802-817. doi:10.1177/1464884911431386

McBride, M., Lowden, K., Chapman, C., & Watson, N. (2018). *Educational needs and experiences of refugee children in Scotland*. Retrieved from http://whatworksscotland.ac.uk/publications/educational-needs-and-experiences-of-refugee-children-in-scotland/

Mulvey, G. (2015). Refugee Integration Policy: The Effects of UK Policy-Making on Refugees in Scotland. *Journal of Social Policy, 44*(2), 357-375. doi:10.1017/S004727941500001X

Ndofor-Tah, C., Strang, A., Phillimore, J., Morrice, L., Michael, L., Wood, P., & Simmons, J. (2019). *Home Office Indicators of Integration framework 2019*. Retrieved from http://sro.sussex.ac.uk/id/eprint/84107/1/__smbhome. uscs.susx.ac.uk_dm50_Desktop_Morrice%20Home%20Office.pdf

New College Lanarkshire. (2016). Welcome to Scotland. A Guide to Scots Law.

OCHA. (2019). Humanitarian Needs Overview. Retrieved from https://hno-syria.org/#key-figures

Pagani, C. (2014). Diversity and social cohesion. *Intercultural Education, 25*(4), 300-311. doi:10.1080/14675986.2014.926158

Phillimore, J. (2012). Implementing integration in the UK: lessons for integration theory, policy and practice. *Policy & Politics, 40*(4), 525-545. doi:10.1332/030557312X643795

Phillimore, J., & Goodson, L. (2008). Making a Place in the Global City: The Relevance of Indicators of Integration. *Journal of Refugee Studies, 21*(3), 305-325. doi:10.1093/jrs/fen025

Phillips, D. (2006). Moving Towards Integration: The Housing of Asylum Seekers and Refugees in Britain. *Housing Studies, 21*(4), 539-553. doi:10.1080/02673030600709074

Piętka-Nykaza, E. (2015). 'I Want to Do Anything which Is Decent and Relates to My Profession': Refugee Doctors' and Teachers' Strategies of Re-Entering Their Professions in the UK. *Journal of Refugee Studies, 28*(4), 523-543. doi:10.1093/jrs/fev008

Platts-Fowler, D., & Robinson, D. (2015). A Place for Integration: Refugee Experiences in Two English Cities. *Population, Space and Place, 21*(5), 476-491. doi:10.1002/psp.1928

Scottish Government. (2003). The Lifelong Learning Strategy for Scotland.

Smyth, G., & Kum, H. (2010). 'When They don't Use it They will Lose it': Professionals, Deprofessionalization and Reprofessionalization: the Case of Refugee Teachers in Scotland. *Journal of Refugee Studies, 23*(4), 503-522. doi:10.1093/jrs/feq041

Sorgen, A. (2015). Integration through participation: The effects of participating in an English Conversation club on refugee and asylum seeker integration. In *Applied Linguistics Review* (Vol. 6, pp. 241).

Spencer, S. (2011). *The Migration Debate*. Bristol: The Policy Press.

Stone, C. (2018). Utopian community football? Sport, hope and belongingness in the lives of refugees and asylum seekers. *Leisure Studies, 37*(2), 171-183. doi:10.1080/02614367.2017.1329336

Strang, A. B., Baillot, H., & Mignard, E. (2018). 'I want to participate.' transition experiences of new refugees in Glasgow. *Journal of ethnic and migration studies, 44*(2), 197-214. doi:10.1080/1369183X.2017.1341717

Taylor, S., & Sidhu, R. K. (2012). Supporting refugee students in schools: what constitutes inclusive education? *International Journal of Inclusive Education, 16*(1), 39-56. doi:10.1080/13603110903560085

Trevena, P. (2018). Attracting and retaining migrants in post-Brexit Scotland: is a social integration strategy the answer? *SPICe Briefing.*

Williams, L. (2006). Social Networks of Refugees in the United Kingdom: Tradition, Tactics and New Community Spaces. *Journal of ethnic and migration studies, 32*(5), 865-879. doi:10.1080/13691830600704446

Wren, K. (2007). Supporting Asylum Seekers and Refugees in Glasgow: The Role of Multi-agency Networks. *Journal of Refugee Studies, 20*(3), 391-413. doi:10.1093/jrs/fem006

Yap, S. Y., Byrne, A., & Davidson, S. (2010). From Refugee to Good Citizen: A Discourse Analysis of Volunteering. *Journal of Refugee Studies, 24*(1), 157-170. doi:10.1093/jrs/feq036

Yin, R. K. (2014). *Case study research : design and methods* (5th edition. ed.). Los Angeles: SAGE.

September 2020
Volume: 17, No: 5, pp. 583 – 595
ISSN: 1741-8984
e-ISSN: 1741-8992
www.migrationletters.com

MIGRATION
LETTERS

First Submitted: 9 December 2019 Accepted: 25 September 2020
DOI: https://doi.org/10.33182/ml.v17i5.891

Labour Market Impact of Syrian Refugees in Turkey: The View of Employers in Informal Textile Sector in Istanbul

Aysegul Kayaoglu[1]

Abstract

In less than a decade, Turkey has become home to some 4 million Syrians due to the bloody conflict across much of its southern border. That only a fraction of those refugees live in designated camps with the overwhelming majority spread about the country has led to hostile sentiments among some natives who blame Syrians for taking away their jobs. Still, research about the impact of Syrians on Turkish labour market outcomes is too limited. Empirical findings analysing micro-level data find either no impact or just abysmall changes to natives' formal employment rates but rather declines in rates of informal employment. This paper presents the findings of a three-month fieldwork in Istanbul's informal textile sector. Looking at the issue from the view of employers, it shows that "on average" country-level findings of the empirical analysis might be quite simplifying and sometimes inconsistent depending on the context. By just looking at the issue in a specific/neighbourhood setting, namely informal textile sector in a rather homogenous urban neighbourhood where the main competition in jobs are between Kurds and Syrians, this study shows that employment rates of natives declined in that specific field due to other factors independent of the Syrians and interestingly even predating their arrival to Turkey. The war-fleeing migrants are understood to have rather taken jobs no longer desired by the natives and generally paid lower wages than natives for doing them. This study particularly raises the role of skill gaps in the local market, changes in the meaning of work in the local population and informal-formal sector interdependence due to price pressures by global value chains in understanding the effect of refugees on locals' labour market outcomes.

Keywords: *Syrian refugees; labour market; textile sector; informal labour; employers.*

Introduction

Since the civil war began in 2011, millions of Syrians have fled their homes and majority of them migrated to neighbouring countries.(Yazgan *et al.* 2015) As a result, Turkey has become the world's largest refugee shelter with its open-door policy for Syrians. (Togral-Koca 2015; Sirkeci 2017) According to the UNHCR Population Statistics, the highest number of Syrian refugees are living in Turkey (63.9% of Syrian refugees worldwide as of December 2018) and the UNICEF has also declared Turkey the country with the highest number of refugee children in particular. As only a small proportion of this population is hosted in temporary accommodation centres (only 63,518 out of 3.6 million registered Syrians, as of April 2020), social and economic consequences of having this big influx of Syrians in Turkish cities already strained under high level of unemployment and income inequality particularly after 2015 would not be completely unexpected.

[1] Aysegul Kayaoglu, Department of Economics, Istanbul Technical University, Istanbul, Turkey.
E-mail: kayaogluyilmaz@itu.edu.tr.

The recent availability of data about the population distribution of Syrians among Turkey's different regions has allowed researchers to analyse the effect of Syrians on various social, economic and political issues. The impact of Syrians on the natives' labour market outcomes has also received some attention as those migrants have been accused of seizing jobs from natives and suppressing their wages through increased competition. A simplistic theoretical framework suggests that immigration leads to an increase both in labour supply and demand with the former shifting more than the latter, which in equilibrium causes a decline both in natives' wages and employment rates. However, empirical literature offers an ambiguous effect of immigration on natives' labour market outcomes. The early strand of literature argues that immigration has only negligible effects on the wages and employment of the native population in the short run as immigrants were argued to be poor substitutes for the native workers (Antonji and Card 1991; Goldin 1994; Pischke and Velling 1997). Therefore, the effect of immigration on natives' labour market outcomes was argued to prevail only in the long-run (Friedberg 2000; Weiss *et al.* 2003; Cohen-Goldner and Paserman 2011). Borjas *et al.* (1996) criticised those findings as they did not consider the spill-over effects of migration, such as internal displacement of native workers. The second strand of economic literature employed a different theoretical approach, which assumed that immigrants and natives were close substitutes for each other. Unlike the earlier literature, those papers suggested a sizeable effect of immigrants on the labour market outcomes of natives (Card 2001; Borjas 2003; Angrist and Kugler 2003; Borjas and Katz 2007; Card 2009; Ottaviano and Peri 2011).

All those research was, however, dealing with the effect of rather voluntary migration to developed countries in a non-experimental setting, which had various disadvantages about their identification due to self-selection bias and, instrumental variables strategy has been employed to address this problem. The usual way of explaining how the labour market outcome of natives are affected by migration influx (informal/formal employment, labour force participation, unemployment and so on.) is through shares of immigrants at the level of analysis together with some other control variables. However, immigrant sorting into regions with higher economic potentials also causes biased findings in this type of methodologies. Using a quasi-experimental setting in both developed and developing countries, some researchers have investigated the effect of involuntary mass migration flows on the natives' labour market outcomes and the majority of those studies have found either no or just negligible effect. Card (1990), for example, analysed the labour market effect of a sudden 7% increase in the labour supply in Miami and concluded that it had virtually no effect on the wages and unemployment level of less-skilled natives. Hunt (1992), likewise, studied the effect of the 1962 Repatriates from Algeria to France and showed only a minor effect on the unemployment (0.3 percentage points increase) and wages (average annual salaries are found to decrease by at most 1.3%) of non-repatriates.[2]

As the civil war in Syria resulted in a massive refugee outflow, a natural experiment setting was born for analysis of the effect of Syrian refugees on natives' labour market outcomes in a number of neighbouring countries including Turkey. Ceritoglu et al. (2015), for example, used a difference-in-differences strategy at the NUTS2-level in Turkey to investigate the effect of refugee inflow on the labour market outcomes of native population aged between 15 and 64. They find that the likelihood of working in the informal market for natives dropped by 2.2 percentage points in the treatment regions that had over 2 per cent refugee population as a share of its total population and, 1.1 percentage points of that decline are argued to have left the labour force with another 0.7

---

[2] For other examples also see Carrington and de Lima 1996; Friedberg 2001; Mansour 2010; Glitz 2012; Aydemir and Kırdar 2013; Maystadt and Verwimp 2014; Cohen-Goldner and Paserman 2011; Baez 2011; Ruiz and Vargas-Silva 2015.

percentage points staying as unemployed and the remaining 0.4 percentage points switching to a formal job. More interestingly, they found that these effects were not through job separation of natives but rather through diminishing their job-finding probability. Del Carpio and Wagner (2015) used an IV strategy to investigate the effect of Syrians on natives' labour market outcomes and like Ceritoglu et al. (2015) they also studied individuals aged 15 to 64. They claimed that Syrian refugees in Turkey caused a statistically significant effect on the displacement of informal, low-educated and female workers.[3] Moreover, Bagir (2018) found statistically significant and negative effect of Syrian refugee influx on the wages and employment of the low-skilled and less-experienced workers analysing the Household Labor Force Surveys.

Despite economic contributions of Syrians in Turkey[4], they are blamed to have negative economic effects according to the perceptions of native population in Turkey. A particular survey showed that Turkish people were concerned about their labour market conditions being changed after the arrival of Syrians, and a striking 69% of them agreed in 2014 with the statement "Syrians take our jobs" (Erdogan, 2015). When they were asked about their concerns in the future in a following survey in 2017, 51.4% of natives favoured the idea that the Syrians will seize their jobs (Erdogan, 2017). Besides, only 8.2% of the respondents agreed with the statement "Syrian refugees are beneficial for the Turkish economy" in the 2017 Syrian Barometer survey of more than 2,000 natives.

This paper is a humble attempt to understand the effect of Syrians in the informal textile sector and see if the common beliefs in the Turkish society and findings of the regional empirical analyses would also be supported in a micro field study. With this aim, I conducted a three-month fieldwork in 2016 in informal textile ateliers[5] in Kucukkoy, a district of Istanbul famous with sweetshops[6] where the neighbourhood is rather homogenous in terms of its ethnic background and competition for jobs in those ateliers are mainly between Kurdish and Syrian residents. In-depth interviews were completed mainly with the owners of ateliers in order to understand how their production and hiring/firing has changed after the arrival of Syrians. However, interviews were also conducted with both Turkish/Kurdish and Syrian employees[7] to triangulate the information taken from employers about the salaries and working conditions. Although this study cannot be generalised to all the sectors in Turkey or even over the textile sector in different regions, it aims to contribute to the literature by reflecting on the issue from a unique point of view – that of employers in the informal sector.

Background

The inflow of Syrians to Turkey was rather at low levels in late 2011 (it was 8,000 in December 2011) but the figures rapidly grew since 2012 and reached to 3.6 million in April 2020. The

---

[3] Also see Akgündüz et al. (2015), Binatlı and Esen (2016), Koyuncu (2016), Lordoğlu and Aslan (2015), ORSAM and TESEV (2015), Korkmaz (2017).

[4] For example, World Bank (2015) report shows that 26% of the newly established firms in 2014 had either Syrian ownership or capital.

[5] There were also a few registered ateliers but either some of their workers did not have social security registry or they were employing Syrian refugees in the time of fieldwork.

[6] Atışalanı, Esenler and Merter are also districts with lots of textile ateliers (both formal and informal) who pay in weekly/montly basis. Çağlayan is another district of textile ateliers but they usually work on daily basis. In other words, they pay their workers daily given the number of pieces they complete in a day and they have worse working conditions. All these regions are famous with employing Syrian refugees.

[7] It was too difficult to talk with employees as there was always a time pressure in their work as they were paid according to their performances which was measured by the number of pieces they were completing. For those, I had a chance to talk, I either talk to them during their lunch or tea/coffee breaks or while they were working.

introduction of identity cards for Syrians in December 2014 made it easier to measure the total population of Syrians living outside the camps though it is widely suspected that even 3.6 million remains an underestimation as there are believed to be Syrians living in Turkey without any registration due to various concerns[8]. In addition to enabling a more proper count of Syrian refugees in Turkey, these cards also provide direct access to health, education and aid. However, the cards are provided given the province Syrians reside in and they are invalidated if their holders move to another province without the approval of the Directorate General of Migration Management within the Interior Ministry in Ankara. This also means that Syrians who live in a province other than where they are registered can neither benefit from the free public services nor apply for a work permit.

In January 2016, Syrians are allowed to apply for work permits. Its conditions are explained in the law 'Work Permits of Foreigners Under Temporary Protection' (*Geçici Koruma Sağlanan Yabancıların Çalışma İzinlerine Dair Yönetmelik*) published in the Official Gazette. It is stated that Syrians under temporary protection are able to apply for a work permit six months after getting their temporary protection ID cards. However, those working in the agricultural sector are exempted from the work permit application. There are also eligibility rules related with the firm they plan to work. For example, the total number of Syrians in a firm that will employ a Syrian worker with a work permit cannot be more than 10% of native workforce. There are also restrictions of employing Syrians in small firms. The legislation stipulates that only one Syrian refugee can be employed formally at firms with a size of less than 10 employees. These quotas can be eliminated only if the firm owner proves that there is a scarcity of native workers able to work in the same position with Syrian worker for the previous four weeks of work permit application. Furthermore, it must be noted that those work permits are not permanent and the application must be renewed at each time Syrian workers change their work places. Besides, not Syrians but the company owners are asked to apply to the provincial head office of the Turkish Employment Agency Directorate General. So, in fact, the Syrian work permit provided by Turkish authorities should rather be seen as a 'permit to employ Syrians'. Strikingly, the total number of Syrians with a work permit is only 34,573 as of April 2020.[9] Saying this, the majority of Syrians in Turkey work in the informal sector without any social security registration and insurance. In addition to working in the informal sector, as Kayaoglu and Erdogan (2019) present, employment rate of Syrian refugees in Turkey is around 40 percent where half of those employed work either in irregular/seasonal jobs or as unpaid family workers.

Data and Methodology

Empirical analyses in this paper use the primary data collected during three-month fieldwork (between April and June 2016) in the neighbourhood of Kucukkoy in Istanbul where it is impossible to escape the deafening noise of textile machines used in small and medium-size informal ateliers scattered around. I talked with the owners of nine ateliers and also had conversations with twenty-one Syrian and twelve native textile workers. The average age of Syrian interviewees was 22, although it was 34 for the native sample. Moreover, the proportion of female workers in the native sample was much higher than the Syrian sample. Only two individuals in the Syrian sample were women. This was mainly because of the comparatively low levels of Syrian women in the research

---

[8] See Deniz et al. (2016) who argued that many Syrians in the border cities were afraid of being labeled as traitors by their secret service once they will be registered in Turkey. Therefore, those who had a plan to return Syria were preferring not to register.

[9] See https://multeciler.org.tr/turkiyede-calisma-izni-verilen-suriyeli-sayisi/

field. During the interview, a 19-year-old Syrian man from Aleppo who once had a dream of becoming a doctor gave a clue about this gender imbalance:

> "The life style here in Turkey is very different than ours. For example, here women are working side by side with men. It is not appropriate for us [*Syrians*]. We prefer our women to stay at home and take care of domestic work. If they work, they should work in places where there are only women. But Istanbul is very expensive. It is not possible to maintain a family life with just one wage. If you see a Syrian woman working outside, you would be right to assume that their financial situation is extremely bad."

However, this view is rejected by a Syrian Kurdish woman aged 32 who was working in one of the informal textile ateliers. She claimed that this kind of view depends on the culture and argued that Syrians from Aleppo, particularly from rural areas, are more conservative. Still, among nine ateliers that were visited, only two Syrian women workers were observed and the rest of Syrian workers were men, with a sizable proportion being below age 18.

Since it is very difficult to enter in the informal businesses for a fieldwork, personal links are used to find connections. A childhood friend was chief-worker in one of the ateliers and he helped me to build a trust with his employer who was my first interviewee. He then referred me to the owner of another atelier and a longer chain of interviewees emerged in the same manner. Apart from this snowballing technique, random data collection was also used but it was more difficult to get the consent of employers in those ateliers as they were suspicious of my motivations and worried that I could report them to authorities. Visits to the ateliers are ended when saturation is reached, in order words, after realising that owners or managers of those ateliers were giving similar answers to research questions. During the fieldwork, the views of owners in hiring and wage-setting decisions for Syrians are questioned. Qualitative content analysis is employed to categorise and identify major themes from the narratives which are presented below.

Saying this, one must also note the limitations regarding the sample. First of all, the data is just collected in one district therefore its results should not be generalised for the impact of Syrians in other districts and sectors. Second, the study focuses on the viewpoints of employers as the reseach question of this paper was to understand how Syrians changed the employment and payment behaviours of firm owners. Therefore, employees are only interviewed shortly[10] to triangulate the already collected data about their wages and working conditions. Thus, the their full views are missing in this study and a planned future research will focus on their aspects.

Still, the paper has two main contributions. First, it addresses an important issue in a field which is comparatively very difficult to collect data and, it is the first study analysing the effect of Syrians in the informal sector in Turkey using a qualitative data. Second, it aims to contribute and give insight to the existing studies about the role of migrants in the local labour markets by looking at the issue with a different lens, namely forced migration and informal economy nexus.

Hiring Decisions of Textile Atelier Owners

When employers are asked about the widely-argued displacement of native workers because of Syrians, interestingly all of them suggested that they were already seeing their workers quit textile

---

[10] Another reason of conducting shorter interviews with employees was their very tight work schedules. Informal employees working in the field area had only two 10-minute breaks before and after the lunch break. Moreover, their lunch break was maximum 1 hour. As they were also working non-stop, it was not possible to conduct longer interviews. Moreover, except 2 employees, the researcher is not allowed to talk with employees during the work hours.

jobs before the arrival of Syrians. Majority of employers turned out being thankful for the presence of Syrians since they argued to have difficulty filling up positions domestically before. For example, a 38-year old manager with an experience of almost 15 years in the textile sector has put it as bluntly as the following:

> "When the Syrians came, no replacements or transfers happened. We had too few a workforce before Syrians. So, we had a low production capacity. Syrians added a supportive force to production. In short, we didn't lay off workers because of Syrians... We need skilled labour at contracted sewing business. It makes no difference if by Turks or Syrians, what really matters to us is that we could produce as much as we are supposed to." (manager, 38 years old, male)

Besides, they have argued that the young generation in Turkey does not want to work in the textile sector and as the textile work requires good physical health on top of apprenticeship training, firms are preferring to employ the young population though there is not enough labour supply among natives, as employers claim. For example, a 65-year old business owner who started to work as a textile employee himself during his childhood and later built his own atelier gave the following testimony in visible disgust towards young native labor force:

> "My girl, I'm 65 years old and I'm still working but youngsters don't. Let's go outside now together and we'll see many of them drinking beer, smoking pot or taking drugs. People say there's unemployment in Turkey. Not at all! Go ask all firms and they will complain of scarcity of workers. I would hire the next Syrian coming through this door because there are no Turkish workers in the market anymore. No workers, really! People got used to being comfortable elsewhere." (65 years old owner, male)

However, these accusations of employers should be approached with caution considering the working conditions in these ateliers. Both native and Syrian employees complained about the working conditions but stated that they have no other options. Workers do not have social security registration and their wages are generally lower than or equal to minimum wage. Moreover, Syrian refugees, but particularly those who do not have temporary protection cards, are paid much lower than natives. In some cases, their payments are even delayed or at worst not paid. These wage differences between Syrians and natives are also documented by Aksu Kargın(2018) in the case of Hatay and Gaziantep provinces. Apart from lower payment without insurance, these ateliers do also have worse working conditions which operate generally in the basements. A Kurdish employee in one of these underground ateliers told his situation openly;

> "Look at this place. Who will be willing to work here? I do it because this is the job I do since my childhood. I wish I continued my education so that I would not be in this dust and had a better job." (38-year-old, employee, male)

This problem of labour supply scarcity is even more severe in informal ateliers as they are usually doing sub-production or contract manufacturing (*fason* in Turkish) type of production and, this requires them to have a certain level of production completed at each day otherwise they are not able to get next order from the 'boss firms'[11] as they call it. High price pressure from

---

[11] These are contracted firms who get orders from international companies or from internal market but not able to complete the job themselves due to the price pressure by the ordering firm. So, they order certain stages of the job to different informal textile ateliers who do it cheaper which enables them having enough margin to make profits.

international companies leads formal textile 'boss firms' to work with informal ateliers. For example, if a jacket has to be produced by a maximum 20 TRY (which is set by the international ordering company) and if this order cannot be produced by the formal firm because of their costs, then they work with an informal atelier who agrees to do the job for 12 TRY. This way enables them to keep getting orders and making profits. The field research also found that there are specific employees in formal textile firms who visit informal ateliers and get price offers for a particular order. Thus, the interdependence of formal and informal textile sector breeds the informality in Turkey and causes the price pressure on informal ateliers which is, according to some employers I interviewed, an important reason of low wages they pay for their workers. Decreasing labour supply from the native population partly due to bad working conditions seem to open a door for Syrian refugees to work in these informal jobs as many of them are ready to work at any job to survive in urban areas. Saying this, it was remarkable that all of the employers complained about the lack of labour supply from the native population without mentioning the low wages or bad working conditions in their ateliers which can be illustrated by the quotation below:

> "Frankly, we have difficulty finding Turkish staff in textiles sector since there is scarcity of them looking for a job. We hired Syrians because Syrians came to us looking for a job. We would have hired Turks if they had come. For instance, we replaced 4 Syrians with another 4 Syrians while we hired 2 Turks past month." (38 years old, manager, male)

There were some concerns about the role of retail sector in urban areas and the rise of shopping malls in city centres on attracting the young lower-educated population. The textile atelier owners did generally declare that young people are no more willing to be involved in hard work but rather willing to have a job in shopping malls and be paid the minimum wage anyway. When I compared the 'bad' working conditions in their ateliers with the environment in shopping malls such as being less noisy, shinier, cleaner and less-demanding physically, some employers claimed that those retail sector jobs do not teach the youth any skills. As exemplified in the interview cited below, many of them criticised the young population about their choices:

> "Our fellow citizens here don't work. All of them are at coffeehouses. We can't find new recruits. Nobody wants to develop any skills anymore. They prefer to work as a security guard than at textiles. So much so, it's like we are producing one day but unable to do so the other day. We will end up being more and more dependent on imports eventually."(owner, 37 years old, male)

Interestingly, improving the working conditions did not seem to be on the agenda. It seemed that this working conditions were also faced by employers themselves once they were employees in textile ateliers. This could also be another reason of harshly criticising the youth who are claimed to disfavour textile jobs. Except one case, all the rest were once child labourers in the textile ateliers.

When I tried to understand their hiring decisions and how ethnicity plays a role, I realised that they were all very much profit oriented. In other words, majority of them did not care whether their workers are Syrian or Turkish but they rather have expectations about their daily performances. Given their earlier experiences, on the other hand, some of those atelier owners displayed prejudices about Syrians and their working styles claiming that Syrians are used to live and work in comfort. For example, an informal atelier owner explained this as follows:

"Most of them (Syrians) are not willing to work. They are lazy people like our new generation. They offer bad quality production even if they work and because of that I wouldn't hire Syrians." (owner, 37 years old, male)

There were also various concerns about the work performance of Syrians in comparison with the native workers. All of the ateliers had a very tough work schedule. On average, they start working at 8 am and finish at 7 pm. There is a one-hour lunch break in the afternoon and twice a 10-minute coffee/tea break during the day. Imagine working in a very dark, noisy place filled with a thick smell under such a schedule, you can understand how difficult it is to keep up with this work routine. However, as owners of the ateliers I interviewed had all started to work in textile companies themselves at a very young age (mostly as child workers), it seems that they internalised this work schedule so much that it was rather shocking for them if, for example, Syrians demand extra tea/coffee breaks. One employer stated that:

"Syrians got used to comfort. They wouldn't work like Turkish workers. They are calm and they don't worry if the day's quota is readied or not, if they make money or not. While they were in Syria, they could live with just a single-family member's income. They got used to that comfort." (owner of an informal textile atelier for 5 years, male)

However, this view has been critisized by a 17-year-old Syrian employee who argued that;

"We are not lazy but life conditions in Turkey is so tough. I was a high school student in Syria and was not planning to be an employee in such an atelier. War caused this. My father was a textile worker in Aleppo but there they were starting to work around 11 am and finishing late. So, they were still working long hours but conditions were better and they were paid better. Here we try to obey the rules but not easy to be changed so fast. For example, child labor was not common in Syria. Boys were helping their fathers or working in a firm to learn a profession. Here you see many Syrian children working with very low wages. And, everything is according to tight rules. Even cars are parked in an order. Culture is different here."

In addition to concerns related to work performance of Syrians, there were also some considerations about the insecurity or risk of hiring a Syrian refugee. It was sometimes about the lack of registration in Istanbul or concerns about how the survival strategies of Syrian workers handicapping them as they try to decide about their production plan. For example, they complained a lot about low levels of loyalty by refugees as they were argued to change work places often if they are offered slightly higher wages elsewhere. Interestingly, low wages or Syrian refugees hardship living in Istanbul in crowded families were not questioned. Employers had rather positioned themselves as people who made favours to Syrians and gave a 'bread' to them and, therefore expecting loyalty in return of whatever their wages. You can see those feelings clearly from the quote below:

"I don't hire Syrians. Not because they don't do any work but because they quit and go elsewhere the moment they are offered 50 lira more. They are opportunistic. They want higher salaries. For instance, I had a Syrian machine operator and I was paying him 500 lira a week. He was offered 550 elsewhere and he left, letting me down." (owner of the atelier for 16 years, male)

This lack of trust towards Syrian workers created extra roles for the previous or well-performing 'loyal' Syrian workers because they act as job finders for their fellow Syrian friends. Employers are found to prefer hiring new Syrians through already established contacts. Those early workers, irrespective of their ages, have usually better knowledge of Turkish language which also makes them a bridge between employers and Syrian employees. Thus, they at least help solve the problems related with the language at the early periods of employment. These issues are often raised in my interviews and the following quotes might help to understand their role better:

> "I wouldn't hire a Syrian now because it doesn't work out. There were two kids once. I didn't know one of them was Syrian while I was hiring him. He spoke Kurdish well. Then I learned he was Syrian. Later, my Kurdish-speaking staff quit and that Syrian boy was left here. We cannot communicate with him anymore, losing time trying to explain him all the work." (owner of the atelier for 16 years, male)

> "When hiring, we apply standard procedures for Turks like asking for a clean criminal record but we cannot do the same with Syrians. Current Syrians bring fellow Syrians in for a job. So, it's mostly through such recommendations for them." (a 38 years old manager with an experience of almost 15 years in the textile sector, male)

In terms of the substitutability of Syrians in those textile ateliers, many employers argued that they never can be seen as substitutes to the native workers because they always have a concern in their minds about the uncertainties of hiring them. Interestingly, employers did not seem to question their low payments to Syrians or having an efficiency wage to make sure they stay long term in their ateliers. They were rather willing to have them work at the condition that is offered by the employer. If Syrians bargain about their wages, they were even accused of being cunning and, as one interviewee put it, 'learning the rules' in Turkey. Overall, employers were also not sure about long-term stay of Syrians in Turkey and this, as they argued, prevents them from hiring more Syrians in their workforce. In other words, employers I interviewed were not willing to hire Syrian refugees as workers but they were feeling obliged to do it simply because of low labour supply from the native population, as you can also understand from the statement below:

> ""We could have expanded our Syrian workforce to cut salary and thus expenses but it wouldn't be wise to build an only-Syrian workforce since they don't have papers. It's like they may work here for two days and tell us they are going to Germany on the third. Or they would go back home once the war is over. Imagine a statement on an armistice or the end of war coming out, there wouldn't be a single Syrian left here. We would experience a 50% drop in production when every other Syrian goes home in such a scenario. And even if we could replace them with Turks, it would take time to train the newcomers." (owner of an informal textile atelier for 12 years, male)

The Effect of Syrian Refugees on the Wages of Native Workers

In addition to learning more about the hiring process and current problems of those small ateliers, I also wanted to understand how the Syrian influx affected the wages of natives. In that aspect, there were interesting findings. Although the popular belief suggests a negative effect of Syrians on the wages of native employees[12], the labour process in the informal textile sector seem

---

[12] Syrian Barometer 2017 and 2019 show that majority of natives have negative perceptions about the impact of Syrians on the labor market. Moreover, as listed in the Section 1, microeconometric analyses provide evidence of the negative wage effect of Syrians on the low-educated, less-experienced workers who are mainly employed in the informal sector.

to work in a different way. Wages are already low in those informal jobs[13] and there is an obvious lack of labour supply which makes it difficult, if not impossible, to decrease the wages of native workers by employers as they are in need of keeping their already hired workers to be able to finish their daily production on time.

Moreover, I found out that some native employees asked to have higher wages when they see that a Syrian employee starts working next to them with almost the same wage. There were even cases where Turkish employees quit because the employer rejected to give a pay raise to them after recruiting Syrians. These kinds of reactions and demands for a wage increase by native workers put employers in difficult positions, as they argued, in terms of hiring Syrians:

> "Most Syrians are lazy. And since it is like that, Turks began to complain about being paid the same although they are far more productive, asking for pay raises. We were negatively affected as a result." (owner, 5 years of experience, male)

> "It turned out bad that they came. How so? Skilled workers got angry and quit because of them. Why? Once a Syrian comes, you kind of have to hire him to increase production or just hire him because you are sorry for what happened in Syria. You say ok let me give him this much of salary and he would work. Then your current employees start to complain about how much that Syrian is paid although he is not skilled at the job first. I lost 5-6 workers because they got angry like that. Alas, we already gave them pay raise from 1100 to 1300 Turkish lira a month but then the government raised the minimum wage to far above. How could we cope with that?" (owner, 12 years of experience, male)

As it can be understood from the quotations above, salaries paid to native employees were already low and in many cases lower than the minimum wage. Although employers of informal textile ateliers blame Syrians for native's demand of a higher wage, native workers interestingly claimed that their low wage is not because of Syrians but because of employers who do not pay enough. One interviewee even mentioned his sorrow for Syrian workers because, according to him, they are paid so low and cheated by employers. Thus, the interviews with employees showed that, on the one hand, wages of natives did not increase because Syrians were ready to work at lower prices, and this led some natives quit their jobs. And, on the other hand, Syrian employees argued that they are paid lower than their native colleagues and, in some cases, their payments are postponed for months or not paid at all. Not being paid on time causes these workers to stay in those ateliers with a hope to get their payments. Saying this, the accusation of some employers about Syrians unexpectedly changing their workplaces and therefore abruptly crippling their production capacity is questionable.

Moreover, although the employers I interviewed argued that they pay all of their workers according to their experience and performance, and not by their ethnicity, they mentioned that there are aware of the abusive behaviours of some other employers in the sector. Many interviewees, for example, argued that there are textile firms where Syrians are paid very low wages or required to continue working in ateliers although not being paid on time. One employer said:

---

[13] The field research with workers showed that females (whether Syrian or not) are paid always lower compared to males even if they do similar jobs. On the other hand, the wage is usually lower than the legal minimum wage except in cases where the worker has an expertise or experience. Moreover, our field data showed that Syrian male/female workers are paid lower than native men/women..

"I hear stories of employers who hire Syrians for 2-3 months and don't pay them their promised salaries, citing bankruptcy as an excuse." (owner of an atelier since 5 years, male)

Some employers also claimed that labour market conditions of Syrians are changed through gaining more experience and skill in the textile ateliers as if it should not be the case. Syrians are critisized for bargaining over their wages and asking for more. Saying this, it must be noted that the wages offered to Syrians, as observed in the research field, were always lower than their native counterparts. The following quotes are plainly summarising those views of employers:

"Syrians conditionally accept our salary terms. For instance, if we promise them 800 lira a month, they want 900 lira next month. And we do agree to pay raises if their performance gets better. When they first came to Turkey, they were OK with whatever we offered but now they aren't like that. Now they have a self-confidence and experience of having lived here for so long. Because Syrian-seeking firms increased in number, now they think they could find a job elsewhere. Still, the unskilled among them are accepting anything." (owner, 12 years of experience, male)

To sum up, although there were concerns about losing native workforce, increasing level of uncertainties due to employing Syrians and low performance of them, employers had a consensus that there is overall a positive effect of Syrians on their sector because they were able to complete their daily orders thanks to them. However, they have many concerns about the future of their businesses such as lower amount of orders from abroad or low profit margins due to price pressure from the international companies. Those employers who were hiring Syrian workers claimed that employing Syrians was in fact a coping strategy for them in such a business environment as can be seen in the following statement:

"If the Syrians hadn't come, half the ateliers in textiles were closed down and the sector would have been ruined today. So, it was very good for Turkey that they actually did come" (owner, 65 years old, male)

Conclusion

Understanding the labour market effect of Syrian refugees in Turkey is crucial because the popular beliefs about their negative effects both on wages and employment of natives increase tensions in the society. Empirical evidence so far argues that on average Syrians had small but negative employment effects on informal, low-educated and women workers in Turkey. Moreover, those studies suggested that job finding the probability of those groups decreased because of Syrian influx into the country.

This study does not challenge macro-level studies but instead aims to understand the labour process and effects of Syrian refugees in the informal textile ateliers in Istanbul and to see how empirical findings which present 'on-average' findings could be different in various contexts such as industry, informality and neighbourhood of firms. The micro findings can be very different from each other. This study suggests that neighbourhood, sectoral conditions and firm dynamics are all related to the effect of Syrian refugees on the wages and employment of natives.

The testimonies presented in this paper suggest that Syrians did not cause a decrease in the wages of natives, but they, in fact, in some exceptional cases even caused an increase. However, lower wages paid to Syrians resulted in zero or small increases in the wages of natives, and this resulted in quits of native workforce in some cases. Therefore, although employers have argued that Syrian workers have not replaced native workers, lower labour supply of natives for bad working conditions and Syrians' vulnerabilities causing them to accept lower payments caused a higher proportion of Syrians than natives. Therefore, although some employers had concerns about employing Syrians, they seemed to be obliged to hire them due to lack of labour supply from the native population. Syrian workers are eventually argued to have improved the production in those ateliers, and their entrance into the country is rather welcomed by the owners of informal textile ateliers, at least in this regard. It is important to note that employers that are interviewed did not provide any views about improving their work conditions, and they were complaining about the workers who are not willing to work in their ateliers. They somehow internalise these working conditions and argue that these conditions were what they had since their childhood as child workers. Thus, it seems that exploitation of both native and Syrian employees will continue unless inspections for these informal ateliers increase and a voluntary disclosure scheme give them an incentive to formalise and offer better working conditions to employees. Decreasing the level of informality is a very long-term process considering the high level of it in Turkey. Therefore, during the transmission phase, it should also be ensured that employees are paid regularly as promised. This is particularly important for Syrian workers as they do not have any legal institution to ask for their rights since they are employed informally and, in many cases, without a temporary identity card.

Acknowledgements

I would like to thank participants of the Istanbul Policy Center Conference on Migration, Social Transformation and Differential Inclusion in September 2018, seminar participants in the Department of Political Science at Boğaziçi University and two anonymous reviewers for their valuable and constructive comments.

References

Akgündüz, Y., Van Der Berg, M. and Hassink, W. (2015). 'The impact of refugee crises on host labor markets: the case of the Syrian refugee crisis in Turkey'. *IZA Discussion Papers*, No. 8841.

Aksu Kargın, I. (2018). 'An Assessment of the Refugees' Access to Labor and Housing Markets and Healthcare Services in Turkey from Syrian Refugees' Perspective'. *Border Crossing*, 8 (1): 220-236.

Aydemir, A., and Kirdar, M. (2013). 'Quasi-experimental impact estimates of immigrant labor supply shocks: the role of treatment and comparison group matching and relative skill composition'. *European Economic Review*, 98: 282-315.

Baez, J. E. (2011). 'Civil wars beyond their borders: The human capital and health consequences of hosting refugees'. *Journal of Development Economics*, 96(2): 391-408.

Bağır, Y. K. (2018). 'Impact of the Syrian refugee influx on Turkish native workers: An ethnic enclave approach'. *Central Bank Review*, 18(4): 129-147.

Binatli, A. O., and Esen, O. (2016). 'Suriyeli Mültecilerin Bölgesel İşgücü Piyasalarına Etkisi'. In Yildirim, E. (ed.) *Ortadoğudaki Çatışmalar Bağlamında Göç Sorunu*, Efil Yayınevi, pp. 1-11.

Borjas, G. J., Freeman, R. B. and Katz, L. F. (1996). 'Searching for the Effect of Immigration on the Labor Market'. *National Bureau of Economic Research*, No. w5454.

Card, D. (1990). 'The impact of the Mariel boatlift on the Miami labor market'. *ILR Review*, 43(2): 245-257.

Carrington, W. J. and De Lima, P. J. (1996). 'The impact of 1970s repatriates from Africa on the Portuguese labor market'. *ILR Review*, 49(2): 330-347.

Ceritoglu, E., Yunculer, H. B. G., Torun, H. and Tumen, S. (2017). 'The impact of Syrian refugees on natives' labor market outcomes in Turkey: evidence from a quasi-experimental design'. *IZA Journal of Labor Policy*, 6(5).

Cohen-Goldner, S. and Paserman, M. D. (2011). 'The dynamic impact of immigration on natives' labor market outcomes: Evidence from Israel'. *European Economic Review*, 55(8): 1027-1045.

Del Carpio, X. V. and Wagner, M. (2015). 'The impact of Syrians refugees on the Turkish labor market'. *The World Bank Policy Research Working Papers*.

Deniz, C.A., Ekinci, Y. and Hülür, A. B. (2016). *Bizim Müstakbel Hep Harap Oldu: Suriyeli Sığınmacıların Gündelik Hayatı*. Istanbul Bilgi University Press.

Erdoğan, M. M. (2014). *Suriyeliler: Toplumsal Kabul ve Uyum Araştırması*. Hacettepe Universitesi, Göç ve Siyaset Araştırmaları Merkezi Raporu (HUGO).

Erdoğan, M. M. (Ed.). (2017). *Kopuştan Uyuma kent mültecileri: Suriyeli mülteciler ve belediyelerin süreç yönetimi: İstanbul örneği*. Marmara Belediyeler Birliği Kültür Yayınları.

Friedberg, R. M. (2001). 'The impact of mass migration on the Israeli labor market'. *The Quarterly Journal of Economics*, 116(4): 1373-1408.

Glitz, A. (2012). 'The labor market impact of immigration: A quasi-experiment exploiting immigrant location rules in Germany'. *Journal of Labor Economics*, 30(1): 175-213.

Hunt, J. (1992). 'The impact of the 1962 repatriates from Algeria on the French labor market'. *ILR Review*, 45(3): 556-572.

Kayaoglu, A., and Erdogan, M. M. (2019). 'Labor Market Activities of Syrian Refugees in Turkey'. Economic Research Forum Working Papers (No. 1290).

Korkmaz, E. E. (2017). 'How do Syrian refugee workers challenge supply chain management in the Turkish garment industry'. University of Oxford, *International Migration Institute Working Papers 133*.

Koyuncu, A. (2016). 'Nimet mi? Külfet mi? Türkiye'nin Suriyeli Sığınmacıları ve Göç Ekonomisi Üzerine Bir Derkenar'. In Esen, A. and Duman, M. (ed.) *Türkiye'de Geçici Koruma Altındaki Suriyeliler: Tespitler ve Öneriler*. Istanbul: Dünya Yerel Yönetim ve Demokrasi Akademisi Vakfı (WALD) yayınları, pp. 107-130.

Lordoğlu, K., & Aslan, M. (2015). Araştırma - Saha Notları: Beş Sınır Kenti ve İşgücü Piyasalarında Değişim: 2011-2014. *Göç Dergisi*, 2(2), 249-267. https://doi.org/10.33182/gd.v2i2.565

Mansour, H. (2010). 'The effects of labor supply shocks on labor market outcomes: Evidence from the Israeli–Palestinian conflict'. *Labour Economics*, 17(6): 930-939.

Maystadt, J. F. and Verwimp, P. (2014). 'Winners and losers among a refugee-hosting population'. *Economic development and cultural change*, 62(4): 769-809.

Sirkeci, I. (2017). 'Turkey's Refugees, Syrians and refugees from Turkey: a country of insecurity'. Migration Letters, 14(1): 127-144.

Oytun, O. and Gündoğar, S. S. (2015). 'Suriyeli sığınmacıların Türkiye'ye etkileri raporu'. *Orsam-Tesev Raporu*, 195: 1-40.

Ruiz, I. and Vargas-Silva, C. (2015). 'The labor market impacts of forced migration'. *American Economic Review: Papers and Proceedings*, 105(5): 581-86.

Togral-Koca, B. (2015). 'Deconstructing Turkey's "Open Door" Policy towards Refugees from Syria'. Migration Letters, 12(3): 209-25.

Yazgan, P., Utku, D. E. and Sirkeci, I. (2015) 'Syrian Crisis and Migration'. Migration Letters, 12(3): 181-192.

September 2020
Volume: 17, **No**: 5, pp. 597 – 608
ISSN: 1741-8984
e-ISSN: 1741-8992
www.migrationletters.com

MIGRATION
LETTERS

First Submitted: 28 August 2019 Accepted: 28 January 2020
DOI: https://doi.org/10.33182/ml.v17i5.845

Integration Measures within the Reform of the Common European Asylum System: The Unsolved Limbo of Asylum Seekers

Laura García-Juan[1]

Abstract

The European Union has proved to be ineffective in covering the needs of millions of people who seek asylum, while trying to satisfy the security claims of the Member States. The EU institutions have decided to reform the Common European Asylum System to coordinate the procedures, requirements, and conditions for acceptance, aiming to harmonise the national legislative frameworks. One of the most notorious aspects is the extension of the integration measures and conditions to asylum seekers. Nonetheless, the new rules still fail to offer a solution for those asylum requests that are going to be denied after long waiting periods even if the applicants have benefited from the integration programs. In order to avoid such legal implications for the long-term asylum seekers, this article encourages the EU institutions to adopt an ultimate solution, even if a bit creative, that would be coherent with the goals of the CEAS reforms.

Keywords: *CEAS; Dublin System; integration policy; integration measures; European Union.*

Introduction

For the European Union (EU), the governing of migration flows has been the main topic on its agenda and strategic programs for over a decade, which has allowed this issue to reach an advanced stage. On 13 May, 2015, the European Commission issued the European Agenda on Migration, whose introduction coincided with the sharp increase of the number of asylum seekers in the EU (Petracou *et al.*, 2018: 2). This agenda proposed immediate measures for dealing with the crisis in the Mediterranean. All measures have been taken, and will continue to be taken, in the following years to manage all aspects related to migration in a more effective way. With regard to the long and medium terms, the Commission suggested guidelines in four political respects: 1- Reducing the incentives for irregular migration; 2- Border management, which involves saving lives and securing external borders; 3- Europe's duty to protect: a strong common asylum policy; and 4- A new policy on legal migration. These pillars set new priorities for integration policies and optimise the benefits of migration for the people involved as well as for the countries of origin (European Commission, 2015).

The EU has historically been concerned regarding the arrival of immigrants to its territory; however, such concern has grown in the past few years with the massive entrance of mixed flows

[1] Laura García-Juan, PhD in Human Rights, Democracy and International Justice from the Human Rights Institute of the University of Valencia (Spain). Associate Professor and Head of Research of the Faculty of Law and Political Sciences of the Universidad Pontificia Bolivariana, Medellin, Colombia. Email: laura.garciaj@upb.edu.co.

Acknoweldgement: This article is the result of the Research Project "Exploring new paths in comparative migratory law that promote citizen coexistence and democratic values" (Ref. 069C-04/18-37), financed by the Universidad Pontificia Bolivariana and led by the Law Research Group (COL0008924). We appreciate all the support provided by the Integrated Centre for the Development of Research of the UPB.

of immigrants and refugees. The launching of the European Union Global Strategy in June 2016 proves this.[2] However, not only the management of such flows but also the acceptance and accommodation of new arrivals into the European societies have been a challenge and a key aspect in the political agenda of the EU. In 2004, European institutions understood that immigration was not an isolated or temporary phenomenon; instead, it involved a considerable number of immigrants who ended up settling on a permanent basis. Therefore, since then, the immigrants' integration plays an important role in the EU's plans. Such priority was established when the Justice and Home Affairs Council adopted the Common Basic Principles (CBP) in the framework of the Hague Programme,[3] which were reaffirmed by the institution in 2014 (European Commission, 2016a).

One of the premises that justified these principles was the conviction that the success of the immigrants and their descendants' integration in the host society is an essential aspect of the management of migrations, and at the same time, the migration policies may contribute to the success of the integration policy. However, one of the main errors in the formulation of the Community institutions' (Commission, Council, and Parliament) integration policies and instruments was to put aside asylum seekers, refugees, and beneficiaries of subsidiary protection (López, 2007: 240). This situation began to be remedied with Regulation (EU) No 516/2014, which rules the Asylum, Migration and Integration Fund (European Parliament, 2014), which establishes the guidelines with regard to the effective integration of applicants and beneficiaries of international protection and of re-established refugees (García-Juan, 2015: 100).[4]

The EU institutions were able to reinforce the idea that if the immigrants' flow was canalised in an orderly fashion and correctly managed, the Member States would obtain benefits such as the strengthening of their economies, higher social cohesion, an increase in the sense of security, and more cultural diversity. Similarly, the conviction took root that if the beneficiaries are considered as a whole, the European process would improve and that the EU's position in the world would be reinforced (Bendel, 2005: 23). The Council understood that the effective management of migrations by each of the Member States would result be in everyone's interest, bearing in mind that the development and application of the integration policy is a fundamental responsibility of each of the states individually, more than the EU as a group (Sebastiani, 2017: 55). But at the time, the fact that the EU was about to experience an unprecedented crisis regarding refugees and asylum applicants, which is still growing today, was unknown.

The debate regarding the extent and level of Community competences in immigrant integration policies was put on hold with the Treaty of Lisbon as, in the Treaty, the European institutions were conferred an active role in integration but did not assume any specific competence that may

---

[2] In contrast to the Global Strategy for the European Union's Foreign and Security Policy established in 2016 *"Shared Vision, Common Action: A Stronger Europe,"* the migration policy failed to appear within the European Security Strategy in the period 2003–2015 *"A Secure Europe in a Better World."* But thirteen years later, migration is one of the key points of the new global strategy (See European Council, 2016). Far more complete than the previous document and with clearly international hopes, the new strategy understands migrations as a challenge and as an opportunity and acknowledges the key role that migrations play in a scenario where security can change unexpectedly.

[3] The Hague Programme: Strengthening Freedom, Security and Justice in the European Union, Official Journal of the European Union (OJEU) C 53/1, March 3, 2005.

[4] As I am writing this article (August 2019), the European Commission is accepting applications for funding through the Asylum, Migration and Integration Fund to support the integration of third-country nationals. A total of €21.5 million is available through the various calls for proposals.

anticipate a communitarization.[5] This way, as the harmonisation regarding these matters on the 28 internal legal systems is excluded, each state was granted the liberty to rule according to its own decisions, which spawned a diversity of models and approaches. This Treaty refers to promote "the integration of third-country nationals residing legally in their territories", but do not say a word about asylum seekers integration measures or policies.

The reforms set forth in the Common European Asylum System (hereinafter CEAS) pay significant attention to integration as well as the extension of the integration measures to the asylum seekers. This approach is something new that is worth to put the focus on. The first part of this paper offers an overview of the CEAS and the Dublin System. The second part revises the principal reforms, which are currently being negotiated among the European institutions, incisively analysing those affecting integration. The third part focuses on a particular aspect of the CEAS reform: measures and requirements for integration of asylum seekers.

The Common European Asylum System in the context of the refugee crisis

The growing and intense migration influx into Europe in the past few years has made refugees, asylum seekers, and international immigrants to become one of the central issues of current political debate (Tocci, 2017: 491). The pressure on Dublin's system and the increasing, incoherent plans suggested in relation to migration are emphasising the need, among the Member States, to revisit the role of European institutions in the handling of this political subject. In fact, some states have accused the European Commission, the Parliament, and the Council of imposing regulations that have a negative effect upon them. However, at the same time, the EU claims that countries such as Italy and Greece are not complying with the existing rules. The solidarity between states has been rather scarce, and flagrant violations of human rights have been documented. Such situations have led to a series of questions with regard to the rules and ethics that apply to handling of migration Ceccorulli & Lucarelli, 2017: 96).

The countries that constitute the EU have their own national legislations that apply the common framework in very different ways. These divergences have, in the past few years, spawned increasing tension between the countries that defend the free movement of people within the EU and those that demand stricter controls at international borders, thus showing themselves as weak, disorganised, and fragmented before public opinion and the international community, which is something they were not used to (Chaban & Elgström, 2014: 174).

To avoid possible disagreements or inconsistencies in the use and meaning of the terms, this article shall employ the word "immigrant" as a means of representing the person who has voluntarily abandoned their home to seek a job and a better life in another country for their own and their family's welfare. This includes those who cross international borders because it is their own decision, with legally issued permits or visas or without them. In this sense, the term "regular immigrants" (legal ones or those who migrated under regular administrative conditions) stands for both the former ones and for those who remain in the host country with all authorisations in order. "Irregular immigrants" (illegal ones or those who migrated under irregular administrative conditions) shall include those in the second group and those who have decided to remain in the

---

[5] Article 79 of the consolidated version of the TFUE, in point 4 states: "The European Parliament and the Council, acting in accordance with the ordinary legislative procedure, may establish measures to provide incentives and support for the action of Member States with a view to promoting the integration of third-country nationals residing legally in their territories, excluding any harmonisation of the laws and regulations of the Member States." (OJEU C 83, 03/30/10).

host country even though they do not have the required authorisations in order.[6] In both cases, these definitions shall exclude those who move around the country with such intents and purposes but whose nationality is that of a EU Member State as these are considered to be citizens of the EU and thus entitled to free movement.

Within the CEAS framework, the term refugee shall encompass people fleeing from wars, prosecution, or natural disasters to save their lives (because of necessity, not voluntarily). Although the United Nations Convention on the 1951 Refugee Law includes a restricted definition of the term, it is interpreted here in a broader sense than it is in other international agreements such as the 1969 OAU Convention Governing the Specific Aspects of Refugee Problems in Africa and the 1984 Cartagena Declaration on Refugees. Along these lines, an asylum seeker is a refugee who has initiated the administrative proceedings to be granted the right of asylum. If the authorities finally acknowledge that right, the petitioner shall legally acquire refugee status.

These points having been made, it is worth remembering that never before have the EU's migration policies been subject to such levels of criticism nor have they raised such a debate not only within the institutions and the Member States but also within the international community. The incompatibility of the so-called "Fortress Europe", together with the self-proclaimed goal of contributing to a fairer world, creates a gap between what the EU does and what it wishes to represent (Cortés, 2013: 112). Moreover, regulating migration flows and their consequences represents a particularly serious challenge for this supranational entity. The migration responsibility is shared between the EU and its Member States, but the efforts for agreeing on common policies have become highly polemical because of the different ways in which countries apply the European regulations (Lucarelli, 2014: 4).

This research is focused on a relatively new aspect of the CEAS: the importance of the integration of the asylum applicants and international protection beneficiaries as understood in the CEAS reform. When the 2004 Basic Common Principles of Integration were established, they all made reference to immigrants who were legal residents and none referred to refugees, asylum seekers, or beneficiaries of any kind of international protection (Illamola, 2011: 162). Because of this, the extended integration treatment is surprising. In that year, integration was defined as a "dynamic, two-way process of mutual accommodation by all immigrants and residents of Member States". The 6th principle proclaims that "Access for immigrants to institutions, as well as to public and private goods and services, on a basis equal to national citizens and in a non-discriminatory way is a critical foundation for better integration" (European Commission, 2005). However, the formal declaration of these principles has still not solved the matters related to the effective and careful assessment of individual cases, which is an essential aspect of the right to asylum.

What happens in a daily basis is that the receiving country tags incomers as refugees, economic immigrants, regular or irregular immigrants, asylum seekers, and so on and applies certain prior selection criteria, such as nationality and country of origin. From this tag or category, migrants are

---

[6] Although the term has been broadly criticized by several fields for not being legally acknowledged, these migrants shall also be referred to with the expression "economic migrants" as this is a term generally used by the specialized doctrine and by the EU institutions and other international organizations. See McDowell, L. (2009). The Manual on the Criteria for Determining the Refugee Status by virtue of the 1951 Convention and the 1967 Protocol on the Refugee Law, enacted in 1992 by the United Nations High Commissioner for Human Rights, contains the following definition: "Migrants are people who, for different reasons included in the Convention, voluntarily abandon their country in order to settle somewhere else'. They may be motivated by the desire of making a change or embarking on an adventure, for family reasons or personal matters. If exclusively motivated by economic matters, it shall be referred to as an economic migrant and not a refugee. However, the distinction between economic migrants and refugees is sometimes confusing..." (paragraphs 62 and 63).

forced to take different administrative paths that lead them to different situations, depending on the group under which they have been classified. For example, if someone who considers themselves to be a refugee or has been *a priori* classified as such initiates asylum proceedings, they shall, from that moment onward, be subject to the EU's asylum and refugee rules until the petition is granted (Moldovan, 2018: 83). Moreover, if an economic migrant requests a residence permit, their administrative situation will be completely different and they shall be subject to the immigration laws of the country where the proceedings have been initiated. Once the process has begun, the former shall be protected by the *non-refoulement* principle, but the latter shall not. In principle, they are both "condemned" to follow the path of the blanks that they filled in when completing the form, without having any correspondence with the detailed and effective analysis of each specific case, which is what lends sense to the creation of the refuge (Menéndez, 2016).

Once the refugee status or immigrant status as a legal resident is acquired, the country that has granted the relevant permit starts to consider another aspect: integration. As previously said, integration policies are a matter, the approach and development of which correspond entirely to the EU Member States, with the applicable Community Directives being limited to suggest (without imposing) certain strategies or solutions. Here we shall center upon the treatment given to integration in the CEAS with regard to asylum seekers, although some references shall be made to the concept in relation to legal residents.

The reform of the Common European Asylum System with regard to integration

Focusing on the foundations of the complete integration policy of the EU by far exceeds the aim of this paper. Nonetheless, it is worth mentioning that the "integration" concept was formulated to deal with the peculiarities and identities of immigrants and refugees with the purpose of facilitating their inclusion in the education systems of the Member States and making feasible their access to the labour market (Joppke, 2007).

The integration of immigrants and refugees, its regulations, and the creation of related public policies, including those issued by European institutions and the Member States themselves, is another aspect of migrations' governance that has been heavily criticised in Europe. Once again, we are apparently facing the dilemma between what is being said and what is actually being done (Acosta, 2012: 158). In different forums, the instrumentalism of the so-called "integration measures and conditions" has been censured, and its misuse for dubious immigration selection plans has been condemned (Groenendijk, 2004: 117). In this section, we study the evolution of this key aspect in the CEAS and the treatment given by the proposed reforms to the integration measures and conditions that apply to applicants and beneficiaries of international protection in the envisaged reform.

The CEAS is a set of EU rules developed between 2011 and 2013 that establish the common procedures to deal with international protection applications and to receive and resettle refugees and asylum seekers. However, since this system is governed by Directives rather than Regulations, the 28 states have produced protocols and regulatory provisions that differ significantly from one state to the other as they opted to follow the recommendations of European institutions in an unequal manner (Chetail, 2016a: 24). Not determining that refugees have the legal duty to seek asylum in the first Member State they arrive at is one of the CEAS's main problems. Consequently, many refugees try to reach other places, where they have relatives or friends who may receive them. Nevertheless, the so-called Dublin system states that Member States may send asylum seekers back to the country through which they entered the EU as long as the said country has an efficient asylum regime (Weber, 2016: 37). Here we find an inconsistency that the reform addresses in an unsuccessful way (Chetail, 2016b: 594).

The migration and refugee crisis suffered by most EU countries has revealed the need to review the legal reforms introduced in the CEAS during those years. Although one of the main purposes of the said modifications was to achieve further harmonisation regarding procedures and requirements, the practice has demonstrated that considerable differences, which are still difficult to unify, continue to exist.[7] The main consequence is that the "secondary movements" of refugees and *asylum shopping* are usual practices, both of refugees and asylum seekers, which still hinder the efficient and organised management of international protection applications (Thielemann & Armstrong, 2013: 159).

In 2016, the European Commission encouraged a series of reforms, the objective of which is to harmonise the asylum procedures in all Member States by establishing common agreements to address the unequal implementation of the CEAS and the problems pertaining to the Dublin system. The ultimate goal is to offer a law not only suitable to any third-country national who needs international protection but also to ensure the fulfilment of the principle of *non-refoulement*. The whole system proceeds on the basis of articles 67.2 and 78 of the Treaty on the Functioning of the European Union, as well as Article 18 of the Charter of Fundamental Rights of the EU. Neither of these two legal instruments provides a definition for the words "asylum" or "refugee," referring, in both cases, to the 1951 Geneva Convention and its 1967 Protocol (Rossi, 2017: 53).

European institutions are conducting negotiations to make the said reforms. On 6 April, 2016, in Brussels, the European Commission presented the Communication entitled "Towards a Reform of the Common European Asylum System and Enhancing Legal Avenues to Europe" (European Commission, 2016b). The proposed priorities are five, namely, 1- Establishing a sustainable and fair system for determining the Member State responsible for asylum seekers; 2- Reinforcing the EURODAC system; 3-Further harmonising the CEAS rules to ensure more equal treatment across the EU and reduce unjustified pull factors; 4-Preventing secondary movements within the EU to ensure the functioning of the Dublin mechanism; and 5-Transforming the European Asylum Support Office into the EU's asylum Agency. Three months later, on 13 July, 2016, the Commission presented the second package of reforms consisting of a Directive proposal and two Regulation proposals, the objective of which is to reinforce the priority mentioned in the third place, that is, further harmonising the system rules to ensure a more equal treatment across the EU.[8] Nowadays, the negotiations are still ongoing. However, they are in a dead end in view of the last report issued by the Presidency of the Council of Europe addressed to the Permanent Representatives Committee, dated February 26, 2019.[9]

---

[7] Even though the CEAS is one of the most protective asylum systems in the world, it is characterized by the Member States' difference in treatment regarding asylum seekers and asylum applications per se. Some of these differences comprise the terms for administrative proceedings, reception conditions, term of duration of the residence permits granted, and unequal access to integration programs. See Schittenhelm, K. (2019).

[8] The three texts under discussion are: 1- Proposal for a Directive of the European Parliament and of the Council laying down standards for the reception of applicants for international protection [COM(2016) 465 final]; 2- Proposal for a Regulation of the European Parliament and of the Council on standards for the qualification of third-country nationals or stateless persons as beneficiaries of international protection, for a uniform status for refugees or for persons eligible for subsidiary protection and for the content of the protection granted and amending Council Directive 2003/109/EC of 25 November 2003 concerning the status of third-country nationals who are long-term residents [COM(2016) 466 final]; 3- Proposal for a Regulation of the European Parliament and of the Council establishing a common procedure for international protection in the Union and repealing Directive 2013/32/EU [COM(2016) 467 final].

[9] Council of the European Union (JAI). Note from Presidency to Permanent Representatives Committee/Council [Document ST_6600_2019_INIT]. Brussels, 26 February 2019.

With that second package, the Commission would have completed the reform of the CEAS by adopting three new proposals: a) replacing the asylum procedures Directive with a Regulation, harmonising the current disparate procedural requirements in all Member States, and creating a genuine common procedure; b) replacing the asylum requirements Directive with a Regulation and setting uniform standards for the recognition of people in need of protection and the rights granted to beneficiaries of international protection; c) revising the previous Reception Conditions Directive with another Directive to further harmonise reception conditions in the EU, increase applicants' integration prospects, and decrease secondary movements.

By means of an accelerated examination procedure (fast-track), these reforms propose the dismissal of asylum applications of those who are not expected to be recognised as beneficiaries of international protection, for it is highly likely that they would be considered unfounded. This category includes, among other cases, those whose country of origin has been classified as "safe" by the EU[10] and also when there is existing reasonable grounds to believe that a third country is safe for the applicant. This means that an application may be dismissed when the determining authority establishes that "there is a connection between the applicant and the third country in question on the basis of which it would be reasonable for that person to go to that country, including because the applicant has transited through that third country which is geographically close to the country of origin of the applicant," and when "the applicant has not submitted serious grounds for considering the country not to be a safe third country in his or her particular circumstances".[11]

In other words, asylum applications submitted by Albanians, Bosnians, Macedonians, Kosovars, Montenegrins, Serbians, and Turks may be dismissed by means of accelerated procedures, as well as applications submitted by nationals of other countries who have crossed a safe country on their way to the EU and cannot prove that staying in such country did not jeopardise their life or physical integrity. According to the foregoing, if the reform of the CEAS is passed in its current wording, the sense of the right to asylum itself in the European Union would lack meaning.

Pursuant to the literalness of the proposed regulations, an individual's nationality or the accidental circumstance of choosing one route instead of another on their way to the EU will define the result of their application in advance. Clearly, this is not in line with the detailed and meticulous assessment of each concrete case and personal circumstances, which constitutes the very basis of the right to asylum. In this scenario, it is possible to foresee that the hopes of millions of refugees and asylum seekers of being granted refugee status in Europe will end up completely shattered. In spite of this, we must also consider those people whose applications are regulated by the CEAS currently in force. What happens with the people who are official asylum applicants and have not yet received a reply by the competent authority? They have been authorised to remain in the country of the EU that is dealing with their application but in what conditions are they living? Can adults

---

[10] International law and the EU legislation on asylum procedure consider that a country is safe when it has a democratic system and when, generally and consistently, no persecution, punishment, torture, inhuman or degrading treatment, violence threat, or armed conflicts exist. There are still 12 EU Member States (Austria, Belgium, Bulgaria, Czech Republic, Germany, France, Ireland, Luxemburg, Latvia, Malta, Slovakia and United Kingdom) that have their own lists of safe countries. Nevertheless, the EU is suggesting that a unique list be used, according to which, all Member States should apply the same criteria. European institutions have estimated that 17% of the total number of asylum applications submitted before the EU derives from citizens of the 7 countries included in this unique list (Albania, Bosnia and Herzegovina, Republic of Macedonia, Kosovo, Montenegro, Serbia, and Turkey). Furthermore, it is proposed that the applications of nationals of "safe" countries be assessed through a fast-track procedure to unblock the system and expedite the decisions of grounded applications.

[11] See article 45.3 COM(2016) 467 final "The concept of safe third country".

work legally in the labour market? Do children have access to regular education systems? Did they have access to the reception and integration programs offered by the different public administrations and other private entities?

These asylum seekers are in an uncertain life situation, in a legal limbo, without receiving an answer from the CEAS. In the following paragraphs, we go through the way in which integration measures and conditions have been addressed in the reforms that are currently subject to negotiation in the EU's main institutions.

Integration measures and requirements

Although both terms are used indistinctively in the different translations on Community rules, here the expression "integration requirements" will be used to refer to specific *compulsory* requirements that the Member States may demand (before leaving the country of origin or upon arrival) of the relatives with whom reunification has been sought. They also refer to the *compulsory* requirements that may be stipulated to renew the temporary residence permit or to acquire a permanent one (called "long-term residence permit") in order to acquire the nationality of the country of residence or to retain the benefit of the material conditions for its acceptance. Here the term "integration measures" will be used when referring to agreements, programs, circuits, or devices in which migrants *voluntarily* participate (involving economic immigrants, refugees, asylum applicants, and beneficiaries of subsidiary protection) to access specific rights.

Such integration measures and requirements comprise courses, tests, and other kinds of examinations in which the level of mastery over the language of the host community is assessed, as well as knowledge regarding regulations, history, costume, and principles of the Member State to which the application is filed regardless of the purpose. In some European countries, these are called cultural integration courses (Van Niejenhuis, Ottenb & Flachea, 2018).

The main normative instruments of the EU that refers to the integration measures and requirements are as follows: the Council Directive on the right to family reunification[12] and the Council Directive concerning the status of third-country nationals who are long-term residents.[13] The scope of application of the former comprises both the resident legal immigrants as well as beneficiaries of refugee status, although in this second scenario the regulation fails to allow the imposition of integration conditions prior to departure. The second directive is applied to resident legal immigrants in any of the 28 Member States of the EU but not to the applicants or beneficiaries of international protection.

From the analysis of the CEAS regulation and the reforms planned, the following inferences can be made. The Directives still in force are limited with regard to integration, considering other special needs and the particular challenges of integration to which the beneficiaries of international protection are faced with to be guaranteed the effective exercise of their rights and benefits. Likewise, it is requested that such individuals be considered in the integration programs that the beneficiaries are assigned to. However, the said Community rules fail to allude to the integration measures and requirements. While Directives 2013/32/EU and 2013/33/EU fail to mention such

---

[12] Council Directive 2003/86/EC of 22 September 2003 on the right to family reunification (OJEU October 3, 2003).
[13] Council Directive 2003/109/EC of 25 November 2003 concerning the status of third-country nationals who are long-term residents (OJEU January 23, 2004).

issue,[14] Directive 2011/95/EU simply establishes that Member States have to guarantee their international protection beneficiaries access to integration programs that they consider fit considering the specific needs but leaving out total freedom with regard to its structure. Besides, the said access is limited to those who are already beneficiaries of the refugee or subsidiary protection status.[15]

Unlike these Directives, in the reformed texts of 2016, the integration of international protection beneficiaries is a key and crosscutting issue in the entire regulation. Accordingly, such reforms would amend what was pointed out above regarding the historical omission of this group in the Community acquis with regard to integration, as well as to the minor importance given to integration in the European Community law enforced regarding asylum and refuge (Kancs and Lecca, 2018: 2601). The texts being discussed deal with "effective integration and participation of all, refugees or legal migrants".[16] Referring to the said integration as being inclusive is relatively new for the EU, since, as stated in the introduction, in 2014, the Regulation on the Asylum, Migration and Integration Fund achieved it for the first time (García-Juan, 2015: 134).

The expected reforms emphasise the need of increasing the applicants' integration perspectives not only for those already having refugee status or subsidiary protection but also for those cases where there is a possibility of applications being accepted. To achieve this, it is suggested that the asylum applicants be able to work and obtain their own income as soon as possible (between three and six months from the application's initial filling) even while their applications are being processed. Also, compulsory integration measures are mentioned for the first time, the nonfulfillment of which may lead to benefit substitution, reduction, or withdrawal of the material reception conditions.

The proposal establishing the requirements for the acknowledgment of international protection considers it to be essential for Member States to promote the integration of its beneficiaries into their societies. It states the scale and scope of the rights and obligations and offers incentives for its active integration but at the same time allows the 28 members (soon to be 27) to grant some kind of social assistance with the condition of effective participation of these beneficiaries in the integration measures in accordance with the Action Plan on the integration of third country nationals (European Commission, 2016c). Nevertheless, when dealing with integration, this document refers exclusively to immigrants and refugees from third countries who are legally residing in the EU.[17]

The 2016 Action Plan encourages the enforcement of integration measures prior to departure to prepare the resettlement of refugees in order to comply with the European Commission suggestions related to resettlement programs (Caponio, 2018: 2059). The argument employed is that providing support to people from third countries as soon as possible in their migration process has

[14] Respectively: Directive 2013/32/EU of the European Parliament and of the Council, of 26 June 2013, on common procedures for granting and withdrawing international protection; and Directive 2013/33/EU of the European Parliament and of the Council, of 26 June 2013, laying down standards for the reception of applicants for international protection.

[15] See article 34 of the Directive 2011/95/EU of the European Parliament and of the Council, of 13 December 2011, on standards for the qualification of third-country nationals or stateless persons as beneficiaries of international protection, for a uniform status for refugees or for persons eligible for subsidiary protection, and for the content of the protection granted.

[16] It is likely that the New York Declaration for Refugee and Migrants, signed by 193 Member States of the United Nations on September 19, 2016, is the reason of such specific reform. By means of this declaratory document, the signatory countries assumed the commitment of sharing in a more equal way the responsibility for the refugees of the world by means of the application of the Comprehensive Refugee Response Framework. One of its aims is to improve the self-reliance and integration of refugees with measures encouraging access to education and work.

[17] Integration measures may be language classes, civil integration courses, professional formation courses, and similar courses related to employment.

contributed to successful integration.[18] As stated above, this 2016 Plan was more restrictive in terms of the scope of integration programs than the SECA reform texts handled in Brussels.

Another new and relevant aspect of the CEAS reform is the possibility for those who were given refugee status or subsidiary protection but, for whatever reason, no longer enjoy this status, to have three months to request another legal status, for example, regular resident immigrant for working reasons. It is important to highlight that such a possibility is only offered to those who at some time benefited from international protection, but it does not include those who were asylum seekers or who were "labeled" refugees from the start but never had a favourable decision on their file. What is true is that the economic impact of alternative refugee integration policies in the EU still is unknown (Kancs and Lecca, 2018: 2628).

Conclusion

The treatment given to integration in the CEAS reform that is pending in the EU's institutions has evolved in two directions. The first one is positive in that the implementation of policies and integration instruments has been extended to cover asylum seekers whose files are pending when, according to the regulations in force, this is limited to those who already are international protection beneficiaries. The second one is negative as the very basis of the right to asylum are being put at risk by making the mere possibility of requesting for it conditioned on factors such as nationality or the path selected to reach EU countries. Furthermore, the possibility of obligatorily applying integration measures and requirements to the beneficiaries of international protection is real for the first time. Moreover, these are conditions that must be met to obtain certain reception and assistance benefits.

Nonetheless, the reforms do not offer an ultimate solution to asylum applicants in a legal limbo either, that is, for those with a pending application either because they are not in the country where the right to asylum was enforced or because the outcome of the application is unknown. What will happen to those participants in the integration programs for asylum seekers that finally will receive a rejection resolution on their application? How much money and institutional effort will be wasted on these cases? No specific mechanism has been foreseen for solving the problem of millions of people wandering EU territory without a defined legal statute, without the possibility of working under legal terms, and without a clear idea of what their rights and duties are.

The applicability of integration policies aimed at asylum applicants as it has been established within the CEAS reforms exceeds the limits established by the current Community regulations, which restrict the concept to mean third-country nationals who are legal residents and beneficiaries of some kind of international protection. Hence, the very moment of being a bit creative is now. The proposal is that the CEAS reforms include at least a mechanism that allows long-term asylum seekers to change their migrant status to that of immigrants for working reasons so that they can request a working residence permit as long as they meet certain integration requirements. The EU cannot waste a minute.

---

[18] The CEAS reform establishes certain limits for the application of compulsory integration measures for international protection beneficiaries in the individual cases of excessive difficulties, which is the result of the Judgment of the Court (Second Chamber) of 4 June 2015, Case C-579/13.

References

Acosta, D. (2012). "En Attendant Godot or the EU Law Limits to Integration Conditions". In: Y. Pascouau and T. Strik (eds.) *Which Integration Policies for Migrants? Interaction between the EU and its Member States*, Nijmegen: Wolf legal Publishers.

Bendel, P. (2005). "Immigration Policy in the European Union: Still bringing up the walls for fortress Europe?". *Migration Letters*, 2 (1): 20-31. https://doi.org/10.33182/ml.v2i1.18

Caponio, T. (2018). "Immigrant integration beyond national policies? Italian cities' participation in European city networks". *Journal of Ethnic and Migration Studies*, 44 (12): 2053-2069. https://doi.org/10.1080/1369183X.2017.1341711

Ceccorulli, M. and Lucarelli, S. (2017). "Migration and the EU Global Strategy: Narratives and Dilemmas". *The International Spectator,* 52 (3): 83-102. https://doi.org/10.1080/03932729.2017.1332850

Cortés, F. (2013). "La posibilidad de la justicia global. Sobre los límites de la concepción estadocéntrica y las probabilidades de un cosmopolitismo débil". *Revista de Estudios Sociales,* 46: 109-118. https://doi.org/10.7440/res46.2013.11

Chaban, N. and Elgström, O. (2014). "The Role of the EU in an Emerging New World Order in the Eyes of Chinese, Indian and Russian Press". *Journal of European Integration,* 36 (2): 152-169. https://doi.org/10.1080/07036337.2013.841679

Chetail, V. (2016a). "The Common European Asylum System: Bric-à-brac or System?". In: V. Chetail, P. De Bruycker and F. Maiani (eds.) *Reforming the Common European Asylum System. The New European Refugee Law*, Leiden: Brill. https://doi.org/10.1163/9789004308664

Chetail, V. (2016b). "Looking Beyond the Rhetoric of the Refugee Crisis: The Failed Reform of the Common European Asylum System". *European Journal of Human Rights*, 28 (5): 583-602.

European Commission. (2016a). Communication from the Commission to the European Parliament, the Council, the European Economic and Social Committee and the Committee of The Regions 'Action Plan on the integration of third country nationals' [COM(2016) 377 final, page 2].

European Commission. (2016b). Communication from the Commission to the European Parliament and the Council "Towards a Reform of the Common European Asylum System and Enhancing Legal Avenues to Europe" [COM(2016) 197 final].

European Commission. (2016c). Communication from the Commission to the European Parliament, the Council, the European Economic and Social Committee and the Committee of the Regions— *Action Plan on the integration of third country nationals* [COM(2016) 377 final].

European Commission. (2015). Communication from the Commission to the European Parliament, the Council, the European Economic and Social Committee and the Committee of the Regions: 'A European Agenda on Migration' [COM(2015) 240 final].

European Commission. (2005). Communication from the Commission to the Council, the European Parliament, the European Economic and Social committee and the Committee of the Regions —A Common Agenda for Integration— Framework for the Integration of Third-Country Nationals in the European Union [COM (2005) 389 final–not published in the official journal].

European Parliament. (2014). Regulation (EU) No. 516/2014 of the European Parliament and of the Council, of 16 April 2014, establishing the Asylum, Migration and Integration Fund, amending Council Decision 2008/381/EC and repealing Decisions No. 573/2007/EC and No. 575/2007/EC of the European Parliament and of the Council and Council Decision 2007/435/EC.

Fassi, E. and Lucarelli, S. (2017). *The European Migration System and Global Justice: A First Appraisal*. GLOBUS Report /1 ARENA Report 2/17. http://www.globus.uio.no/publications/reports/2017/2017-01-report-migration.html (accessed 17 July 2019).

García-Juan, L. (2015). "Medidas y condiciones de integración de inmigrantes: una propuesta europea difícil de articular en España". *Migraciones,* 38: 87-110. https://doi.org/10.14422/mig.i38.y2015.004

Groenendijk, K. (2004). "Legal Concepts of Integration in EU Migration Law". *European Journal of Migration and Law,* 6 (2): 111-126. https://doi.org/10.1163/1571816042885969

Illamola, M. (2011). "Los Principios Básicos Comunes como marco de la política de integración de inmigrantes de la Unión Europea y su incorporación en la política española de inmigración". *Revista de Derecho Comunitario Europeo,* 38: 155-182.

Joppke, C. (2007). "Beyond national models: Civic integration policies for immigrants in Western Europe". *West European Politics,* 30 (1): 1-22. https://doi.org/10.1080/01402380601019613

Kancs, D. and Lecca, P. (2018). "Long-term social, economic and fiscal effects of immigration into the EU: The role of the integration policy". *World Economy*, 41 (10): 2599-2630. http://doi.org/10.1111/twec.12637

López-Pich, P. (2007). "La política de integración de la Unión Europea". *Migraciones,* 22: 221-256.

Lucarelli, S. (2014). "Seen from the Outside: The State of the Art on the External Image of the EU". *Journal of European Integration,* 36 (1): 1-16. https://doi.org/10.1080/07036337.2012.761981

McDowell, L. (2009). "Old and New European Economic Migrants: Whiteness and Managed Migration Policies". *Journal of Ethnic and Migration Studies*, 35 (1): 19-36. https://doi.org/10.1080/13691830802488988

Menéndez, A. (2016). The refugee crisis: between human tragedy and symptom of the structural crisis of European integration. Conference at the University of Bologna, Political Science Department. Bologna: 6 December 2016.

Moldovan, R. (2018). "Towards a common European Union immigration policy: Navigating a difficult obstacle course". *Online Journal Modelling the New Europe,* 28: 74-104. http://doi.org/10.24193/OJMNE.2018.28.05

Petracou, E. V., Domazakis, G. N., Papayiannis, G. I. and Yannacopoulos, A. N. (2018). "Towards a common European space for asylum. *Sustainability*, 10: 1-17. http://doi.org/10.3390/su10092961

Rossi, E. (2017). "Superseding Dublin: The European asylum system as a non-cooperative game. *International Review of Law and Economics,* 51: 50-59. https://doi.org/10.1016/j.irle.2017.06.003

Schittenhelm, K. (2019). "Implementing and Rethinking the European Union's Asylum Legislation: The Asylum Procedures Directive". *International Migration*, 57 (1): 229-244. http://doi.org/10.1111/imig.12533

Sebastiani, L. (2017). "¿Para quién y para qué son buenas las buenas prácticas? Unión Europea, integración de (in)migrantes y despolitización/tecnificación de las políticas hegemónicas: un estudio de caso". *EMPIRIA. Revista de Metodología de las Ciencias Sociales,* 36: 39-62. https://doi.org/10.5944/empiria.36.2017.17858

Thielemann, E. and Armstrong, C. (2013). "Understanding European Asylum cooperation under the Schengen/Dublin system: a public goods framework". *European Security,* 22 (2): 148-164. https://doi.org/10.1080/09662839.2012.699892

Tocci, N. (2017). "From the European Security Strategy to the EU Global Strategy: Explaining the Journey". *International Politics,* 54 (4): 487-502. https://doi.org/10.1057/s41311-017-0045-9

Van Niejenhuis, C., Ottenb, S. and Flachea, A. (2018). "Sojourners' second language learning and integration. The moderating effect of multicultural personality traits". *International Journal of Intercultural Relations*, 63: 68-79. https://doi.org/10.1016/j.ijintrel.2018.01.001

Weber, F. (2016). "Labour Market Access for Asylum Seekers and Refugees under the Common European Asylum System". European Journal of Migration and Law 18 (1): 34-64. https://doi.org/10.1163/15718166-12342089.

September 2020
Volume: 17, **No**: 5, pp. 609 – 620
ISSN: 1741-8984
e-ISSN: 1741-8992
www.migrationletters.com

MIGRATION
LETTERS

First Submitted: 3 April 2020 Accepted: 6 May 2020
DOI: https://doi.org/10.33182/ml.v17i5.949

Hukou System, Horizontal, Vertical, and Full Job-Education Mismatch and Wage Progression among College Graduates in Beijing, China

Donghong Xie[1]

Abstract

This article investigates college graduates in Beijing, China, and asks, First: Whether college graduates without local hukou are prone to educational mismatch? Second: What role does the hukou system play in the educational mismatch? And third: Whether college graduates without local hukou are willing to lower their wages in order to get a hukou? I use the Beijing College Students Panel Survey (BCSPS), and multinomial logit models and the linear regression analyses are conducted. I find that college graduates with (without) local hukou through job are more likely to be vertical and full mismatch than locals, and those who obtain a hukou through job have a higher full mismatch. After considering the educational mismatch, there is no significant difference in monthly wages between college graduates (not) having a hukou by work and locals.

Keywords: *college graduates; educational mismatch; wage; Beijing; China*

Introduction

As one of the most important redistributive institutions, the household registration (*hukou*) system has received much attention from all sectors of society in China (Cheng and Selden,1994). The *hukou* system required all Chinese households to be registered in the locale where they resided and categorized as either agricultural or non-agricultural (rural or urban) status (Wu,2019). Transforming one's *hukou* status from rural to urban is a central aspect of upward social mobility (Wu and Treiman,2004).

With the implementation of the household contract responsibility system, rural areas release a large number of surplus labourers. At the same time, with the reform of urban and rural economic system, non-agricultural industries develop rapidly, creating a large number of employment opportunities. Under the combined effect of push and pull, numbers of floating population, leaving inland villages to pursue economic opportunities in coastal cities, continue to increase and the scale expands rapidly. However, *hukou* registration status plays an important role in affecting not only rural floating population return on human capital but also their offsprings' educational opportunities (Chan and Buckingham, 2008; Cheng and Selden, 1994; Wu et al., 2015; Wu and Zhang, 2018; Wu, 2019).

The household registration system is the main reason for the different status treatment in the labour market. Due to the heterogeneity of household registration, local people and outsiders are treated unequally. Through education, workers gain knowledge and skills, and more education means more human capital and high labour productivity. In order to reduce the losses caused by

---

[1] Donghong Xie, School of Sociology and Population Studies, Renmin University of China, Beijing, China, 100872. Email: xiedonghong@ruc.edu.cn.

household registration discrimination, outsiders without local *hukou* may invest more in education to improve their competitiveness in employment, which may distort the human capital return mechanism of workers, especially in megacities like Beijing, Shanghai and Shenzhen. *Hukou* in these cities is related to a lot of social welfare and public resources, such as children's schooling, college entrance examination, housing, social security, etc. Therefore, college graduates without local *hukou* may work in jobs unrelated to their educational background and/or below their skill level and accept low wages to get a *hukou* in megacities, creating the much-discussed job-education mismatch.

The present study adds to the literature by looking into the well-known *hukou* advantages through the lens of job-education mismatch, proposing and testing two models. First, I examine the likelihood of job-education mismatch for college graduate with a local *hukou* and without a local *hukou* compared to natives. Second, I explore the relationship between job-education mismatch and wages, testing whether this relationship differs by *hukou*. This study is among the first to distinguish between vertical mismatch (overeducation), horizontal mismatch (relatedness between educational field and job), and full mismatch (both horizontal and vertical mismatch), explore the important role of *hukou* in educational mismatch, and examine their effects on wages.

The distinction between different types of mismatch is important since each represents different (albeit related) aspects of labour market disadvantage and therefore has unique policy implications. Some highly skilled college graduates, for example, may work in their field but at a lower level than their education would otherwise predict. Others may work unrelated to their field of study, forcing them to change occupations altogether. Both possibilities have distorted the return on human capital. The conclusions in this article provide a better understanding of how the various types of job-education mismatch affect college labour market integration.

Vertical and Horizontal Job-Education Mismatch

The existence of a potential discrepancy between educational attainment and the"skills" actually used at their jobs has been a major concern for social scientists and economists since the 1970s. A large body of literature highlights the implications of the gaps and its measurement (Banerjee et al., 2019; Nieto and Ramos, 2017; Mavromaras et al., 2013; Sirkeci et al., 2018; Saunders 2015; Johnston et al., 2010). There are objective and subjective methods to measure the level of correspondence, named vertical mismatch, between educational degree and the educational degree required to perform that job properly.

The first approach, of objective measurement and two strategies, consists of comparing the actual educational achievement with an objective education needed (Muñoz et al., 2018). The first strategy is job analysis (JA), a systematic evaluation method and an assignment educational level. Workers with a higher educational degree than the assignment educational level are considered as over-educated, while with a lower educational degree than the required level are regarded as under-educated. However, the standards are not updated every year, producing annual bias (Hartog, 2000). The second strategy, known as realized matches (RM), consists in defining at least one standard deviation from the mean or mode of others in their occupation. Educational achievement above one standard deviation is considered to be over-educated. A drawback of this method is that it is driven by demand and supply forces and also ignores variations (Leuven and Oosterbeek, 2011).

The second approach -of a subjective measurement approach (SA) - consists of asking the workers about the educational requirement by the company or the level required for job. Variations of this approach are asking workers directly whether they are matched, whether they are using their skills sufficiently, or whether they require a extra training to deal with the tasks. Like many subjective evaluation methods, respondents may overstate or understate the requirements.

However, a form of job-education mismatch receiving less attention in the literature is horizontal mismatch, the disagreement between a worker's field of study and his or her occupation (Banerjee et al., 2019). Like vertical mismatch, horizontal mismatch also has two measurements-JA and SA. By standardized occupational classifications-such as O*Net and NOC, the job analysis method compares the required educational fields to major (Wolbers, 2003). Like JA method of vertical mismatch, updating standards is a major issue. Respondents are asked how closely their educational field is related to the job they do named SA method. A potential disadvantage is that workers' perceptions of horizontal match are by definition subject to self-report bias (Banerjee et al., 2019).

Several studies have simultaneously examined both vertical and horizontal job-education mismatch. Banerjee et al. (2019) compared the horizontal, vertical, and full job-education mismatch among white natives, white immigrant and racial minority immigrant and find immigrants, especially racial minority immigrants, are more likely to be full mismatch; Meronin and Vera-Toscano (2017) tested the persistence of vertical mismatch and full mismatch among recent graduates and evidence showed no real differences between vertical or full overeducation.

Job-Education Mismatch among College Graduates

Human capital is one of the key factors in the determination of labour market performance. Consistent with this theory, researchers have found that job-education mismatch is a major source of labour market disadvantage for migrants. Migrants and native residents may differ in childhood environment, cultural adaptation and family background, which may affect their job-education match.

All studies on migrants' job-education mismatch have focused on vertical mismatch (overeducation), but in practice, mismatches involve both vertical and horizontal mismatch. Banerjee et al. (2019) have found immigrants (particularly racial minorities immigrants) who are unable to find work related to their educational background are more likely to accept work unrelated to their major. In a word, immigrants (particularly racial minorities immigrants) are more likely to be full mismatch than white native-born Canadians. Using microdata from the 2007 wave of the Adult Education Survey (AES), Nieto et al. (2015) found immigrants are more likely to be skill mismatch than natives, and the difference is much larger for vertical mismatch, wherein the difference is higher for the origin of immigrants. Therefore, analyzing only vertical mismatch may overlook an important aspect of migrant labour market.

Household Registration and Graduate Floating Population in China

Compared with developed countries, China's household registration system, which restricts population mobility, had a profound impact on the labour market for a long time (Wu and Zheng, 2018). Besides the functions of population registration and management, the current household registration system is closely related to resource allocation and distribution. Therefore, different *hukou* status are bound with different welfare benefits (Gerber, 2000; Wu and Xie, 2003). As a result, *hukou* in big cities often becomes a scarce commodity in the job market (Song, 2016).

The key task of building a new type of urbanization in 2019 calls for further reform of the household registration system, focusing on settling rural migrant workers in cities and towns. Abolishing restrictions on permanent residence in small and medium-sized cities with 1 million permanent residents; restrictions in cities with 1 to 3 million residents will be lifted completely; cities with 3 to 5 million residents will fully relax household registration requirements, and abolish the household registration restrictions for key groups. However, megalopolises such as Beijing and Shanghai still control the population size and screen outstanding talents by setting up *hukou* threshold. The *hukou* policy has been gradually tightened in recent years, and the number of college graduates settling down has dropped.

Take Beijing for example: Beijing's settlement channels are divided into nine categories: fresh graduates; international students; talent introduction; postdoctoral outbound; relatives; corporate executives; college student village official; national award for voluntary bravery and national civil servants. For college graduates, fresh graduates and college student village official are major ways to achieve local *hukou* in Beijing. Of course, a fair and reasonable return on human capital is also important for college students. Getting a college degree is the result of long-term investment in human capital by individuals, families and society. It reflects the benefit of human capital investment and has an important impact on the quality of life for college students and their families. However, due to the restrictions of the household registration system, as well as the welfare of the household registration itself, college graduates may look for jobs that do not match their major or even educational background to get a local *hukou* in Beijing.

Conceptual Framework and Hypotheses

In this study, I examine vertical, horizontal, and full mismatch among college migrants with a *hukou* and without a *hukou* compared to natives. I also investigate the effect of each type of mismatch (vertical, horizontal, full) on wages. I hypothesize the following. First, consistent with previous studies (Wald and Fang, 2008; Chiswick and Miller, 2009; Joona et al., 2014), college graduates without a local *hukou* will be more likely to experience job-education mismatch than their counterparts. Second, college graduates who obtained a *hukou* through job will be more likely to face full (horizontal and vertical) mismatch. *Hukou* related benefits will cause college migrants to have much difficulty in finding work commensurate with their level of education and/or their field of study. Third, I expect that vertical job-education mismatch will be associated with greater wage disadvantage than horizontal mismatch, and full mismatch will be associated with the greatest wage disadvantage.

Data and Methods

This study is based on the data from the Beijing College Students Panel Survey (BCSPS). The baseline survey was conducted in 2009, with the population of interest being the full-time first year and third year undergraduate students at all 54 public universities affiliated with the ministry of education, other ministries, or the Beijing municipal government. For the first-year college attendees in the baseline survey, the follow-up data of the BCSPS accumulated longitudinal information across the entire 4-year college duration from 2009 to 2012. For the third-year college attendees in the baseline survey, the follow-up data of the BCSPS accumulated longitudinal school information from 2009 to 2010 and labour market information from 2011 to 2012. In 2013, a fifth round of the survey was conducted on the college graduates of the previous first and third years, respectively, with a total sample size of 2,603, including the mismatch between education and job, household change and labor market performance.

We use the fifth round of the survey and the sample is restricted to college graduates who are working in Beijing, as Beijing's *hukou* is related to a wide range of social welfare and public resources. There are opportunities differences between Beijing registered population and non-Beijing registered population. Therefore, Beijing can act a typical case to explore the impact of the household registration system and job-education mismatch. Despite its merits, it is important to note that the survey is selective, as it only examines college graduates in Beijing. Great caution would be essential in any attempt to generalize this study's conclusions to the general populations, including those with no college educational degree.

For first outcome variable, the likelihood of job-education mismatch, I examine the likelihood of vertical, horizontal, and full mismatch of college graduates. Therefore, I run three separate models: (1) only horizontal mismatch (horizontal mismatch but vertical match), (2) only vertical mismatch (vertical mismatch but horizontal match), and (3) full mismatch (horizontal mismatch and vertical mismatch). The three categories are mutually exclusive. The horizontal mismatch is measured using a question in the BCSPS that asks how closely the respondent's job is related to his or her educational field, where 1= "strongly disagree," 2= "disagree," 3= "neutral," 4= "agree," and 5= "strongly agree". Those who answer neutral and below are considered to be horizontal mismatch. The vertical mismatch is measured using a question in the BCSPS that asks the education requirement of their current job. The level of education required for job below her/ his educational degree is considered as vertical mismatch. Respondents who are both horizontal and vertical mismatch are considered as full mismatch.

The key explanatory variable in the first analysis is the migration status. This variable is constructed from two separate questions in the BCSPS. The first question asks respondents to identify their origin province of the college entrance examination. Those whose origin province of the college entrance examination are not Beijing but work in Beijing are defined as migrants. The second question asks respondents that whether your organization or company provide a *hukou*. From these two questions, I construct a single set of two dummy variables representing: (1) migrant getting a *hukou* by work, (2) migrant not getting a *hukou* by work. To model the determinants of an education–occupation mismatch, multinomial logistic regression is employed since there are four categories (only horizontal mismatch, only vertical mismatch, full mismatch and full match (reference group)) of the dependent variable. The coefficients of the model represent changes in the log odds of being in each education–occupation mismatch category compared to the reference category corresponding to a unit change in the corresponding independent.

My second analysis examines the wage effects of horizontal, vertical, and full mismatch on migrant who (not) getting a *hukou* compared to natives. There are two main sets of explanatory variables: (1) migration status and (2) horizontal, vertical, and full job-education mismatch. I also examine the interaction between migration status and job-education mismatch to test whether the wage effect of each type of mismatch has different effects. For both outcome measures, the control variables are age, gender, occupation, non-agricultural household, graduate student, Party membership, father's education and father's Party membership.

Results

Descriptive Results

Table 1 indicates descriptive statistics of selected variables for natives, migrant getting a *hukou* by work, and migrant not getting a *hukou* by work. Looking into the likelihood of job-education mismatch, I find that about 20 percent of native-born college graduates are full job-education match, higher than migrant without a *hukou* (13.1%) and migrant with a *hukou* (3.3%); 38.5% of natives experience horizontal mismatch without vertical mismatch; that is, they work in a job not related to their educational field yet commensurate with their years of education.

Table 1. Descriptive statistics of selected variables for natives, migrant without a *hukou*, and migrant with a *hukou*.

Variable	Natives	Migrant without a *hukou*	Migrant with a *hukou*
Match type			
Full match	0.202	0.131	0.033
Only horizontal mismatch	0.385	0.303	0.355
Only vertical mismatch	0.183	0.189	0.185
Full mismatch	0.230	0.377	0.427
Age (years)	24.61	24.90	24.90
Male	1.585	1.560	1.411
Non-agricultural	0.696	0.611	0.726
Graduate student	0.044	0.143	0.532
Party membership	0.296	0.360	0.597
Father's education	12.53	11.67	13.23
Father's Party membership	0.321	0.320	0.492
Industry			
The second industry	0.153	0.143	0.170
Banking and finance	0.195	0.114	0.145
The IT industry	0.148	0.354	0.177
Other industries	0.504	0.389	0.508
N	405	175	124

The disparity in job-education mismatch becomes more apparent when I examine full mismatch. Only about 23 percent of natives are both horizontal and vertical mismatch. In contrast, nearly 38 percent of migrant without a *hukou* and 43 percent of migrant with a *hukou* report full mismatch. In other words, college graduates, especially those who have a *hukou* by work, are more likely to work both in jobs unrelated to their field of expertise and in jobs less than their years of education.

Likelihood of Job-Education Mismatch

I model the likelihood of horizontal, vertical, and full job-education mismatch using multinomial logistic regression. The results are presented in Table 2.

Table 2 presents a number of interesting findings. First, as shown in Column 1, the coefficient for migrants is 0.45, not significant. Dividing migrants into those with a *hukou* and without a *hukou*, the effect changes: comparing with natives in Beijing, the coefficient for migrant with a *hukou* is 1.56, meaning that migrant with a *hukou* is associated with a 378% increase to horizontal mismatch. Second, Columns 2 and 5 show that the estimated effect of migrants on vertical mismatch is substantially larger than native-born college graduates, and migrants are more likely to be vertical mismatch in order to obtain a *hukou*. Third, compared with locals, the likelihood of full mismatch is higher for migrants, and those migrants with *hukou* are more likely to be full mismatch.

Table 2. Multinomial logistic regression estimates of the likelihood of an education–occupation mismatch

	Model 1			Model 2		
	Horizontal Mismatch	Vertical Mismatch	Full Mismatch	Horizontal Mismatch	Vertical Mismatch	Full Mismatch
Migrant	0.449	0.753*	1.150***			
	(1.615)	(2.457)	(4.094)			
Ref. group: Natives						
Migrant without a *hukou*				0.101	0.447	0.778**
				(0.337)	(1.349)	(2.592)
Migrant with a *hukou*				1.564**	1.792**	2.319***
				(2.711)	(2.955)	(4.017)
Age	0.039	0.238*	0.057	0.058	0.256*	0.080
	(0.404)	(2.180)	(0.563)	(0.596)	(2.322)	(0.784)
Male	0.466+	0.151	0.116	0.533*	0.208	0.196
	(1.934)	(0.559)	(0.466)	(2.195)	(0.763)	(0.779)
Urban	-0.329	-0.212	-0.449	-0.336	-0.218	-0.455
	(-1.133)	(-0.650)	(-1.492)	(-1.155)	(-0.668)	(-1.512)
Graduate	1.098*	0.514	0.914+	0.758	0.206	0.536
	(2.223)	(0.953)	(1.827)	(1.498)	(0.370)	(1.036)
Party membership	-0.188	-0.097	-0.197	-0.224	-0.128	-0.237
	(-0.712)	(-0.330)	(-0.715)	(-0.844)	(-0.432)	(-0.854)
Father's education	0.003	-0.051	-0.002	-0.003	-0.056	-0.010
	(0.065)	(-0.991)	(-0.052)	(-0.076)	(-1.096)	(-0.213)
Father's Party membership	0.205	0.410	0.246	0.203	0.408	0.244
	(0.710)	(1.259)	(0.815)	(0.698)	(1.244)	(0.801)
Industry						
Banking and finance	-0.829+	0.086	-0.785	-0.831+	0.087	-0.787
	(-1.816)	(0.160)	(-1.645)	(-1.815)	(0.161)	(-1.644)
The IT industry	-0.826+	-0.530	-0.557	-0.760+	-0.471	-0.481
	(-1.855)	(-0.975)	(-1.232)	(-1.699)	(-0.863)	(-1.059)
Others industries	-0.861*	0.175	-0.893*	-0.889*	0.151	-0.926*
	(-2.179)	(0.373)	(-2.181)	(-2.244)	(0.321)	(-2.255)
cons	-0.177	-5.596+	-0.463	-0.637	-6.019*	-1.024
	(-0.070)	(-1.930)	(-0.175)	(-0.248)	(-2.060)	(-0.383)
N						704

Note: t statistics in parentheses. $+p < .1$, $*p < 0.05$, $**p < 0.01$, $***p < 0.001$.
Source: Authors calculations using BCSPS2013.

Taken together, these results from multinomial logistic regression models reveal that migration status led to the education–occupation mismatch, which includes horizontal mismatch, vertical mismatch and full mismatch. Differences in mismatch between those migrants having a *hukou* and not having a *hukou* are also probably due to *hukou* per se. The household registration system interferes with and even distorts the human capital return mechanism of college migrants. In order to get the welfare on *hukou*, college floating population have to take jobs that do not match their major background or even educational degree.

Wage Effects of Job-Education Mismatch

Next, I model the wage effects of each type of job-education mismatch and examine how these effects differ by *hukou* status (see Table 3). Compared Model 3 to Model 5, I have two findings. First, after accounting for a vector of other wage-determining characteristics, migrants face an initial monthly wage advantage of 33.9 percentage points compared to natives while migrants with a *hukou* face a larger initial wage advantage (34.8%) than those without a *hukou* (33.4%). This was not unexpected. It's easy for natives to find work while college migrants who want to stay in Beijing have to go through a series of selection, and only the elite can stay in Beijing. Second, vertical mismatch and full mismatch will lower the individual's wage, yet only vertical mismatch's effect is significant. Compared with full match, vertical mismatch is associated with a 22-percentage point decrease in monthly wage.

Table 3: OLS regression models on determinants of logarithmic monthly earnings among three categories

	Model 3	Model 4	Model 5	Model 6
Migrant	0.339^{***}	0.234		
	(5.064)	(1.323)		
Horizontal mismatch	0.024	0.022	0.023	0.022
	(0.258)	(0.204)	(0.248)	(0.200)
Vertical mismatch	-0.218^{*}	-0.245^{+}	-0.219^{*}	-0.246^{+}
	(-2.111)	(-1.930)	(-2.114)	(-1.932)
Full mismatch	-0.154	-0.246^{*}	-0.156	-0.245^{*}
	(-1.621)	(-2.046)	(-1.626)	(-2.037)
Migr # Hori		0.039		
		(0.189)		
Migr# Vert		0.106		
		(0.468)		
Migr # Full		0.219		
		(1.056)		
Migr without a *hukou*			0.334^{***}	0.278
			(4.469)	(1.479)
Migr with a *hukou*			0.348^{***}	-0.019
			(3.625)	(-0.047)
Migr without a *hukou* # Hori				-0.021
				(0.092)
Migr without a *hukou* # Vert				0.082
				(0.326)
Migr without a *hukou* # Full				0.161
				(0.710)
Migr with a *hukou* # Hori				0.313
				(0.731)
Migr with a *hukou* # Vert				0.335
				(0.745)
Migr with a *hukou* # Full				0.489
				(1.142)
N	704	704	704	704

Note: t statistics in parentheses. $\dagger p < .1,$ $^{*}p < 0.05,$ $^{**}p < 0.01,$ $^{***}p < 0.001.$
Source: Authors calculations using BCSPS2013.

Figure 1. Predicted logarithmic monthly wages for natives and migrants, dependent on education mismatch. The estimations are based on Model 4 in Table 3.

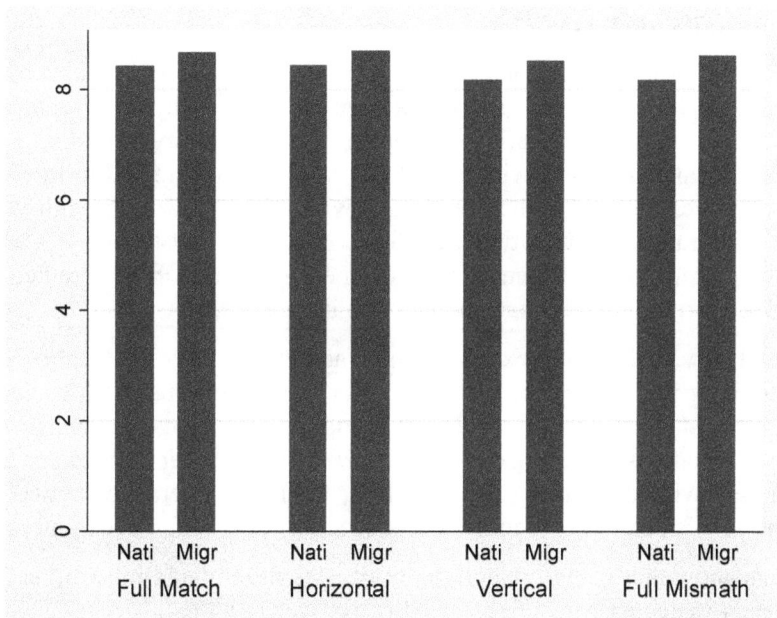

Figure 2. Predicted logarithmic monthly wages for natives and migrants (*hukou*), dependent on education mismatch. The estimations are based on Model 6 in Table 3.

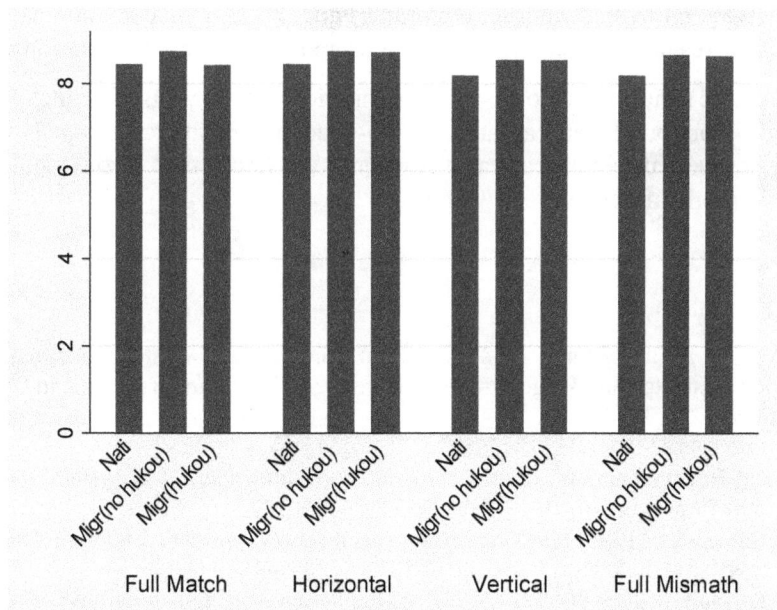

Adding the interaction between migration status and job-education mismatch to test whether the wage effect on each type of mismatch has different effects, I get some interesting findings

(Figure 1 and Figure 2). Whether or not educational mismatch occur, the wages of migrants are higher than natives, but not significant. Migrants who not having a Beijing *hukou* have higher wages than their counterparts, while the effect was not significant.

Discussion and conclusion

This study examines the incidence and wage effects of horizontal, vertical, and full job-education mismatch for college migrants (not) getting a *hukou* by work compared to natives in Beijing. My analysis of job-education mismatch yields two key findings. First, both college migrants with a local *hukou* and without a local *hukou* are more likely to be vertical and full mismatch than natives. Second, college migrants with a local *hukou* through work have a higher full mismatch. These findings show that the effects of the *hukou* system on job-education mismatch between the three groups are different. Natives can easily find a job and are better matched, while migrants need to sacrifice their human capital to achieve a job.

The second part of the study examines the wage effects of job-education mismatch. Here, I have three important findings. First, vertical mismatch and full mismatch by itself result in wage disadvantage. Second, college migrants face an initial monthly wage advantage of 33.9 percentage points compared to natives while migrants with a *hukou* face a larger initial wage advantage (34.8%) than those migrants without a *hukou* (33.4%). Third, adding the interaction between migration status and job-education mismatch shows that there is no significant difference in monthly wages.

The results show that many college migrants accept unrelated jobs to get a local *hukou*, but this does not lead to a decrease in their wages. In other words, although migrants have an educational mismatch in order to obtain the *hukou*, they are not willing to sacrifice their wages and benefits. These findings highlight the importance of disaggregating the various types of job-education mismatch experienced by college migrants. Most previous studies of job-education mismatch have focused exclusively on overeducation (Wald and Fang, 2008; Chiswick and Miller, 2009; Sharaf, 2013), which may result in misleading conclusions and policy recommendations.

Although these results are inconsistent with previous findings on migrants' wage disadvantage, the unpacking of horizontal, vertical, and full job-education mismatch provides further insight into the underlying causes of human capital distortions. We know that vertical and full mismatch by themselves differently affect workers' wage.

References

Banerjee, R., Verma, A., and Zhang, T. (2019). Brain Gain or Brain Waste? Horizontal, Vertical, and Full Job-Education Mismatch and Wage Progression among Skilled Immigrant Men in Canada. *International Migration Review*, 53(3),646-670.
   https://doi.org/10.1177/0197918318774501
Chan, K. W., and Buckingham, W. (2008). Is China abolishing the *hukou* system? *The China Quarterly*, 195(9),582-606. https://doi.org/10.1017/S0305741008000787
Cheng, T., and Selden, M. (1994). The origins and social consequences of China's *hukou* system. *The China Quarterly*, 139(9),644-668. https://doi.org/10.1017/S0305741000043083
Chiswick, B. R., and Miller, P. W. (2009). The international transferability of immigrants' human capital. *Economics of Education Review*, 28(2),162-169.
   https://doi.org/10.1016/j.econedurev.2008.07.002

Gerber, T. P. (2000). Educational stratification in contemporary Russia: Stability and change in the face of economic and institutional crisis. *Sociology of Education*, 10,219-246. http://doi.org/10.2307/2673232

Hartog, J. (2000). Over-education and earnings: where are we, where should we go? *Economics of education review*, 19(2),131-147. https://doi.org/10.1016/S0272-7757(99)00050-3

Johnston, R., Sirkeci, I., Khattab, N., & Modood, T. (2010). Ethno-religious categories and measuring occupational attainment in relation to education in England and Wales: a multilevel analysis. *Environment and planning A*, 42(3), 578-591.[https://www.researchgate.net/publication/46559803_Ethno religious_categories_and_measuring_occupational_attainment_in_relation_to_education_in_England_a nd_Wales_a_multilevel_analysis]

Joona, P. A., Gupta, N. D., and Wadensjö, E. (2014). Overeducation among immigrants in Sweden: incidence, wage effects and state dependence. *IZA Journal of Migration*, 3(1),9. https://doi.org/10.1186/2193-9039-3-9

Leuven, E., and Oosterbeek, H. (2011). Overeducation and mismatch in the labor market. *In Handbook of the Economics of Education* (Vol. 4, pp. 283-326). Elsevier. https://doi.org/10.1016/B978-0-444-53444-6.00003-1

Mavromaras, K., McGuinness, S., O'Leary, N., Sloane, P., and Wei, Z. (2013). Job mismatches and labour market outcomes: panel evidence on university graduates. *Economic Record*, 89(286),382-395. https://doi.org/10.1111/1475-4932.12054

Meroni, E. C., and Vera-Toscano, E. (2017). The persistence of overeducation among recent graduates. *Labour Economics*, 48,120-143. https://doi.org/10.1016/j.labeco.2017.07.002

Muñoz de Bustillo, R., Sarkar, S., Sebastián, R., and Antón, J. I. (2018). Education mismatch in Europe at the turn of the century: Measurement, intensity and evolution. https://mpra.ub.uni-muenchen.de/85779

Nieto, S., and Ramos, R. (2017). Overeducation, skills and wage penalty: Evidence for Spain using PIAAC data. *Social Indicators Research*, 134(1), 219-236. https://doi.org/10.1007/s11205-016-1423-1

Nieto, S., Alessia, M. A. I., and Ramos, R. (2015). Educational mismatches in the EU: Immigrants vs natives. *International Journal of Manpower*, 36(4), 540-561. https://doi.org/10.1108/IJM-11-2013-0260

Saunders, B. (2015). Overeducated and over here: skilled EU migrants in Britain. *Transnational Press London*.

Sharaf, M. F. (2013). Job-education mismatch and its impact on the earnings of immigrants: evidence from recent arrivals to Canada. *ISRN Economics*, *2013*. https://doi.org/10.1155/2013/452358

Sirkeci, I., Acik, N., Saunders, B., & Přívara, A. (2018). Barriers for highly qualified A8 immigrants in the UK labour market. *Work, employment and society*, 32(5), 906-924.

Song, Y. (2016). *Hukou*-based labour market discrimination and ownership structure in urban China. *Urban Studies*,53(8),1657-1673. https://doi.org/10.1177/0042098015576861

Wald, S., and Fang, T. (2008). Over-educated immigrants in the Canadian labour market: Evidence from the workplace and employee survey. *Canadian Public Policy*, 34(4),457-479. https://doi.org/10.3138/cpp.34.4.457

Wolbers, M. H. (2003). Job mismatches and their labour-market effects among school-leavers in Europe. *European Sociological Review*, 19(3),249-266. https://doi.org/10.1093/esr/19.3.249

Wu, L., and Zhang, W. (2018). Rural migrants' homeownership in Chinese urban destinations: Do institutional arrangements still matter after *Hukou* reform. *Cities*, 79(9),151-158. https://doi.org/10.1016/j.cities.2018.03.004

Wu, X. (2019). Inequality and social stratification in Post socialist China. *Annual Review of Sociology*, 45(6),363-382. https://doi.org/10.1146/annurev-soc-073018-022516

Wu, X., and Treiman, D. J. (2004). The household registration system and social stratification in China: 1955–1996. *Demography* ,41(2), 363-384. https://doi.org/10.1353/dem.2004.0010

Wu, X., and Xie, Y. (2003). Does the market pay off? Earnings returns to education in urban China. *American Sociological Review*, 6,425-442. https://doi.org/10.2307/1519731

Wu, J., Yao, X., and Zhang, J. (2015). Is *Hukou* discrimination between urban and rural areas vanishing? Evidence from the reform period 1989–2011. *Econ. Res. J* 11,148-160.

Wu, X., and Zheng, B. (2018). Household registration, urban status attainment, and social stratification in China. *Research in Social Stratification and Mobility* 53,40-49. https://doi.org/10.1016/j.rssm.2017.11.002.

September 2020
Volume: 17, **No**: 5, pp. 621 – 638
ISSN: 1741-8984
e-ISSN: 1741-8992
www.migrationletters.com

MIGRATION
LETTERS

First Submitted: 1 February 2020 Accepted: 5 May 2020
DOI: https://doi.org/10.33182/ml.v17i5.694

Understanding the Reconstruction of Personal Networks Through Residential Trajectories

Olga Ganjour[1], Eric D. Widmer[2], Gil Viry[3], Jacques-Antoine Gauthier[4], Vincent Kaufmann[5] and Guillaume Drevon[6]

Abstract

This article examines how residential trajectories influence the spatiality and composition of personal networks. Three mechanisms are considered: the addition of spatially close network members, the selection of spatially distant network members, and the substitution of spatially distant network members by spatially close ones. An ego-centred network analysis combined with sequence analysis of residential experiences is used to capture the personal networks and the residential trajectories of individuals from two birth cohorts in Switzerland. A series of regression models test the association between the types of personal networks that individuals develop, in terms of both spatial dispersion and composition, and their residential trajectories. The results show that individuals who moved far away from their place of birth are embedded in large and diversified personal networks, which include spatially distant relatives, local nuclear family members, and local friends. On average, individuals who experienced residential migration have larger and more diverse personal networks than individuals who stayed close to their place of birth. The addition mechanism accounts for much of this greater diversity.

Keywords: *residential migration; residential trajectories; personal networks of migrants; network spatiality; social integration; social relationships*

Introduction

The increased geographical mobility of globalised societies may have paradoxical effects on personal networks and consequently on social integration; such effects have – so far – been overlooked. There is a large and relevant literature on the personal networks of migrants, which considers, in particular, the types and amounts of social support activated at a distance (for instance, Mulder & Van der Meer, 2009; Mulder & Cooke, 2009). Evidence on the social support or social capital of migrants (broadly defined as resources stemming from social networks) does not end the

[1] Olga Ganjour (Corresponding author), Department of Sociology, University of Geneva, 1205 Geneva, Switzerland. E-Mail: olga.ganjour@unige.ch.
[2] Eric D. Widmer, Department of Sociology, University of Geneva, 1205 Geneva, Switzerland. E-mail: eric.widmer@unige.ch
[3] Gil Vry, School of Social and Political Science, University of Edinburgh, EH8 9LN, Edinburgh, UK. E-Mail: gil.viry@ed.ac.uk
[4] Jacques-Antoine Gauthier, Laboratory of Urban Sociology (LaSUR), École Polytechnique Fédérale de Lausanne, 1015 Lausanne, Switzerland. E-mail: Jacques-antoine.gauthier@unil.ch.
[5] Vincent Kaufmann, Laboratory of Urban Sociology (LaSUR), École Polytechnique Fédérale de Lausanne, 1015 Lausanne, Switzerland. E-Mail: vincent.kaufmann@epfl.ch.
[6] Guillaume Drevon, Life Course and Inequality Research Centre, University of Lausanne, 1015 Lausanne, Switzerland. E-Mail: guillaume.drevon@epfl.ch.

debates related to their social integration, as the variety of personal networks plays out not only in terms of support received or provided, actual or potential (Herz, 2015; Magdol & Bessel, 2003), but also in terms of the composition of such networks (Lubbers et al., 2010). On the one hand, since the classical work of Litwak (1960), it has been confirmed that geographical mobility is associated with the lasting presence of extended family. The decision to move is rooted in family practices and obligations (Cooke, 2008). Family members are largely present in the composition of migrants' personal networks, despite increasing distances (previous works by the authors, 2017; 2018). On the other hand, several authors argue that distance reduces the normative control of the family (Coleman, 1988; Larsen Axhausen & Urry, 2006) and creates opportunities for "networked individualism" (Wellman et al., 2005, p.165) away from role requirements (Allan, 2001). Thus, personal networks of migrants are expected by some to include a large number of spatially close non-family members and to weaken relationships with the spatially distant family of origin (Ryan, 2007), while others stress the lasting importance of family relationships.

This study tackles the spatiality of personal networks, which is the extent to which such networks are localised or spread out in space. Such spatiality is a crucial component of social integration that has not yet received the attention it deserves, in particular regarding its association with network composition. The role of family relationships in shaping network spatiality indeed deserves further scrutiny. In this article, we first stress the specificity of family relationships in personal networks as such relationships may survive at a distance while also having the potential to be recreated locally. We then describe three spatially sensitive mechanisms of development of personal networks, which may account for their diversity when facing migration: the *addition* of spatially close network members to spatially distant network members, the *selection* of spatially distant network members, and the *substitution* of spatially distant network members by spatially close ones. Residential migration captures the longstanding change in the geographical location of individuals across either national borders (international migration) or between regions within a country (internal or inter-regional migration) – and results in redefining the spaces of daily life (Niedomysl, 2011). We define migrants as individuals who have moved and lived far from their birthplace, in other regions of the country, or in different countries, for a significant period of their lives.

Based on a representative sample of 830 adults from two birth cohorts of individuals living in Switzerland, we assess the extent to which such mechanisms, in relation to family versus non-family relationships, may account for the diversity of personal networks of migrants compared with non-migrants. The discussion stresses the crucial importance of family relationships for understanding the reconstruction of the personal networks of migrants and makes some suggestions for social policies.

The special character of family relationships

Previous studies have confirmed that residential migration is a complex and collective action involving family, kinship, and local communities (Larsen, Axhausen & Urry, 2006; Cooke, 2008; Ryan, 2004). In Switzerland, many people prefer to commute, even if it costs much more time and money than to move homes (previous work by the authors, 2011). Evidence from the literature shows that such choices are motivated by the risk of dissolving family and friendship relationships (Green & Canny, 2003; Vignal, 2002). The continuity of support at a distance and sharing the decision to move with family members can be explained by the special character of family relationships, an explanation that supposes intergenerational solidarity (Bengston & Roberts, 1991) and responsibilities due to the emotional and practical support shared between family members (Finch & Mason, 1993; Mason, 1999; Morgan, 2013). The definition of a "local family entourage" (Bonvalet & Mason, 1999) characterises the family solidarity that goes beyond the household. These findings are echoed in recent studies focusing on "transnational" families. When migrants face situations in which their local support and local relationships are poor, then distant sources of support and interactions are likely to be activated, even over long geographical distances (Ackers, 1998; Baldassar, 2007; Bryceson & Vuorela, 2003). However, geographical distance influences negotiations about family solidarity. For example, it establishes the limits up to which family members can be asked for practical and emotional support (see, for example, Mulder & Van der Meer, 2009; Mulder & Cooke, 2009). There is also a difference in the readiness and capacity of family members to provide support at a distance. For example, fathers and siblings are less supportive than mothers and children, especially sons, if they live far away (Mulder & Van der Meer, 2009).

Residential migration enlarges personal network geographies (Larsen, Axhausen & Urry, 2006) and provides spatially dispersed personal networks (Wellman, 2001; previous work by the author), including spatially widespread relatives (parents and siblings) and spatially close voluntary kin (e.g., friends) (previous works by the authors, 2017; 2018). The development of technologies, such as mobile phones and high-speed transport, facilitates the maintenance of family relationships at a distance. Contrary to expectations, it does not decrease the role of family members' physical visits for "network activation" (Urry, 2012). According to Mason (2004), visits activate kinship networks over a long distance through the sharing of kinship biographies, doing things together, and negotiating about propriety, morality, and exchange in kin relationships.

Although spatial dispersion has become a feature of families in contemporary mobile societies, relatively little is known about how residential migration shapes the presence of family relationships with regard to other types of relationships in personal networks. From the literature, we hold that the reconstruction of personal networks due to migration progresses through three mechanisms: the *addition* of spatially close network members to spatially distant network members, the *selection* of spatially distant network members, and the *substitution* of spatially distant network members by spatially close network members. The next sections shortly describe such mechanisms.

Addition of spatially close network members to spatially distant network members in personal networks of migrants

The network literature stresses that migrants combine spatially distant strong relationships with family members and nearby weak ties with non-family members (Wellman & Wortley, 1990). It was found that residential migration reinforces the boundaries between family and non-family members in the composition of personal networks. Particularly, residentially mobile individuals are embedded in more transitive support networks, in which network members are highly interconnected, whereas immobile individuals are fostered in highly centralised and less dense support networks characterised by the presence of family members and friends (previous work by the authors, 2012). The social characteristics of migrants, such as age, level of education, and socio-economic status, strongly influence the spatial dispersion of families (Mulder & Kalmijn, 2006; Carasco et al., 2008). The average distance to all family members is greater for young, university-educated, middle-class individuals than for older, less educated and working-class people. The networks of highly educated individuals are balanced between weak ties and far-flung ties with family and friends living elsewhere and connected through communication technologies and social visits (Urry & Elliott, 2010). Along the same lines, Ryan (2007, 2011) showed that the creation of local relationships is less likely for lowly educated immigrants who have problems with language acquisition and who stay bound to their community of origin within the host country. For example, mothers with children use local friends for tangible support and local knowledge (Ryan, 2007). Thus, the development of local support may influence the extent of support at a distance.

Spatially distant relationships with family members and spatially close relationships with non-family members should be established due to their specific activation for support. The creation of spatially close new relationships with non-family members is warranted because it is unreasonable for practical support or mutual co-presence to have only spatially distant contacts (Larsen, Axhausen & Urry, 2006). Activated by normative commitments, face-to-face meetings, phone calls, and regular visits, family relationships are less sensitive to distance than are relationships with friends, which are more likely to be weakened when distance increases (Bonvalet & Mason, 1999; Coenen-Huther, Kellerhals, Von Allmen, 1994; Lubbers et al., 2010; Pollet, Roberts, & Dunbar, 2013; Wrzus, Hänel, Wagner, & Neyer, 2013; previous work by the authors, 2018). Thus, geographical proximity is related to weak relationships because strong relationships have stronger foundations on which to exist at a distance (Carrasco, Miller, & Wellman, 2008; Wellman & Wortley, 1990).

Some studies connect residential trajectories with other life trajectories to explain the creation of new weak ties or the maintenance of old strong ties. For instance, young adults leaving school and entering the job market tend to reduce their number of weak ties but to increase the overall homogeneity of those ties, as one prefers to maintain intensive relationships with those who are the "same as oneself" (Bidart & Lavenu, 2005). The beginning of a romantic relationship initially favours the addition of new weak relationships shared with the partner. However, when the couple comes to live under the same roof, the number of their network members drops. In addition, the inclusion of friends in personal networks depends on the age of the respondents. Evidence from the British Household Panel Survey showed that young respondents choose friends outside the family, whereas old respondents choose friends within the family (Pahl & Pevalin, 2005).

Overall, the personal networks of migrants include spatially distant and close-by network members due to the migrants' needs for support and on the basis of their social-demographic characteristics and life-course stage. Consequently, an *addition effect* is revealed by the combination of spatially close non-family members and spatially distant family members in the personal networks of migrants.

Selection of spatially distant significant network members in personal networks of migrants

Previous studies have demonstrated that residential migration is associated with the selection of social relationships. The strongest, more intimate relationships with kinship members are maintained over a distance, whereas weaker ties are eliminated (see, for example, Bonvalet & Mason, 1999; Grossetti, 2007). A recent relocation may lead people to focus on a small, emotionally intimate group rather than maintain relationships with a large number of less intimate individuals (Bidart & Lavenu, 2005). A decline in the number of network members depends on the background of migrants and their ability to replenish their networks rapidly. Those who easily adapt to a new social situation are more likely to be open to new sources of personal relationships and are able to create new relationships. The selection of relationships may also be influenced by resources that are necessary for maintaining ties at a distance (previous works by the authors, 2002). A study conducted in the United States observed that residential migration, which is often related to social mobility and socio-economic status, could be considered an explanatory factor of kinship solidarity (Johnson, 2000). Highly educated people are more likely to be geographically mobile, so they have fewer opportunities to interact with kin than less educated people.

The selection of spatially distant family members predominantly concerns vertical relationships with parents and children. These relationships are more resistant and hence survive at greater distances than relationships with friends, collaterals (siblings, cousins, etc.), and weaker relations (neighbours, colleagues, and other acquaintances) (Bonvalet & Mason, 1999; Coenen-Huther, Kellerhals, Von Allmen, 1994). The selection of relationships may be extended to spatially close family members, including members of the nuclear family, such as partners and children. The selection of relationships at a distance depends on the functions that are fulfilled by these connections. Emotional relationships (Wellman & Wortley, 1990) and the relationships reinforcing the symbolic importance of family (Johnson, 2000) are more selected than the relationships activated by practical support, which are more likely to be replaced by local connections (Wellman & Wortley, 1990).

Friends are less likely to be concerned with selection at a distance because friendship ties are shaped more strongly by individual negotiation than normative expectations of support. Furthermore, maintaining friendship relationships at a distance mostly requires actions (Cronin, 2015) and occasional meetings (Larsen, Axhausen & Urry, 2006). Thus, a *selection effect* is revealed by the presence of spatially distant kin members, such as parents and children, in the personal networks of migrants.

Substitution of spatially distant significant network members by spatially close network members in personal networks of migrants

Residential migration was also found to foster turnover in personal relationships (e.g., Lubbers et al., 2010). This mechanism relates to the substitution or replacement of spatially distant family members, for example, parents, by spatially close family members, uncles and aunts, or by spatially close non-family members, friends, and colleagues. The effect of substitution was confirmed in previous studies, particularly concerning those who provide support to mobile individuals (Mulder & Van der Meer, 2009) and their network composition (Magdol & Besel, 2003). It was found that the practical support and companionship provided by family members are more likely substituted by non-family members with increasing geographical distance from the place of birth (Herz, 2015; Mulder & Van der Meer, 2009). However, non-family members are less likely to substitute for family members with regard to emotional support (Herz, 2015; Magdol & Bessel, 2003). Using panel data on Argentinian migrants in Spain, Lubbers et al. (2010) showed that the structure and composition of migrants' social networks barely change after migration; networks have hardly added Spanish members over time, and they have become only slightly stronger in terms of closeness. In this case, turnover in personal relations was associated with stability in the composition and structure of the networks. Individual characteristics and the length of residence hardly influence the change of networks over time (Lubbers et al., 2010). However, other studies have shown that the length of residence is an additional condition that influences the substitution of kin relationships by non-kin relationships in the personal networks of migrants (Magdol & Bessel, 2003). A recent long-distance relocation impedes exchanges with kin to a greater degree than with non-kin members. However, over time, spatially close non-kin members compensate for the lack of spatially distant kin members (Magdol & Bessel, 2003).

Substitution may also concern friendship relationships because they require more meetings and negotiations (Allan, 1998) as well as their engagement in practical support (Ryan, 2007). However, a qualitative study conducted in the UK showed that intimate friendship ties remain strong after residential migration and are not replaced by new local relationships (Cronin, 2015). Staying in touch with friends at a distance is performed not only through meetings but also through the expression – at a distance – of "sensibilities of friendship" (Cronin, 2015, p. 679). Thus, a *substitution effect* is revealed by an overrepresentation of spatially close kin and non-kin members in the personal networks of migrants.

From this evidence, we hypothesise that residential migration shapes personal networks through addition, selection, and substitution effects. An addition effect is visible when spatially close family members and friends are added to spatially distant ones. A selection effect is present when some specific network members living far away, such as parents or children, are overrepresented in personal networks of migrants compared to other network members. A substitution effect occurs when spatially close relatives and friends are strongly overrepresented in personal networks of migrants compared to spatially distant relatives and friends. Note, however, that these three mechanisms can occur simultaneously and do not exclude each other. This paper aims to gain insight into the presence of such constitutive mechanisms of personal networks using a large and representative dataset of people living in Switzerland, with detailed information on their personal networks and migration trajectories.

Data

We use data from the Family tiMes survey, which includes a representative sample collected in 2011 of 803 individuals from two birth cohorts (1950–1955 and 1970–1975) living in Switzerland. The Family tiMes data offer a unique opportunity to analyse how personal networks are related to life-course trajectories, such as residential migration trajectories because it includes both ego-centred network data and biographical data based on life history calendars. The study combines ego-centred network analysis with sequence analysis of residential experiences from the place of birth.

Ego-centred network data

The ego-centred network consists of a focal actor, termed *ego*, and a set of network members, termed *alters*, who are tied to the ego (Wasserman & Faust, 1999). A free-listing technique was used to delineate the respondents' significant personal relationships (see above). This technique has been used in several surveys devoted to core networks (Marsden, 1987), migrant networks (Herz, 2015; Herz et al., 2019; Lubbers, 2011), and family interdependencies through the Family Network Method (FNM) developed by one of the author's previous works (Author, 1999; 2013; 2000). Respondents were asked to provide a list of persons who were very important to them during the past year, even if the respondent did not get along with them. "Who are the individuals who, over the past year, have been very important to you, even if you have not gotten along well with them?" They were instructed that the term "important" referred to people who have played a role, either positive or negative, in their life during the past year (previous works by the authors, 1999; 2006). This elective citation of significant network members is important for the consideration of personal networks, which not only include individuals closely linked by blood or marriage but also include more inclusive relationships, including friends and non-kin. The personal network size is limited to 19 significant network members. The respondents were also asked to describe the type of relationships they had with these people, choosing from the following categories: partner, children, parents, siblings, kin members (grandparents, grandchildren, relatives-in-law, uncles and aunts, cousins, nephews and nieces, godparents), friends, and other non-kin members (colleagues, employees, servants, hospital personnel, comrades-in-arms, neighbours, etc.). On that basis, we recoded the variable of personal networks into seven categories: partners, children, parents, siblings, kin members, friends, and other non-kin members.

Spatiality of personal networks data

We computed the geographical distance between the respondent and any significant alter using seven categories: respondent did not cite any significant alter; respondent and alter live in the same household or in the same municipality; respondent and alter live in different municipalities within a distance smaller than 10 km; respondent and alter live within a distance between 11 km and 40 km; respondent and alter live within a distance between 41 km and 100 km; respondent and alter live within a distance between 101 and 500 km; and alter lives abroad. The legal and symbolic distance created by national boundaries encouraged us to use this last category. We then computed the measure of distance for aggregated categories of alters: partners, children, parents, siblings, kin members, friends, and other non-kin members. If the respondent cited two significant network members of the same category, for example, a sister and a brother (who both belong to the sibling category), we computed the average distance between the respondent and the two network members. If the respondent cited three or more significant network members of the same category, for example, two sisters and one brother, or three friends, we took into account the maximum distance among these relatives. In this latter case, we aimed to increase the presence of spatially distant collaterals or friends in personal networks, as according to a study conducted in France (Ogg & Bonvalet, 2004), there is a strong duality in the presence of collaterals and kin relatives in personal networks: one part often lives near, whereas another part lives quite far away.

Life history calendar data

Retrospective life history calendars are used to collect longitudinal data in the survey study. While longitudinal panel surveys are the best means of studying the life course as a process, the life history calendar allows researchers to retrospectively reconstruct this process (Freedman, D. et al. 1988). The respondents were asked: "Now, I would like to know where you have lived throughout your life. Please consider only periods of at least six months." For each semester of age, the life history calendar records the respondent's postcode, tracking their successive places of residence from birth until the time of interview. The road distance (in km) between each place of residence and the respondent's birthplace was inferred using routing software modelling the Swiss road network and recoded into five categories (1. 0–10 km, 2. 11–40 km, 3. 41–100 km, 4. 101–500 km and 5. abroad).

Results

Typology of personal networks in terms of composition and spatiality

We ran a Multiple Correspondence Analysis (MCA) on the variables measuring the geographical distance between the respondent and their significant network members. This exploratory method provides a better understanding of how the response categories are interrelated and can be used to identify underlying patterns (Abdi & Valentin, 2007). Following the standard practice for MCA analysis, we retained five dimensions, which explain the maximum of the variance (Husson et al., 2009). To describe these structuring dimensions, we used the cross-validation procedure or correlations between the variables considered in MCA and the dimensions (Josse & Husson, 2016). We then performed a hierarchical cluster analysis using the Ward method (Ward, 1963) on the scores of MCA to build a typology of networks in terms of both composition and spatiality.[7] This procedure allows us to go beyond the consideration of one dimension of spatiality and additionally takes into account the composition. The number of clusters was set to six on the basis of standard quality indices.[8]

Table 1 describes the six types of personal networks in terms of composition and spatiality by the percentage of citations of each category of significant network members. The first type, "Local family network" (28%), includes individuals who predominantly cited family members who are spatially close to them (less than 10 km) as significant network members. They are strongly oriented to their partners and cited spatially close children and parents. In this type, siblings, other kin/non-kin members, and friends are largely absent. Focusing on the nuclear family and spatially close parents, this type of personal network excludes other kin and non-kin ties. The mean network size is limited to three individuals who live close to the respondents. The average distance from the respondents to them is 9 km.

The second type labelled "Local friendship network" (27%) includes respondents who cited a very limited number of spatially close network members as significant. When they do so, they predominantly cite spatially close friends and no parents, no children, and no other relatives. In addition, these individuals hardly cited the partner as significant. The mean size of the network is approximately three individuals, all of whom live relatively close to the respondents. The average distance from the respondents to them is approximately 16 km.

We named the third type "Nearby extended network" (19%) as it includes networks of respondents who cited alters who live at quite a distance from them (41–100 km) or spatially close (less than 10 km). They cited children and parents who belong to these two categories of distance. In both cases, they cited siblings or other kin. They also mentioned both spatially close (less than 10 km) and distant friends (41 to 100 km). Individuals in this group frequently cited their partner as a significant network member. The mean network size is about four network members, living on average 29 km from the respondents.

The fourth type labelled "Nationally extended network" (8%) includes individuals who cited their children, parents, siblings, and extended kin who live far from them (101–500 km) within Switzerland. Individuals in this group rarely cited a partner as significant. Most of the cited friends also live far from them (101–500 km). The mean size of the network counts about five individuals living on average 93 km from the respondents.

The fifth type labelled "Internationally extended network" (16%) includes individuals who cited parents, siblings, and extended kin who live abroad. They also cited children and friends who live either spatially close or abroad. Overall, individuals belonging to this type cited both spatially close and distant children and friends and spatially distant members of the family of origin: parents, siblings, and other kin. They rarely cited their partner as significant. The mean network size counts about four individuals living abroad at an average of 209 km from the respondents.

---

[7] We used the missMDA package in R for dealing with missing values in MCA. The missing values are imputed as categories corresponding to the mean of non-missing values for each variable (Josse & Husson, 2016).

[8] We used the WeightedCluster package in R (Studer, 2013); according to Point Biserial Correlation (PBC), ASW index, CH and CHsq, partitioning in 6 groups is the best solution.

The sixth network type, which we call "Residual type" (2%), due to the small number of cases, was not contributed in the analysis.

Table 1. The description of types of personal networks in terms of composition and spatiality by citation of network members at a distance in %, mean size of networks, and mean distance between respondent and network members.

	Type 1 Local family network N=222, 28%	Type 2 Local friendship network N=213, 27%	Type 3 Nearby extended network N=154, 19%	Type 4 Nationally extended network N=68, 8%	Type 5 Internationally extended network N=130, 16%	Type 6 Residual type (excluded from the analysis) N=16, 2%
Mean size of network	3.47	2.68	4.47	4.60	4.35	5.00
Mean distance between respondent and significant alters, km	8.95	15.69	28.54	92.90	208.79	43.93
Standard deviation	28.28	42.27	25.64	63.28	125.61	73.74
Citation of significant alters at the distance						
Partner				40		
0	10	70	8	59	28	31
1	90	29	88		67	69
2				1	1	
3			2			
4		1	2		2	
5						
6					2	
Children				63		
0	29	87	68	3	49	75
1	3			22	15	6
2	55	4	7	6	16	13
3	8	7	11	4	4	
4		2	11	2	3	6
5	5		3		2	
6					11	
Parents				53		
0	75	96	51		59	47
1				9		47
2	22	2	19		2	
3	3	2	19	4	1	
4			11	29	5	
5				4		
6					34	6

Table 1. Continued.

	Type 1 Local family network N=222, 28%	Type 2 Local friendship network N=213, 27%	Type 3 Nearby extended network N=154, 19%	Type 4 Nationally extended network N=68, 8%	Type 5 Internationally extended network N=130, 16%	Type 6 Residual type (excluded from the analysis) N=16, 2%
Sibling				49		
0	91	85	55		64	38
1						38
2	9	8	9	2	2	
3		7	15	4	2	6
4			20	46	3	
5						
6			1		30	18
Kin				86		
0	84	90	80		80	75
1						13
2	14	7	2	2	4	6
3	2	3	8	2		
4			10	12		
5						
6					16	6
Friends				44		
0	91	43	45		60	25
1				9		63
2	6	32	20	12	12	
3	2	21	15		3	
4	1	3	20	35	3	6
5		1			1	
6					22	6
Non kin				89		
0	97	79	94		82	81
1				4		19
2	2	11	1		4	
3	1	9	3	2	2	
4		1	2	5	8	
5						
6					4	

Note: 0-is not cited as significant; 1- lives in the same household/same municipality, 2- lives at a distance less than 10 km; 3- lives at a distance 11–40 km; 4-lives at a distance 41–100 km; 5- lives at a distance 101–500 km; 6-lives abroad.

Typology of residential trajectories

Sequence analysis techniques are used to capture chronological variations of behaviours such as residential migration at an individual level. Residential trajectories include past and present locations and their characteristics. We constructed types of residential trajectories using sequence analysis to holistically apprehend residential choices from a life course perspective (Heinz et al. 2009). The core programme of sequence analysis may be described in four steps: 1. Constructing sequences of states, 2. Comparing the sequences 3. Grouping the sequences into meaningful types and 4. Associating these types with some variables of interest (Gauthier J.-A., et al., 2014). Once constructed, the individual sequences are then systematically compared to one another using the optimal matching metric, which quantifies the degree of dissimilarity between all pairs of individual sequences (Kruskal, J., 1983). Next, a clustering procedure is applied to the distance matrix containing the dissimilarity scores to group similar sequences together and produce a typology of migration histories (Ward, J. H., 1963). Standard quality indices are used to help identify the number of groups present in the data (Rousseeuw, 1987). The typology of residential trajectories is used here as an explanatory categorical variable in regression models, while the types of personal networks are included as the dependent variables. Using the same quality indices as for the typology of personal networks, we retain five meaningful types of residential trajectories. Sequence analysis resulted in five types of residential trajectories (Figure 1). A description of the types based on the mean number of semesters spent in each residential category is presented in Table 2.

Figure 1. Typology of residential trajectories from the place of birth

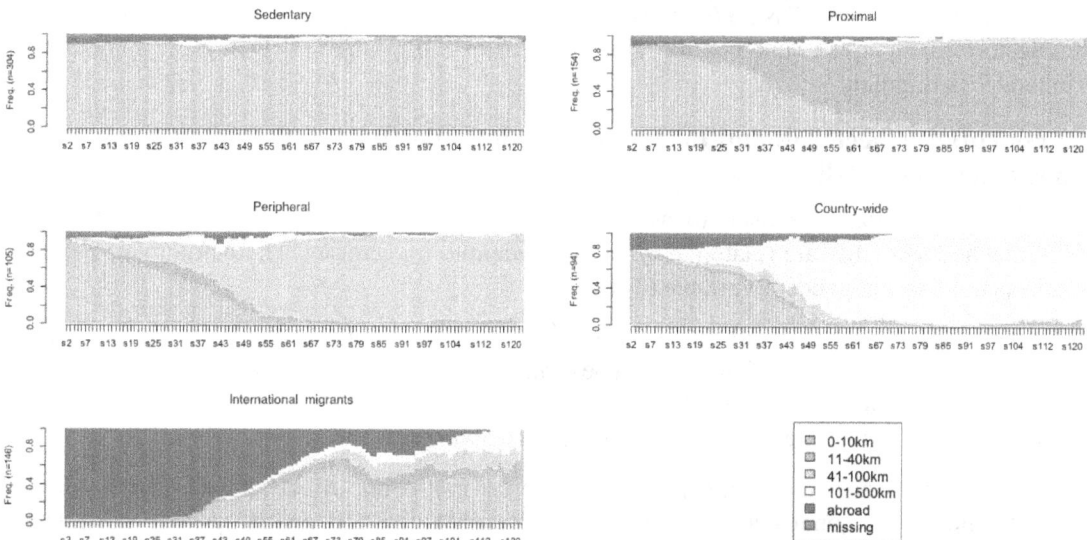

Table 2. Mean time and standard deviation (SD) in semesters spent at each stage by type of residential trajectory

	0-10km	11-40km	41-100km	101-500km	Abroad	Total
Sedentary (N=304)	87.6 (21.4)	3.7 (8.0)	1.9 (5.3)	1.5 (4.4)	3.1(9.3)	97.8
Proximal (N=154)	36.2 (16.2)	48.6 (23.7)	4.1 (8.8)	2.1 (5.3)	2.3 (7.4)	93.3
Peripheral (N=105)	28.8 (15.4)	6.0 (10.8)	60.4 (22.2)	4.2 (7.7)	2.8 (6.2)	102.2
Country-wide (N=94)	26.9 (16.2)	2.8 (7.9)	4.6 (9.1)	61.4 (22.8)	6.5 (12.1)	102.2
International migrants (N=146)	21.4 (16.8)	3.9 (10.0)	3.2 (10.4)	3.0 (9.7)	56.6 (17.9)	88.1

The first type, "Sedentary" (38%), is composed of individuals who have spent most of their life in their birthplace or at a distance of up to 10 kilometres from it. The mean time spent in the category of distance 0-10 km is 87.6 semesters or approximately 44 years. The individuals grouped in the second type, "Proximal" (19%), moved – mainly between the ages of 16 and 30 years – to locations that are up to 11-40 kilometres away from their birthplace. The mean time spent in this category of distance is 48.6 semesters or approximately 24.5 years. In the third type, "Peripheral" (13%), relocation occurs slightly earlier (between ages 15 and 25) and at a distance of 41-100 km from the birthplace. The mean time spent in this category of distance is 60.4 semesters or approximately 30 years. The fourth type, "Country-wide" (12%), reveals a similar pattern regarding the timing of move but is characterised by a relocation within Switzerland at a distance of 101-500 km from the birthplace. The mean time spent in this category of distance is 61.4 semesters or approximately 30.7 years. Finally, the fifth type, "International migrants" (18%), is composed of individuals who migrated to Switzerland, mainly between the ages of 15 and 35. Most of these individuals did not subsequently move far from their first location in Switzerland. The mean time spent in the category "abroad" is 56.6 semesters or approximately 28 years. We consider individuals with trajectories of types "Country-wide" and "International migrants", as well as, to some extent, "Peripheral," as migrants.

Residential trajectories and their relationship to personal networks in terms of composition and spatiality

Logistic regressions are used to assess how the types of personal networks in terms of composition and spatiality are related to types of residential trajectories. The typology of personal networks is used as a dependent variable (Table 3).

People who have many local relationships may have been reluctant to move, arguing for a reverse direction of causality. As network types may shape migration behaviours in return, these regression models cannot be regarded as strictly causal but rather as a way to test the association between residential trajectories and types of personal networks.

Two types of factors that could potentially have a mediating effect between the residential trajectories and the personal networks in terms of composition and spatiality were considered: respondents' socio-demographics and the length of residence in the last region. For socio-demographics, categorical variables were created to control for sex, age, level of education, activity rate and citizenship. For the length of residence in the last region, a continuous variable was created (mean=28.6, SD=17.07). The length of residence in a given place was found to be important for the reconstruction of migrants' personal networks (Cachia & Jariego, 2018; Bidart & Lavenu, 2005; Magdol & Bessel, 2003). However, the reconstruction of personal networks is not a linear process, and major changes in personal networks occur in the first years after migration (Bloem et al., 2008). For this reason, the variable of the length of residence was dichotomised between those who have lived in the last region more than five years versus those who have lived there less than five years.

The results from the regression models show that there is a strong association between the types of residential trajectories and types of personal networks. Individuals who mainly cited their co-resident partner and children (type "Local family network") lived most of their lives close to their place of birth. They are more likely to have a low level of education and are employed full time.

Table 3. The association between the types of personal networks in terms of composition and spatiality and the types of residential trajectories from the place of birth: The results of logistic regression (beta-coefficients)

	Type 1	Type 2	Type 3	Type 4	Type 5
	Local family network	Local friendship network	Nearby extended network	Nationally extended network	Internationally extended network
Residential trajectories (Ref. Sedentary)					
Proximal	-.69**	.37.	.77**	-1.64*	-.56
Peripheral	.17	-1.13***	.77**	.33	.28
Country-wide	-.37	-1.07**	-.01	2.04***	.18
International migrants	-.74*	-.39	-.68	-.07	1.65***
Length of residence in the last region (Ref. more than 5 years)					
Less than 5 years	-0.52	-0.01	-0.28	1.50**	-0.02
Sex (Ref. Male)					
Female	-.25	-.09	.16	.16	.12
Birth cohort (Ref. 1950-55)					
1970-75	-.14	-.42*	.44*	.30	.18
Level of education (Ref. Low secondary)					
Upper secondary	-.62	-.09	2.88**	-1.80*	.17
Vocational	-.33	-.41	2.78**	-.75	-.03
Tertiary	-.62*	-.51	2.42*	-.29	.44
Activity rate (Ref. Full-time)					
Part-time (51-80%)	-1.20**	-.17	.64	-.49	.64
Part-time (50% or less)	-.27	.08	-.48	.71	.54
Self-employed	.11	-.45.	-.01	.59	.21
Non-active	-.03	-.08	-.01	.20	.08
Citisenship (Ref. Foreigner)					
Swiss	-.46	.40	.92	1.44*	-.75*

Note: N=731, . p<0,1, * p<0,05, ** p<0,01, *** p<0,001.

Individuals who cited very few alters (type "Local friendship network") stay close to their places of birth during their whole lives. Their networks did not widely include members of their family of origin and the nuclear family. These individuals are embedded in networks dominated by spatially close friends (less than 10 km away) and friends within a radius of 40 km. They predominantly belong to the birth cohort born in 1950–1955. Note that the presence of friendship ties and the lack of family ties in their personal networks are not associated with residential migration.

Individuals who mainly cited relatives and friends within a 100-km (type "Nearby extended network") have mainly lived at a periphery of up to 100 km from their place of birth. They more often belong to the birth cohort born in 1970–1975 and have a comparatively high level of education. Individuals from this group are embedded in larger and diversified networks compared to the previous groups, with the presence of either spatially close partners, relatively close (less than 10 km) parents, children and friends, or spatially distant parents, children, siblings, other kin, and friends within a radius of 100 km. The inclusion of spatially distant members of the family of origin and of friends is completed by the presence of local nuclear family members and friends, thus highlighting an addition effect. However, it does not confirm a selection effect, which would be revealed by a limited presence of relatives, such as parents and children, who live distantly. Siblings, other kin members, and friends who live within a distance of 11–40 km and 41–100 km are also present in their personal networks. The results also do not confirm a substitution effect because spatially close relatives and friends are not largely present in their personal networks in comparison with relatives and friends who live far away.

Individuals who mainly cited spatially close and distant relatives and friends up to 500 km away (type "Nationally extended network") mainly lived far away (between 101 and 500 km from their place of birth). Individuals belonging to this group moved recently (less than 5 years ago) to their current region of residence. The presence of spatially close relationships with non-family members and spatially distant relationships with family relatives and friends confirms an addition effect. This effect is visible quite soon after moving (less than 5 years). A substitution effect is not confirmed because spatially close family members and friends are not overrepresented in their personal networks in comparison to family members and friends who live far away. A selection effect is not confirmed because spatially distant siblings, other kin, and friends are widely present.

Individuals who mainly cited relatives and friends who were either spatially close or lived abroad (type "Internationally extended network") were mainly born outside of Switzerland. They are embedded in internationally dispersed networks, including a spatially distant family of origin and local nuclear family members. They maintain friendship ties both at a distance and locally. The presence of spatially close children and friends, as well as children, parents, sibling, other kin, and friends living abroad, confirms an addition effect. However, a selection effect is not confirmed because siblings, other kin members, and friends living abroad are also present in their personal networks. The results do not confirm a substitution effect because spatially close family members and friends are not largely present in their personal networks in comparison with relatives and friends who live distantly.

Overall, the results show that migrants, including "Peripheral", "Country-wide" and "International migrants" tend to be embedded in large and spatially dispersed personal networks. They maintain long-distance relationships with their family of origin and friends. They also create local ties with children and friends. Individuals who stayed close to their place of birth are predominantly embedded in smaller and more local networks composed of local nuclear family members, parents or local friends. Migrants rebuild their networks mainly through the addition of spatially close relationships, predominantly with children and friends, as well as by maintaining spatially distant relationships with parents, siblings, other relatives, and friends. Selection and substitution effects are less salient for the reconstruction of personal networks in the case of residential migration.

Conclusion

This study examined the influence of residential trajectories on the composition and spatial dispersion of personal networks. It was found that individuals who lived far away from their place of birth are involved in larger, more diversified and more geographically spread out networks in comparison to weakly mobile or immobile individuals. The latter are embedded in small networks, either with a dominance of spatially close nuclear family members or spatially close friends. Individuals who moved more than 40 km away from their place of birth cited spatially distant parents, siblings, kin, and friends as significant much more often. They also cited spatially close children and friends more often. Thus, residential migration is associated with the addition of spatially close ties and the maintenance of ties with spatially distant alters, particularly with the family of origin and friends.

Controlling for respondents' socio-demographic characteristics, individuals belonging to the birth cohort born in 1970-75 and individuals with a high level of education are more likely to be embedded in large and more geographically extended networks than individuals born in 1950-55 and individuals with a lower level of education. Individuals who moved recently are embedded in large and nationally dispersed configurations. However, the effect of the length of residence on personal networks is not systematically confirmed for individuals who moved at proximity or for international migrants.

The reconstruction of personal networks due to migration was expected to be accounted for by three different mechanisms: addition of spatially close network members, selection of spatially distant network members, and substitution of spatially distant network members by spatially close network members. Among these effects, the addition of new spatially close network members had the strongest impact on the reconstruction of personal networks due to migration. Such addition was reflected by the development of diversified personal networks characterised by the presence of spatially close members of the nuclear family and spatially close friends and distant kin members. A selection effect was not confirmed by the analysis because migrants were embedded in networks with a large presence of spatially distant siblings, other kin, and friends. In addition, the results did not confirm a selection effect towards the nuclear family, known as "family centredness" (Bott, 1971). A substitution effect is not confirmed either because spatially close family and non-family members did not override spatially distant family and non-family members in migrants' networks. The analysis did not support the hypothesis that residential migration leads to the substitution of spatially distant kin and non-kin ties by spatially close kin and non-kin ties. Overall, our results show that the reconstruction of personal networks due to residential migration is hardly gained through the selection or substitution of relationships. We rather observed an increase in the number of relationships, particularly spatially close friends and spatially distant kinship members.

Our results show that distant relatives, particularly members of the family of origin, are largely present in the personal networks of migrants, whereas they are more likely limited in the personal networks of immobile individuals. This finding fully contradicts the expectation that members of the family of origin are widely present in the personal networks of individuals who remain in their place of birth. Geographical distance positively influences the presence of family members, particularly members of the family of origin. Family networks not only survive but also become larger through the involvement of other relatives, in addition to parents and children, living away. Paradoxically, residential migration, which is often associated in the literature with the creation of more personalised relationships, strengthens the presence of family members, particularly from the family of origin, in personal networks. Thus, the creation of new local relationships does not result in the loosening of distant family ties; rather, these processes go in the same direction. The inclusion of spatially distant family members is responsible for family commitments, which continue to play a major role after moving. Obligations to family and friends involve strong normative expectations towards co-presence and care, which is reflected in meetings and activities with friends and family

(Larsen, Axhausen & Urry, 2006; Ryan, 2004; Urry, 2012). Additionally, the salience of the family of origin in personal networks is explained by the effect of distance, which may reinforce the history of family and family roots in the identity of migrants. The migration experiences produce a cumulative effect on personal networks by the addition of spatially close friends and family members to distant ones. Overall, geographical distance favours the creation of more inclusive family networks. This confirms the results from previous studies, which show that new relationships are primarily formed within already established clusters of ties (Lubbers et al., 2010).

Social and migration policies may be well advised to consider such issues. For instance, policies developed in the UK for promoting the integration of immigrants enforce the creation of spatially close relationships (Ryan, 2011). Policy makers should, however, not forget that a large share of the personal networks of migrants is centred on spatially distant family members, which may increase in emotional and practical importance after migration. Migrants provide relatives with support while being supported by them through a variety of exchanges (Baldassar, 2007) and are involved in strong normative expectations towards family and friends (Larsen, Axhausen & Urry, 2006; Urry, 2012). From this perspective, social policies increasing the fluidity of the circulation of spatially distant family members (visas and regimes of residency) may help migrants to sustain their personal networks and social integration in the long run. Conversely, immobile individuals are embedded in small networks, including either the members of their nuclear family or some friends. They may lack personal relationships and be at risk of social isolation, particularly in the event that they need support.

The study has some limitations related to the static link demonstrated between residential trajectories and personal networks. Based on the data at hand and due to the absence of longitudinal data on personal networks, it was not possible to provide a process-oriented empirical demonstration of the link between migration events and changes in personal relationships. Considering personal networks in terms of composition and spatiality across all the phases of residential trajectories would be helpful for understanding network changes associated with mobility issues. The addition, selection, and substitution of alters are strongly intertwined processes, and it is difficult to disentangle them without longitudinal data. In other words, we cannot characterise individuals' personal networks before moving or at which stage of moving these effects appeared. An additional limitation relates to the fact that we could not consider other dimensions of causality related to migration, such as how personal networks impact the likelihood of moving or staying, or the possibility that some relatives follow migrants. This paper provides nevertheless contribution to the literature by delineating such processes and their effects on the composition and spatiality of migrants' personal networks. Further studies should reconsider such processes using longitudinal network data.

References

Abdi, H. & Valentin, D. (2007). Multiple correspondence analysis. *Encyclopedia of measurement and statistics*, 651-657.

Ackers, L. (1998). Shifting Spaces: Women, Citizenship and Migration Within the European Union. Londres: Polity press.

Allan, G. (1998). Flexibility, Friendship and Family. *Personal Relationships*, *15*(5).

Allan, G. (2001). Personal relationships in late modernity. *Personal relationships*, 8, 325-339.

Baldassar, L. (2007). Transnational families and aged care: the mobility of care and the migrancy of ageing. *Journal of ethnic and migration studies*, 33(2), 275-297.

Bengtson, V. L., & Roberts, R. E. (1991). Intergenerational solidarity in aging families: An example of formal theory construction. *Journal of Marriage and the Family*, 856-870.

Bidart, C., & Lavenu, D. (2005). Evolutions of Personal Networks and Life Events. *Social networks*, *27*(4).

Bloem, B. A., Tilburg, T. G. V., & Thomese, F. (2008). Changes in older Dutch adults' role networks after moving. *Personal Relationships*, 15(4), 465-478.

Bonvalet, C., & Mason, J. (1999). Familles et entourage: le jeu des proximités. In Bonvalet, C. Gotman, A. & Grafmeyer, Y. (Eds). *La famille et ses proches: L'amenagement des territoires*. PUF

Bott, E. (1971). *Family and Social Network*. Tavistock publications: London.

Bryceson, D., and Vuorela, U. (2002). The transnational family: New European frontiers and global networks. Berg Publishers Ltd.

Cachia, R., & Jariego, I. M. (2018). Mobility types, transnational relationships and personal networks in four highly skilled immigrant communities in Seville (Spain). *Social Networks*, 53, 111-124.

Carrasco, J. A., Miller, E. J., & Wellman, B. (2008). How far and with whom do people socialise? Empirical evidence about distance between social network members. *Transportation Research Record*, 2076(1), 114-122.

Coenen-Huther, J., Kelerhals, J., Von Allmen, (1994). *Les réseaux de solidarités dans la famille*. Réalités sociales: Lausanne.

Coleman, J. S. (1988). Social capital in the creation of human capital. American journal of sociology, 94, 95-120.

Cooke, T. J. (2008). Migration in a family way. Population, Space and Place, 14(4), 255-265.

Cronin, A. M. (2015). Distant Friends, Mobility and Sensed intimacy. *Mobilities*, *10*(5).

Finch, J. & Mason, J. (1993). *Negotiating Family Responsibilities*, Routledge, London.

Freedman, D., Thornton, A., Camburn, D., Alwin, D., Young-DeMarco, L., & others. (1988). The life history calendar: A technique for collecting retrospective data. Sociological Methodology, 18(1), 37–68.

Gauthier, J.-A., Bühlmann, F., & Blanchard, P. (2014). Introduction: Sequence Analysis in 2014. In P. Blanchard, F. Bühlmann, & J.-A. Gauthier (Eds.), Advances in sequence analysis: theory, method, applications (pp. 1–17). NY: Springer.

Green, E. A. and A. Canny (2003) Geographical Mobility, Family Impacts. Cambridge: Jo-seph Rowntree Foundation, Policy Press.

Grossetti, M. (2007). Are French networks different? *Social Networks*, 29(3), 391-404.

Heinz, W. R., Huinink, J., & Weymann, A. (Eds.). (2009). The life course reader: individuals and societies across time. Frankfurt: Campus Verlag.

Herz, A. (2015). Relational construction of social support in migrants' transnational personal communities. *Social Networks*, 40, 64-74.

Herz, A., Díaz-Chorne, L., Díaz-Catalán C., Altissimo, A., Samuk Carignani, S. (2019). Are you mobile, too? The role played by social networks in the intention to move abroad among youth in Europe. *Migration letters*, 16(1).

Husson, F., Lê, S. & Pagès, J. (2009). Analyse des données avec R. Presses Universitaires de Rennes.

Johnson, C. L. (2000). Perspectives on American kinship in the later 1990s. *Journal of Marriage and Family*, 62(3), 623-639.

Josse J. & Husson F. (2016). missMDA: a package for handling missing values in multivariate data analysis. Journal of Statistical Software, 70(1), 1-31.

Kruskal, J. (1983). An overview on sequence comparison. In D. Sankoff & J. B. Kruskal (Eds.), Time warps, string edits, and macromolecules. The theory and practice of sequence comparison (pp. 1–44). United States: CSLI Publications.

Larsen, J., Axhausen, K. W., & Urry, J. (2006). Geographies of Social Networks: Meetings, Travel and Communications. *Mobilities*, *1*(2), 261-283.

Litwak, E. (1960). Geographic mobility and extended family cohesion. American Sociological Review, 385-394.

Lubbers, M. J., Molina, J. L., Lerner, J., Brandes, U., Ávila, J., & McCarty, C. (2010). Longitudinal analysis of personal networks. The case of Argentinean migrants in Spain. *Social Networks*, 32(1), 91-104.

Magdol, L., & Bessel, D. R. (2003). Social capital, social currency, and portable assets: The impact of residential mobility on exchanges of social support. *Personal Relationships*, 10(2), 149-170.

Marsden, P. V. (1987). Core discussion networks of Americans. *American Sociological Review*, 52(1), 122-131.

Mason, J. 1999. « Living away from relatives: kinship and geographical reasoning » in S. McRae (Eds.), *Changing Britain: families and households in the 1990s*. Oxford: Oxford University Press.

Mason, J. (2004). Personal narratives, relational selves: residential histories in the living and telling. *The Sociological Review*, 52(2), 162-179.

Morgan, D.H. (2013). Time, Space and Family Practices. In Morgan, D.H. (Eds). *Rethinking Family Practices*. London: Pargrave MacMillan.

Mulder, C. H., & Cooke, T. J. (2009). Family relationships and residential locations. *Population, space and place*, 15(4), 299-304.

Mulder, C. H., & Kalmijn, M. (2006). Geographical distances between family members. *Family solidarity in the Netherlands*, 43-62.

Mulder, C. H., & van der Meer, M. J. (2009). Geographical Distances and Support From Family Members. *Population, space and place*, *15*(4).

Niedomysl, T. (2011). How migration motives change over migration distance: Evidence on variation across socio-economic and demographic groups. *Regional Studies*, 45(6), 843-855.

Ogg, J. & Bonvalet, C. (2004). Les enquêtes sur l'entraide familiale en Europe. *Recherches et prévisions*, 77, 77-85.

Pahl, R., & Pevalin, D. J. (2005). Between family and friends: a longitudinal study of friendship choice. *The British journal of sociology*, 56(3), 433-450.

Pollet, T. V., Roberts, S. G., & Dunbar, R. I. (2013). Going that extra mile: individuals travel further to maintain face-to-face contact with highly related kin than with less related kin. *PloS one*, 8(1), e53929.

Rousseeuw, P. J. (1987). Silhouettes: A graphical aid to the interpretation and validation of cluster analysis. *Journal of Computational and Applied Mathematics*, 20, 53-65.

Ryan, L. (2004). Family matters:(e) migration, familial networks and Irish women in Britain. *The sociological review*, 52(3), 351-370.

Ryan, L. (2007). Migrant women, social networks and motherhood: The experiences of Irish nurses in Britain. *Sociology*, 41(2), 295-312.

Ryan, L. (2011). Migrants' social networks and weak relationships: accessing resources and constructing relationships post-migration. *The Sociological Review*, 59(4), 707-724.

Ryan, L., Sales, R., Tilki, M., & Siara, B. (2008). Social networks, social support and social capital: The experiences of recent Polish migrants in London. *Sociology*, 42(4), 672-690.

Studer, M. (2013). WeightedCluster library manual: A practical guide to creating typologies of trajectories in the social sciences with R.

Urry. J. (2012). Social network, mobile lives and social inequalities. *Journal of transport geography*, 21, 24-30.

Urry, J., & Elliott, A. (2010). Mobile lives. Routledge.

Vignal, C. (2002). "Mobilités, migrations et ancrages face à la délocalisation de l'emploi" Pa-per presented at the AISLF conférence « Mobilités familiales au quotidien », October 10-12, 2002, Lausanne.

Ward, J. H. (1963). Hierarchical grouping to optimise an objective function. *Journal of the American Statistical Association*, 58(301), 236-244.

Wasserman, S. & Faust, K. (1999). Social network analysis: methods and applications. Cambridge: Cambridge University Press.

Wellman, B., Hogan, B., Berg, K., Boase, J., Carrasco, J.A., Côté, R., Kayahara, J., Kennedy, T.L.M., Tran, P. (2005). Connected lives : the project.In Purcell, P. (Ed.), Networked Neighbourhoods. Springer Verlag, London, 161-216.

Wellman, B. (2001). Physical Place and Cyber Place: The Rise of Networked Individualism. *International Journal of Urban and Regional Research*, 25.

Wellman, B., & Wortley, S. (1990). Different strokes from different folks: Community relationships and social support. *American journal of Sociology*, 96(3), 558-588.

Wrzus, C., Hänel, M., Wagner, J., & Neyer, F. J. (2013). Social network changes and life events across the life span: a meta-analysis. *Psychological bulletin*, 139(1), 53.

September 2020
Volume: 17, **No**: 5, pp. 639–649
ISSN: 1741-8984
e-ISSN: 1741-8992
www.migrationletters.com

MIGRATION
LETTERS

First Submitted: 1 February 2019 Accepted: 23 May 2020
DOI: https://doi.org/10.33182/ml.v17i5.693

Spending Level of Displaced Population Returned to La Palma, Cundinamarca (2018): A Machine Learning Application

Jenny-Paola Lis-Gutiérrez[1], Mercedes Gaitán-Angulo[2] and Jenny Cubillos-Diaz[3]

Abstract

This research aims to know the variables allowing to predict the spending level of the displacement victims that returned to La Palma, Cundinamarca. For this purpose, a measurement instrument was divided into four sections: characterisation of the population, restitution of economic rights, patterns of economic distribution and, finally, social innovation initiatives. We applied the instrument to 100 participants, and we use different Machine Learning algorithms to know the variables that allow predicting the level of expenses of the displacement victims that returned to La Palma, Cundinamarca. The findings permitted to observe that, at the aggregate level, the Random Forest and the SMV have a prediction capacity higher than 84%.

Keywords: *Displaced population; expenses; victimising events; Colombia armed conflict; machine learning.*

Introduction

Expenditure is a key component in the welfare measure of a population, so, countries use the income or consumption expenses as indicators of poverty. For this reason, many studies have focused on analysing the methods of consumption data collection and the perceived distribution of expenses to obtain levels of poverty in a region (Beegle *et al.*, 2015; Dang & Lanjouw, 2016; Tarozzi, 2007). As a variable, expenditure is more stable than income since it allows a better classification of households and has been considered the standard variable to measure poverty (Deaton, 2005).

Authors such as Shafir (2017) affirm that facts such as poverty, financial challenges, instability of income, expenses and low level of savings occupy a relevant place in populations that have been victims of violence. The context of poverty goes beyond mere survival and is partly a matter of norms and conceptualisation. In this way, as societies advance and standards evolve, things that were once considered a luxury can become common.

Colombia has suffered an internal armed conflict for decades, being the forced displacement one of the most recurrent victimising events in the country (Lagos-Gallego et al., 2017; García-Chavarro, at al., 2018; Lis-Gutiérrez, et al., 2018a, 2018b). The municipality of La Palma, in Cundinamarca region, was, in the year 2015, one of the most affected territories with 13,848 displaced individuals and 2,698 hectares registered as abandoned (Centro Nacional de Memoria Histórica, 2015). However, at present, this municipality is a pioneer in the restitution of lands and return to the territory of the population victim of those crimes.

[1] Jenny-Paola Lis-Gutiérrez, Fundación Universitaria Konrad Lorenz, Colombia. E-mail: jenny.lis@konradlorenz.edu.co.
[2] Mercedes Gaitán-Angulo, Fundación Universitaria Konrad Lorenz, Colombia. E-mail: mercedes.gaitana@konradlorenz.edu.co.
[3] Jenny Cubillos-Diaz, Fundación Universitaria Konrad Lorenz, Colombia. E-mail: jennyk.cubillosd@konradlorenz.edu.co.

The populations that are victims of events such as displacement, and return to their territories, face difficulties in adapting, especially due to labor inclusion issues (Depetris-Chauvin & Santos, 2018; Dabaieh & Alwall, 2018; Contreras, Blaschke, & Hodgson, 2017) and reconciliation and forgiveness (López-López *et al.*, 2019). These changes in their context transformed their social and economic dynamics; so, the monthly low expenses of the displaced population are usually due to informal jobs that accentuate the conditions of vulnerability to which they are exposed (Falla Ramírez, Chávez Plazas, & Molano Beltrán, 2003). This situation does not improve when returning, since populations, in most cases, take several generations to adapt to their territory again (Lis-Gutiérrez *et al.*, 2019). Therefore, the actions framed in the integral reparation of this type of population must be subject to public policies that recognise the complexity of factors that interact in the economic development of their communities (Lacroix & Zufferey, 2019; Johnson *et al.*, 2019).

As a contribution to this subject, the work of Lis-Gutiérrez, et al., (2018c) applies the machine learning principles to measure the incomes of the displaced population in La Palma, finding that the best algorithms were Decision Tree, AdaBoost and Random Forest, with a predictive level between 80% and 90.6%.

Based on these approaches, this research seeks to know the variables that allow predicting the level of expenditures of the population victim of displacement that returned to La Palma, Cundinamarca in 2018. Answering to this question implies knowing the way in which economic dynamics influence social and territorial development, and understanding how the population expenses are related to the historical conditions of violation to their rights.

In this sense, several machine learning or automatic learning algorithms were used, defining machine learning as "the science of giving meaning to data through algorithms and analytical models […] it allows cognitive systems to learn, reason and interact with us in a more natural and personalised way" (IBM, 2018).

The originality of this work is based in two elements: (i) direct work with the community, and (ii) the use of an analysis technique never used so far to understand the relationship between displacement and population expenditures.

Data and Method

In this section, the data, variables and method used for the analysis are presented.

The variables considered emerged from the information obtained in a fieldwork carried out in the municipality of La Palma between July and September 2018, where 100 volunteers were randomly selected, meeting the following conditions: (i) be resident of La Palma, Cundinamarca in 2018, (ii) be part of the displaced population registered in the Unique Registry of Victims (URV), (iii) be over 18 years old, and (iv) belong to socioeconomic levels 1 and 2.

The calculation of the sample was made based on a population size of N = 8,730 inhabitants of the municipality. Having defined the target population range, with the conditions previously predicted, the next step was to calculate the strength of the sample, using the following formula:

$$n = \frac{Z_\alpha^2 N p q}{e^2(N-1) + Z_\alpha^2 p q} \quad (1)$$

Where

N: is the size of the population or universe (total number of potential respondents) = 8.730

Zα = 95%

e = 10%, is the desired sample error.

p = 50% proportion of individuals who meet the study conditions in the population, given that the exact parameter is unknown, 50% is used.

q = 50% proportion of individuals who do not meet the study conditions in the population.

n: sample size

Only 95 individuals were required to guarantee an error margin of 10% and confidence level of 95%. Given the sample of 100 individuals, the confidence level is 95%, and the error margin is reduced to 9.75%. The instrument applied (survey) received a content validation from three expert judges, and a pilot test was applied to 12 people for testing the understanding level of the instrument. The survey used to collect the information was divided into three sections. The first one was oriented to know the socio-demographic characteristics of the population (age, level of education, place of birth, etc.). The second section was related to questions about the rights restitution process to communities that suffered displacement. And the last one sought to know the type of monthly economic expenses and the economic conditions of the household.

The instrument was applied by two volunteers with experience in handling people in the field. The survey was conducted with presence of the interviewer who completed the instrument, during a period of 23,5 minutes. Each of the participants carried out the survey following the following sequence: (i) reading of the informed consent was completed; (ii) application of the filter for validation of inclusion and exclusion criteria; (iii) reading the general instructions; and (iv) application of the instrument.

The instrument was applied as established in Law 1090 of 2006 (Congreso de la República de Colombia, 2011) about the professional practice of the psychologist, from the ethical and procedural point of view, meeting the following criteria: (i) provide clear information about the type of research carried out, the people responsible for it and the institution for which it was being carried out; (ii) inform about the confidential nature of the information provided and the exclusive use of the investigators; (iii) provide sufficient information about the purpose of the investigation; (iv) inform the average duration of the test, the tasks to be performed, and the non-existence of risk of secondary effects or health damages to the participants; (v) explain the manifest of voluntary participation in the investigation; and (vi) inform that the test could be abandoned at any time on a voluntary basis.

The variables that were analysed in the document were the following (Table 1).

Table 1. Instrument variables

Variable	Typology
What is your place of birth?	Categorical
According to the utility bills of your home, what is your stratum? (This information is found on the service invoice)	Categorical
How old are you?	Numeric
What sex do you belong to?	Categorical

Table 1. Continued.

Actually lives in	Categorical
What is your occupation?	Categorical
How many people make up your home?	Numeric
Of these people, how many are financially dependent on you?	Numeric
What is the maximum level of education you have reached?	Categorical
In what year was you admitted as a victim at Unique Registry of Victims (URV)	Numeric
Why is it registered with the Unique Registry of Victims (URV)?	Categorical
In what year did you have to leave the municipality?	Date
To date, have you received any comprehensive reparation measure?	Categorical
If your answer was *yes*, which of the following measures have been part of this comprehensive repair? [financial compensation, repair individual or collective]	Categorical
If the answer was *financial compensation,* could you specify *yes*?	Categorical
If your answer was "You have already used these resources in other investments" could you describe in which investments?	Categorical
Have you received any kind of accompaniment from the state in the investment or expenditure of these resources?	Categorical
If your answer was *yes*, please describe the type of accompaniment	Categorical
In what year were you beneficiary of the repair?	Date
Was this repair Individual or Collective?	Categorical
Normally, how much are the monthly expenses of this home? [COP 1=0-500.000; 2=501.000 -1.000.000; 3=1.001.000-2.000.000; 4= >2.001.000]	Categorical
Normally, how much do the monthly expenses of the household correspond to? [COP 1=0-500.000; 2=501.000 -1.000.000; 3=1.001.000-2.000.000; 4= >2.001.000]	Categorical
Does any member of the household have credits or debts with entities, relatives, friends or people?	Categorical
If your answer to the previous question was *Yes*, specify the value of the credit or debt	Numeric
Have you used the economic resources of credit in a business initiative?	Categorical

Source: own elaboration.

For information processing, several methods (algorithms) of supervised learning were applied, which are summarised in Table 2.

Table 2. Supervised learning algorithms

Method	Synthesis
AdaBoost	It is an adaptive learning algorithm that combines weak classifiers and adapts to the hardness of each training sample, achieving robust classifiers. Allows binary and multi-class classification.
Random Forest	Uses a set of decision trees for the classification and projection. It is a non-parametric procedure which can be used when: (i) there are correlated variables; (ii) few data; (iii) complex interactions; (iv) missing data.
Support Vector Machines (SVM)	Allows the binary classification and multi-class. Makes use of regression analysis and classification.
Neural network	Makes use of the algorithm for multi-layer perceptron (MLP) with retropropagation. Its advantage is that nonlinear models can be learned.
KNN	This mechanism is for the recognition of non-parametric patterns; it is based on the nearest training instances, being an algorithm of k nearest neighbors. It is also known as lazy learning.

Table 2. Continued.

Naive Bayes	A quick and simple probabilistic classifier based on the Bayes theorem, with the assumption of independence of features. It is assumed that the absence or presence of a characteristic is not related to the presence or absence of another property. Its advantage is that it requires little data for training.
Learning algorithm of the decision tree	It is used for discrete and continuous data. It is based on the prediction of the value of a target variable based on various input variables.

Source: Lis-Gutiérrez & Aguilera-Hernández (2019) and Moros et al., (2019).

Results

In Figure 1, the different learning and prediction algorithms used are shown, and in Figure 2, the precision calculations of the same. It should be noted that the use of the random cross validation option was used. This method consisted of randomly dividing the training and test data set, by means of 10 iterations. The adjustment is obtained from the arithmetic mean of the values obtained for each of the iterations. Figure 3 shows the confusion matrix for each algorithm.

Figure 1. Image of the model representation using Orange

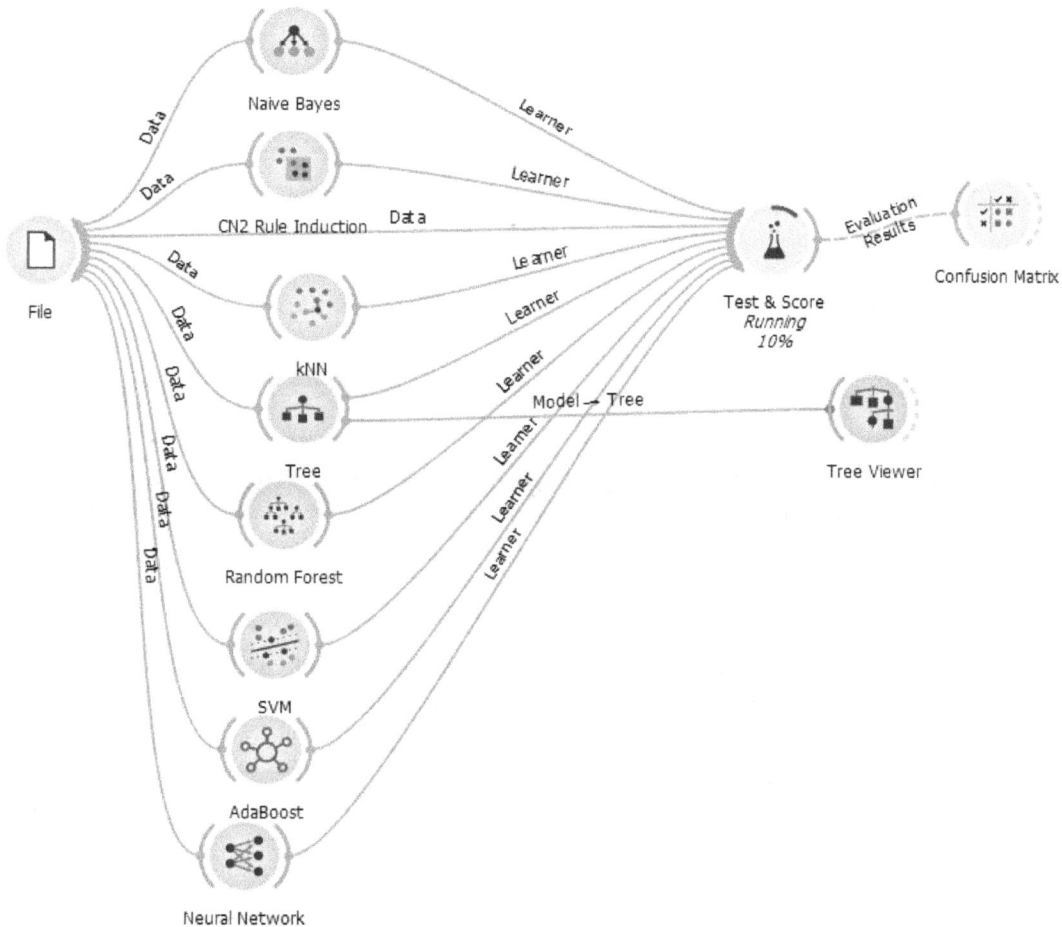

Source: own elaboration using Orange (Demsar, et al., 2013).

Figure 2. Calculation of learning and prediction algorithms for the complete sample.

Test & Score

Settings

Sampling type: Stratified 20-fold Cross validation
Target class: Average over classes

Scores

Method	AUC	CA	F1	Precision	Recall
Random Forest	0.829	0.870	0.863	0.872	0.870
SVM	0.842	0.790	0.765	0.844	0.790
AdaBoost	0.779	0.790	0.792	0.796	0.790
Tree	0.753	0.800	0.795	0.792	0.800
Naïve Bayes	0.817	0.740	0.737	0.750	0.740
Neural Network	0.760	0.740	0.732	0.730	0.740
CN2 rule inducer	0.689	0.710	0.701	0.700	0.710
kNN	0.594	0.600	0.495	0.499	0.600

Source: own elaboration using Orange (Demsar, et al., 2013).

Figure 3. Confusion matrix for each algorithm (complete sample).

Data

Data instances: 100
Features: ID. ¿Cuál es su lugar de nacimiento? ¿Según las facturas de servicios públicos de su casa que estrato es? ¿Cuántos años tiene? ¿A qué sexo pertenece? Actualmente vive en, ¿Cuál es su ocupación?. ¿Cuántas personas conforman su hogar?. ¿De estas personas cuantas dependen económicamente de usted?. ¿Cuál es el nivel máximo de escolaridad titulada que usted alcanzó? ¿En qué año fue admitido como víctima ante el RUV?. ¿Por qué hecho se encuentra registrado ante el RUV?. ¿En qué año tuvo que desplazarse del municipio?. ¿A la fecha cuenta con alguna medida de reparación integral? ¿Si su respuesta fue si ¿Cuál de las siguientes medidas han hecho parte de esta reparación integral? ¿Si la respuesta fue indemnización económica podría especificar si?. Si su respuesta fue "Ya ha hecho uso de estos recursos en otras inversiones" podría describirnos en cuáles inversiones. ¿Ha recibido alguna clase de acompañamiento por parte del estado en la inversión o el gasto de estos recursos?... (total 41 features)

Confusion Matrix

Confusion matrix for Naïve Bayes (showing proportion of predicted)

		Predicted			
		0 a 500,000	1,000,001 a 2,000,000	500,001 a 1,000,000	Σ
Actual	0 a 500,000	84.2 %	20.0 %	39.1 %	61
	1,000,001 a 2,000,000	0.0 %	60.0 %	0.0 %	12
	500,001 a 1,000,000	15.8 %	20.0 %	60.9 %	27
	Σ	57	20	23	100

Figure 3. Continued.

Confusion Matrix

Confusion matrix for CN2 rule inducer (showing proportion of predicted)

		Predicted			
		0 a 500,000	1,000,001 a 2,000,000	500,001 a 1,000,000	Σ
Actual	0 a 500,000	74.6 %	23.1 %	40.0 %	61
	1,000,001 a 2,000,000	4.5 %	69.2 %	0.0 %	12
	500,001 a 1,000,000	20.9 %	7.7 %	60.0 %	27
	Σ	67	13	20	100

Confusion Matrix

Confusion matrix for kNN (showing proportion of predicted)

		Predicted			
		0 a 500,000	1,000,001 a 2,000,000	500,001 a 1,000,000	Σ
Actual	0 a 500,000	63.0 %	20.0 %	66.7 %	61
	1,000,001 a 2,000,000	12.0 %	20.0 %	0.0 %	12
	500,001 a 1,000,000	25.0 %	60.0 %	33.3 %	27
	Σ	92	5	3	100

Confusion Matrix

Confusion matrix for Tree (showing proportion of predicted)

		Predicted			
		0 a 500,000	1,000,001 a 2,000,000	500,001 a 1,000,000	Σ
Actual	0 a 500,000	84.6 %	0.0 %	26.1 %	61
	1,000,001 a 2,000,000	0.0 %	83.3 %	8.7 %	12
	500,001 a 1,000,000	15.4 %	16.7 %	65.2 %	27
	Σ	65	12	23	100

Figure 3. Continued.

Confusion Matrix

Confusion matrix for Random Forest (showing proportion of predicted)

		Predicted			
		0 a 500,000	1,000,001 a 2,000,000	500,001 a 1,000,000	Σ
Actual	0 a 500,000	85.7 %	0.0 %	5.0 %	61
	1,000,001 a 2,000,000	0.0 %	100.0 %	10.0 %	12
	500,001 a 1,000,000	14.3 %	0.0 %	85.0 %	27
	Σ	70	10	20	100

Confusion Matrix

Confusion matrix for SVM (showing proportion of predicted)

		Predicted			
		0 a 500,000	1,000,001 a 2,000,000	500,001 a 1,000,000	Σ
Actual	0 a 500,000	74.4 %	0.0 %	0.0 %	61
	1,000,001 a 2,000,000	6.1 %	100.0 %	0.0 %	12
	500,001 a 1,000,000	19.5 %	0.0 %	100.0 %	27
	Σ	82	7	11	100

Confusion Matrix

Confusion matrix for AdaBoost (showing proportion of predicted)

		Predicted			
		0 a 500,000	1,000,001 a 2,000,000	500,001 a 1,000,000	Σ
Actual	0 a 500,000	83.9 %	0.0 %	32.1 %	61
	1,000,001 a 2,000,000	0.0 %	100.0 %	7.1 %	12
	500,001 a 1,000,000	16.1 %	0.0 %	60.7 %	27
	Σ	62	10	28	100

Figure 3. Continued.

Confusion Matrix

Confusion matrix for Neural Network (showing proportion of predicted)

		Predicted			
		0 a 500,000	1,000,001 a 2,000,000	500,001 a 1,000,000	Σ
Actual	0 a 500,000	77.6 %	0.0 %	40.9 %	61
	1,000,001 a 2,000,000	1.5 %	90.9 %	4.5 %	12
	500,001 a 1,000,000	20.9 %	9.1 %	54.5 %	27
	Σ	67	11	22	100

Source: own elaboration using Orange (Demsar, et al., 2013).

After applying 8 supervised learning algorithms to the survey information, it was possible to identify that:

When considering the average results, the following algorithms have a predictive capacity between 84.4% and 87.2%: Random Forest and SVM; and between 75% and 79.6% had a predictive capacity AdaBoost, Tree, Naive Bayes (Figure 2).

The algorithm with the least predictive capacity was the KNN.

Considering the Figure 3, it is possible to indicate that:

The best algorithms for the prediction of the range of costs between 0 and 500,000 pesos were: (i) Random Forest: 85.7%; (ii) the decision tree: 84.6%; (iii) Naive Bayes: 84.2%; (iv) AdaBoost: 83.9%.

The best algorithms for the prediction of range of expenditure between 500,001 and 1,000,000 pesos were: (i) SVM: 100%; (ii) Random Forest: 85%.

The best algorithms for the prediction of range of expenditure between 1,000,001 and 2,000,000 pesos were: (i) Random Forest: 100%; (ii) SVM: 100%; (iii) AdaBoost: 100%; (iv) Neural Networks: 90.9%; (v) decision tree: 83.3%

The others algorithms do not predict any of the three ranges with an accuracy higher than 80%, therefore, should not be taken into account: KNN y CR2.

Now, the application of the decision tree displaying the variables that allow to predict in 84.6% the population that gets between 0 and 500,000 monthly. Its characteristics are the following: (i) the level of education ranges between primary, secondary or technical support; (ii) have received compensation by the State; (iii) have generally used the resources for housing arrangements and purchase of animals for the farm. Likewise the application of the decision tree displaying the variables that allow to predict in 83.3% the population that gets between 1,000,001 and 2,000,000 monthly. The level of income ranges between 500,000 and 2,000,000 pesos, but most of those who earn between 500,001 and 1,000.000 are located in a rural area.

Conclusions

The variables that allowed explaining the behaviour of the expenses of the victims who returned to La Palma, Cundinamarca were identified. It was possible to establish that the three best supervised learning algorithms, for the average, were at the aggregate level the Random Forest and the SMV emblem with a capacity of prediction, higher than 84%. As in the work of Lis-Gutierrez et al, (2018c), the algorithm with less capacity of prediction was the KNN. The Random Forest, the decision tree, Naive Bayes and AdaBoost: predict the initial income range with a level higher than 83.9% (between 0 and 500,000 pesos, i.e., between 0 and 167 dollars). For the prediction of middle income range (between 500,001 and 1,000.000, i.e. between 167 and 334 monthly dollars), the SVM had a predictive capacity of 100%, followed by Random Forest. With regard to the prediction of middle income range (between 1,000,001 and 2,000.000, i.e. between 334 and 668 monthly dollars), the SVM, the Random Forest and AdaBoost, had a predictive capacity of 100%, followed by the neural networks and the decision tree.

Among the recommendations for future studies are: (i) enlarge the sample, in order to have more predictive power and reduce the error margin from 9.75% to 5%; (ii) replicate this study in other populations, and check if the algorithms identified efficiently predict the income levels of the returning population. In either case, communicating of the findings to the community is required.

Acknowledgements

The authors wish to express their gratitude to the community of La Palma (Cundinamarca).

References

Beegle, K., De Weerdt, J., Friedman, J., & Gibson, J. (2015). Methods of household consumption measurement through surveys: Experimental results from Tanzania. Washington: Banco Mundial.

Centro Nacional de Memoria Histórica. (2015). *Una nación desplazada: informe nacional del desplazamiento forzado en Colombia*. Bogotá: CNMH–UARIV. Retrieved from: http://www.centrodememoriahistorica.gov.co/descargas/informes2015/nacion-desplazada/una-nacion-desplazada.pdf.

Congreso de la República de Colombia (2011). *Ley 1090 de 2006*. Diario Oficial 46.383. Bogotá: Imprenta Nacional.

Contreras, D., Blaschke, T., & Hodgson, M. E. (2017). Lack of spatial resilience in a recovery process: Case L'Aquila, Italy. *Technological Forecasting and Social Change*, 121, 76-88.

Dang, H. A. H., & Lanjouw, P. F. (2016). *Toward a new definition of shared prosperity: A dynamic perspective from three countries.* In Inequality and growth: Patterns and policy (pp. 151-171). Londres: Palgrave Macmillan.

Dabaieh, M., & Alwall, J. (2018). Building now and building back. Refugees at the centre of an occupant driven design and construction process. *Sustainable cities and society*, 37, 619-627.

Deaton, A. (2005). Measuring poverty in a growing world (or measuring growth in a poor world). *Review of Economics and statistics*, 87(1), 1-19.

Demsar, J., Curk, T., Erjavec, A., Gorup C, Hocevar, T., Milutinovic, M., Mozina, M., Polajnar, M., Toplak, M., Staric, A., Stajdohar, M., Umek, L., Zagar, L., Zbontar, J., Zitnik, M., Zupan, B. (2013). Orange: Data Mining Toolbox in Python. *Journal of Machine Learning Research*, 14(Aug), 2349−2353.

Depetris-Chauvin, E. y Santos, R. (2018). Unexpected guests: The impact of internal displacement inflows on rental prices in Colombian host cities. *Journal of Development Economics,* 134, 289-309.

Falla Ramírez, U., Chávez Plazas, Y. A., & Molano Beltrán, G. (2003). Desplazamiento forzado en Colombia. Análisis documental e informe de investigación en la Unidad de Atención al Desplazado (UAID). *Tabula Rasa, 1*, 221-234. Retrieved from: http://www.redalyc.org/pdf/396/39600111.pdf

García-Chavarro, A., Lis-Gutiérrez, J-P., Rincón-Vásquez, J.C., Gaitán-Angulo, M., Cubillos-Diaz, J., Mojica-Sánchez, L. (2018). Caracterización de los hechos victimizantes por región en las víctimas del conflicto armado colombiano.

En J.P. Lis-Gutiérrez, M. Gaitán-Angulo, J. Cubillos-Díaz, L. Mojica Sánchez y L.E. Malagón. *Conflicto y construcción de paz*. Villavicencio: Unimeta.

IBM (2018). Machine learning. Retrieved from: https://www.ibm.com/analytics/es/es/technology/machine-learning/

Johnson, T., von Meding, J., Gajendran, T., & Forino, G. (2019). Disaster vulnerability of displaced people in Rakhine state, Myanmar. In Resettlement Challenges for Displaced Populations and Refugees (pp. 81-91). Springer, Cham.

Lacroix, J., & Zufferey, J. (2019). A Life Course Approach to Immigrants' Relocation: Linking Long-and Short-distance Mobility Sequences. Migration Letters, 16(2), 283-300.

Lagos-Gallego, M., Gutierrez-Segura, J. C., Lagos-Grisales, G. J., & Rodriguez-Morales, A. J. (2017). Post-traumatic stress disorder in internally displaced people of Colombia: An ecological study. *Travel medicine and infectious disease, 16*, 41-45.

Lis-Gutiérrez, J. P., Rincón-Vásquez, J.C., Gaitán-Angulo, M., Cubillos Diaz, J., Vargas, C. (2019). *Hechos victimizantes en Colombia: antes, durante y después de la firma del acuerdo de paz en La Habana*. En: G.A. Campos Avendaño, M.A. Castaño Hernández, M. Gaitán Ángulo y V. Sánchez Mendoza (Compiladores). Diálogos sobre investigación: avances científicos Konrad Lorenz (25-50). Bogotá: Konrad Lorenz Editores. Disponible en: https://blogs.konradlorenz.edu.co/files/book_interactivo_dialogos_en_investigacion.pdf

Lis-Gutiérrez, J.P., Cubillos Díaz, J., Rincón, J.C., Gaitán-Angulo, Lis-Gutiérrez, M., Henao, C., y Balaguera, M.I. (2018a). Ingreso de la población víctimas de desplazamiento que retornó a la Palma Cundinamarca (2018): una aplicación de machine learning. En: J.P. Lis-Gutiérrez, C. Henao y L.E. Malagón-Castro. Técnicas de análisis cuantitativo aplicadas a las ciencias contables y económicas (240-260). Villavicencio: Unimeta.

Lis-Gutiérrez, J-P., Rincón-Vásquez, J.C., Cubillos-Diaz, J., Gaitán-Angulo, M., Mojica-Sánchez L. (2018b). Caracterización de los hechos victimizantes por género en las víctimas del conflicto armado Colombiano. En: Lis-Gutiérrez, et al., *Conflicto y Construcción de paz*. Villavicencio: Unimeta.

Lis-Gutiérrez, J.P. y Aguilera-Hernández, D. (2019). Análisis departamental de las demandas al Ejército colombiano por sus integrantes en calidad de víctimas. En: G. Barbosa Castillo, M. Correa, y A. Ciro Gómez (eds.), Análisis de las demandas de los integrantes del Ejército en calidad de víctimas: una aplicación de "machine learning" (pp. 324-352). Bogotá: Universidad Externado de Colombia.

López López, W., Correa-Chica, A., Sierra-Puentes, M.C., Castañeda Polanco, J.C., Fernández Miranda, G., Durán Jaramillo, M. & Castro-Abril, P. (2019 In press). Armed Conflict Conceptualization of Forgivenness, ReConciliation and Peace: Children's Voices in the Armed Conflict Context. In N. Balvin, & D. J. Christie (Eds.) Children and Peace: From Research to Action. New York: Springer: Peace and Psychology Book Series.

Moros Ochoa, M.A., Lis-Gutiérrez, J. P., Castro Nieto, G.Y., Vargas, C. y Rincón-Vásquez, J.C. (2019). La percepción de calidad de servicio como determinante de la recomendación: una predicción mediante inteligencia artificial para los hoteles en Cartagena. En: G.A. Campos Avendaño, M.A. Castaño Hernández, M. Gaitán Ángulo y V. Sánchez Mendoza (Compiladores). Diálogos sobre investigación: avances científicos Konrad Lorenz (pp. 143-162). Bogotá: Konrad Lorenz Editores. Disponible en https://blogs.konradlorenz.edu.co/files/book_interactivo_dialogos_en_investigacion.pdf

Sierra-Puentes, M., & Correa-Chica, A. (2019 In press). Aspectos socioeconómicos de la población desplazada en Colombia: revisión sistemática. Suma Psicológica, 26(2) http://dx.doi.org/10.14349/sumapsi.2019.v26.n2.1

Shafir, E. (2017). Decisions in poverty contexts. *Current opinion in psychology*, 18, 131-136.

Tarozzi, A. (2007). Calculating comparable statistics from incomparable surveys, with an application to poverty in India. *Journal of business & economic statistics*, 25(3), 314-336.

September 2020
Volume: 17, **No**: 5, pp. 651– 668
ISSN: 1741-8984
e-ISSN: 1741-8992
www.migrationletters.com

MIGRATION
LETTERS

First Submitted: 17 February 2020 Accepted: 2 May 2020
DOI: https://doi.org/10.33182/ml.v17i5.702

From Total Dependency to Corporatisation: The Journey of Domestic Work in the UAE

Rima Sabban[1]

Abstract

Migrant domestic work has played complex, dynamic, and multilevel roles in the evolution of families, and the corporatisation of domestic work across the Gulf Cooperation Council (GCC) countries, particularly the United Arab Emirates (UAE). With the increasing globalisation process in the UAE, migrant domestic work has not only deepened families' critical dependency towards domestic work, but also influenced the state's logic to institutionalise reforms to control, govern, and corporatise domestic works sector in recent years. Using primary and secondary literature sources, this article examines the historical and contemporary evolution of migrant domestic work in the UAE and of the GCC region. It argues that the UAE's domestic work sector has historically transformed from informally structured sector—heavily dependent on the sponsorship of local family structures—to emerging corporatised sector across the UAE labour market. This article presents empirical and theoretical contributions because it highlights the evolving corporatised approach of the state in managing and governing domestic work and its impacts on local family structures in the UAE.

Keywords: migrant domestic work; UAE state; dependency; corporatisation.

Introduction

As a young nation-state in a globalised world, the United Arab Emirates (UAE) has quickly achieved massive, unmatched socioeconomic growth and advancement in the last half century. The UAE, a federation of seven Emirates, comprising *Abu Dhabi, Dubai, Sharjah, Ajman, Um-al-Quwain, Ras al-Khaimah*, and *al-Fujairah*, has transformed from a minor area on the edge of the historical record with limited basic human amenities to becoming an emerging, influential state actor globally (Abdulla 2006). Built on the fortuitous bounty of fossil fuels, the UAE became officially established to unify the governing seven local emirates only nine years after its first oil export, which helped accelerate the UAE economy, society, and labour markets. This has enabled the government to directly support local families' employment and social welfare, transforming the UAE's narrative from total poverty and subsistence living into a modern Cinderella-esque arc of affluence (El Mallakh 1981) (locals and non-locals) (Al Fahim 2006).

As globalisation has shaped mainstream UAE society, it has continued to maintain its tribal family structures, a central unit of society (Heard Bey 2004; Al Sharekh 2007), Acted as a fundamental building block that forms society and its prevailing social structure, the UAE family constitutes the very basis of survival of the culture. While the extended family unit also reinforces and expands the functioning and existence of society. Without these strong cultural and family ties

---

[1] Rima Sabban, PhD, Assistant Dean for Research and Graduate Studies, College Humanities and Social Sciences, Zayed University, Dubai, United Arab Emirates. E-mail: Rima.Sabban@zu.ac.ae.

embedded in the families within the complex social structure, the harshness of the existence in the UAE—especially during the pre-oil discovery period—could not have been structurally sustained. Although the basic notion of "family" in the Emirati context remains central to the very core of the nation's fundamental architecture, the nature of the "family" in the UAE has gone through a series of major changes on a variety of levels (Al-Tarrah 2007) with the advent of wealth and modernity. These specific tangible shifts are largely rooted in multiple and complex social, economic, and political factors that converged to trigger dramatic transformations among local families in the UAE. One of the least anticipated—but most influential—factors in the rapid societal changes in the UAE is the massive influx of Asian and African migrant domestic workers—regulated by governments and facilitated by transnational recruitment agencies—into Emirati households (Sabban 2012a). The arrival of migrant domestic workers accelerated the shift from traditional subsistence living in the UAE and influenced local Emirati households to adapt to more modern conveniences in a global context. Thus, the global migrant emergence and integration of migrant domestic workers into UAE households has profoundly reconfigured the contemporary formation of household structures, cultures, and practices in contemporary Emirati society.

This paper examines the historical and contemporary evolution of migrant domestic work in the UAE. It argues that that the UAE's domestic work sector has historically transformed from informally structured sector—heavily dependent from local family structures—to emerging corporatised sector across the UAE labour market. This paper holds empirical and theoretical contributions because it highlights the evolving corporatised approach of the state in managing and governing domestic work and its impacts on local family structures in the UAE. The study is divided into five key sections. First, I examine the early foundations and the causes of modern migrant domestic work in the UAE. Second, I explore the contemporary structure of the UAE migrant domestic work and its growing corporatisation of the migrant domestic work in the UAE and its evolving role in mainstream UAE society. Third, I dissect the critical costs of migrant domestic work on mainstream UAE society, specifically on local UAE families. Fourth, I explore the growing corporatisation of the migrant domestic work in the UAE and its evolving role in mainstream UAE society. And lastly, I conclude by highlighting future insights on the future role of domestic work in the contemporary formation and continuing dependency of local UAE families on migrant domestic work sector in the UAE.

The Early Years: Historical Foundations

Prior to the state formation of the UAE in 1971, this small corner of the Arabian GCC Peninsula, which consisted of a number of overlapping territories that varied geographically from winding coast to expansive dunes and sprawling mountains, was modestly inhabited by a mixture of Arab tribes, some of whom were nomadic Bedouin and from the surrounding regions, and mostly from India, Iran, and among others. As Table 1 indicates, in the early 1900s, the local population was estimated at no more than 80,000 individuals (Heard-Bey 2001), and the population gradually increased until the oil discovery period, when the local population exploded in response to high international migration of various migrant workers, including domestic workers, into the country (Sabban 2012a).

Table 1. Population Growth and Composition in the uae since 1900

Year	Total	Nationals (%)	Expatriates (%)
1900	80,000	Not available	Not available
1958	86,000	Not available	Not available
1968	180,000	114,000 (63)	66,000 (37)
1975	557,000	201,000 (36)	356,000 (64)
1977	862,000	215,000 (25)	647,000 (75)
1978	950,000	222,000 (23)	787,000 (77)
1979	1,015,000	228,000 (22)	787,000 (78)
1992*	2,012,000	580,000 (29)	1,433,000 (71)
1995	2,411,041	587,330 (24)	1,823,711 (76)
2000*	2,623,000	762,000 (29)	1,861,000 (71)
2005	4,106,427	825,495 (20)	3,280,932 (80)
2010**	8,264,070	947,997 (11.5)	7,316,073 (88.5)
2018***	9,560,748	956,075 (10)	8,604,673 (90)

The local inhabitants heavily relied on the few meagre resources, and considerable ingenuity, to survive the hostile climate in the UAE. As Heard-Bey acknowledges,

> "They [local populations] had developed the means to make all aspects of their seemingly inhospitable environment work for them. Management of these economic resources was harmonised with an age-old social structure producing unique socio-economic responses to the rigors of life in the eastern corner of the Arabian Peninsula" (Heard-Bey 2001)

The above-mentioned "rigours" principally included an absence of basic infrastructures, including roads, schools, hospitals, skilled professionals (that is, doctors, nurses, and engineers), and domestic workers, who were historically considered to be a rare luxury (Heard-Bey 2001). Formal education in the UAE was also neither readily available nor fully accessible to the entire local population (Al Faris 2000), excluding some of the traditional Qur'anic schools and the very few primary schools that were established in the mid-twentieth century (Al Faris 2000; Soffan 1980). As a result, the illiteracy rate exceeded 90 per cent prior to the formation of the UAE (El Mallakh 1981). Moreover, until the 1950s and 1960s, many of the local inhabitants lived in a variety of simple dwellings from goat hair tents and houses made of palm fronds (locally known as '*arish*) or, in some cases, modest constructions made of coral stone with "an upper floor and even an ornate wind tower for comfort during the hot summer months" (Heard-Bey 2001). They also used to live clusters and extended families, and their mode of living has helped families and women sustain itself (Sabban, 2012). Thus, the early historical formation period in the UAE was clearly marked by socioeconomic underdevelopment, and the dependency on foreign migrant workers—specifically migrant domestic work—appears to have been little or almost absent among early local families within mainstream UAE society.

In addition, the local tribal system also played a pivotal role in shaping the local community for centuries, and strengthened the very structure of their society. On an individual level, "tribal 'belonging' is far more reassuring than the comforts of 'home' and the sense of security, which is paramount for people whose social structures are associated with the land they live on" (Heard-Bey 2001). In this particular social system, the family unit was considered to be a fundamental social building block for sustaining all facets of life in mainstream UAE society, ranging from the economy to the political community. The overarching family system provided an embedded structure to maintain the tribal connections and reinforced the complex social roles that eventually shaped the formation of household structures among local families.

In addition, extended family members lived either in the same household as their kin or in close proximity to each other (Sabban 2012a). In fact, local families would help each other in their daily tasks, such as caring for family and children, in times of difficulty or during significant events, including giving birth[2] or falling sick. Additionally, UAE households and families were more directly integrated into the local domestic economy. In the pearl diving era (a vital and high risk means of living before the decline of natural pearls worldwide[3]), men would leave their families for more than three months for employment and would migrate outside of their local communities in order to make the most of the pearling season. During these absences, women were mainly in charge not only the domestic sphere but also of the subsistence economy, making clothing and food, and building houses that were made of palm leaves and/or tents made of processed animal skins or hand-woven fabrics (Al Sayegh 2001; Heard-Bey 2004). The existence of gender-specific roles within local UAE society was not only deeply structured and embedded but also played an integral role in sustaining both the local culture and household structures. However, during this time, women carried much of the burden of domestic duties, ranging from the arts of weaving fishing nets and dyeing the palm leaves used extensively both inside and outside of the domestic arena to caring for animals, along with the more typically associated tasks, such as child rearing and food storage and preparation (Al Sayegh 2001; Heard-Bey 2004). Women, in particular, played a critical role in the overall survival of the local family because "the need to alternate between various economic activities placed great responsibilities on the women during the long periods of time that men were obliged to be away from home" and, therefore, a woman's "contribution earned her a high status in society, and a husband's reputation and honour rested on the conduct of his wife and daughters" (Heard-Bey 2004). These gender-specific social roles therefore configured and defined the local domestic norms, practices, and values among UAE households, reaffirming the critical value of domestic work duties in building the local family, society, and nation.

The gender segregation roles embedded in local households helped to reinforce the early notion and importance of domestic work activities within UAE society (Sabban, 2018). In fact, although hired domestic help or, in some cases, slavery played a role within the local culture, it was often the exclusive reserve of affluent merchant families; therefore, domestic work had little or no impact at all on local households. To an extent, the concept of domestic help from non-family members was

---

[2] Family, friends, and neighbors would support the mother until she regained her strength and was able to return to normal activities. Variations of this practice are still evident among Emirati families today.

[3] Cultured pearls emerged during the 1930s and effectively destroyed the pearling industry that had sustained the local populace and much of the economy for centuries, leaving behind a vacuum that would not be filled until the discovery of oil; this development left the already tenuous subsistence living in disarray.

not a ubiquitous feature of daily life; yet it has recently been observed across every social class, nationality, and family structure across the country. As the country has moved from an aggregate of loosely connected Emirate states to the unified UAE state, this particular concept has eventually transformed the collective understanding that has long lived with the UAE national women.[4]

The Causes of Domestic Transformation

With the discovery of oil, the UAE began to reform its territorial emirate borders and transform into the vibrant cosmopolitan federation that now exists. With the rapid modernisation process, combined with the massive influx of economic wealth and investments in the country's infrastructure, the UAE economy and society quickly transformed. This transformation process initially began with the sudden population growth, as new employment opportunities and the ensuing manpower shortage for building required modern infrastructure helped to create a demand for all types of foreign workers, including domestic workers. More specifically, this particular era shifted the UAE from a subsistence-based economy to one that relied almost exclusively on oil production to thrive, both at the regional and global levels. The following paragraphs highlight how oil wealth helped restructure and transform the nature of UAE society:

With the advent of oil, the Emirates began to "break regional—even international—records in urban development and fast economic growth" (Sabban 2012a). As the UAE embraced the tangible benefits of globalisation, the UAE's economic rankings also increased, to attain one of the highest per capita gross domestic products in the world and the second highest ranking in the region after Saudi Arabia (Ministry of Economy 2016). From an economic standpoint, the dramatic economic shift of the UAE, to an extent, has led to the marginalisation of Emirati families, moving them away from the national economy and their former central role in the mobilisation of labor. Traditional means of employment such as "subsistence agriculture, nomadic animal husbandry, the extracting of pearls and the trade in pearls, fishing, and seafaring" (Shihab 2001) became obsolete or were transferred to imported foreign migrant workers, as the economy diversified and Emiratis began to take on less manual forms of labor. In particular, local UAE nationals began to take on positions that conformed to more westernised concepts of employment, with typical five-day workweeks, eight-hour workdays, and regular salaries. This economic transition and prosperity has eventually created a division:

"A two-tier labour market has emerged in the UAE. At the top is the indigenous labour force, which constitutes about 10 per cent of the total work force. Below this is an unlimited supply of foreign labour. The UAE has reaped benefits from foreign skilled and unskilled workers, who initiated its economic development in the early 1970s and subsequently have come to sustain it" (Shihab 2001)

---

[4] During of the author's fieldwork in the summer of 1993, she interviewed 34 Emirati women who employed domestic workers. Of these, 33 highly praised the value of domestic work because the institution provided an element of social value and afforded the women the opportunity to engage in society. Interestingly, none of the informants—even two decades after the establishment of the federation—felt there was a contradiction between defining their roles in the domestic sphere as the core of their social status and then transferring said related domestic tasks to other, non-Emirati women. This response provides a curious contrast to the long-standing conceptualization and feminist critique of domestic work as a devalued commodity in the market system on which the modern economy is based. "Domestic work has long been the site of contestation since the advent of industrialization, modernization, and women's participation in the work sphere. Domestic work engenders gender tension, class exploitation, and racial manipulation. It has historically been the terrain of domestic violence of different shapes and levels" (Sabban 2014a). For more information, see: Enloe 1990; Jayakody at al. 2008; Mitchel 1974; Oakley 1974; Scott 1986; Smith 1973.

In order to increase national employment in the labor force, women were encouraged and incentivised to participate in the evolving domestic economy, as newer industries were established. The pro-nationalisation policies of the UAE government have increased female labour force participation and integrated them into the modernised workforce in ever increasing capacities, thereby creating a further need for change in the organisation of the domestic sphere. In other words, the UAE government's economic strategy enabled local UAE populations to obtain formalised employment status and increased women's labour market participation, which, to a large extent, drove the labour demand for the domestic work sector to address the growing domestic care deficit within local households.

Although women were still the main responsible figures in the households and families, many factors played important roles in encouraging the importation of domestic workers from abroad, which, in the mid-1980s, became a well-established government immigration system. The *Hareem*[5] system of hierarchy, which had provided support for the young and old within the family for generations by dividing domestic duties among female members of the household,[6] with newly wed woman at the bottom of the hierarchy. Despite the major changes that engulfed the society, UAE women continued to perform the main domestic responsibilities. Although domestic workers started becoming more visible in some families and were taking the place of the newly wed females, they began to accumulate more wealth and participate in the labour market. The prevailing structure of the extended family played a role in both necessitating and sustaining the move into larger, more modernised homes in organised neighbourhoods. However, even as local families started moving out of the existing extended family structure, they continued to support and rely on one another in order to maintain the local culture, customs, and traditional practices.. As new wealth had brought on more responsibilities, families eventually adapted to a more modernised life style by slowly integrating domestic work services to effectively create more efficient household systems (Sabban 2012a; 2014). As daily life in the Emirates became more modern, urbanised, and globalised, the internal structure of local families' households started shifting toward a more nuclear form, and the move to larger modern residences ensured that the employment of domestic workers would inevitably become an imperative option to survive in the contemporary period.

In addition, the (in)dependence[7] period in the 1980s could be potentially viewed as the first period of actual "modernisation" for the family in the UAE and its subsequent metamorphosis from the strictly extended to broadly nuclear (El Haddad 2003; Crabtree 2007; Sabban 2012a). Although the new nuclear families still held strong cultural connections with their extended families by living in close proximity and providing them with multiple forms of domestic help and support, the actual physical and domestic work support lessened or, in some cases, even disappeared in most local households (El Haddad 2003; Sabban 2012a; 2012b). In fact, migrant domestic workers started playing their new household roles and eased the transition of daily life into that of modernity and material wellbeing for entire local families. For newlywed couples or the nuclear family, this new social order provided them with a greater amount of independence and autonomy from the large extended family than had been previously possible, while allowing them to accumulate ample time

---

[5] In this context, *Hareem* (literally, women) refers to the matriarchal system that functioned as the support network among Emirati women, which was, and remains, a major social organizational force. This should not be confused with the *Harem*, that is, the wives and concubines of rulers in the imagined and lived Arab and Islamic world.

[6] The senior matriarch was responsible for the kitchen and other major household decisions; the younger members were provided with lesser tasks to achieve the smooth running of the household.

[7] It is independence for the newly rising nuclear family from the previous structure of the extended family, whereas it is a new form of dependence on domestic workers, which will mark a major transformation in the society.

and space to participate in the labour market, attend social gatherings, initiate entrepreneurial activities, and other related leisure activities. This independence from the local and traditional structure turned out to be a new form of dependence on foreign domestics. The adoption of migrant domestic help enabled families to remain connected with their social relations (that is, extended family, friends, etc.), because they had more time to visit, exchange food, and enjoy quality time with their extended family; they could easily employ domestic workers to do the household work that would have traditionally consumed much of a woman's day (Sabban 2014a; 2014b). Because of the growing dependence on and importance of domestic workers in local UAE households, women were inevitably criticised, particularly in both the English and Arabic[8] media, as the shift to heavy dependence on domestic service became more publicly widespread. These criticisms of women relying on domestic staff to seemingly carry all previous domestic responsibilities and child care[9] arose in both public and private discourse because many perceived such dependency as a form of cultural abandonment of the traditional and cultural women's roles in local UAE society (Khalaf 1987; Khalifa 1986). In other words, the growing dependence on migrant domestic workers was not only viewed as a direct threat—either actual or perceived—to the established cultural domestic norms but also as a negative factor in sustaining women's cultural identity as domestic carriers and protectors (as mothers) of the local culture and nation.

The influx of economic investment has also enabled the state's "revenues to finance huge programs for governmental spending, maintain a huge number of governmental employees, and support the prices of energy, water and other services for their citizens" (Ministry of Economy 2016), while simultaneously providing "the government with the opportunity to undertake ambitious economic development programs" (Faris 1994). The transformative economic shift has also empowered the state to increase its political capacity and reaffirm its domestic sovereign power to govern the local populations. Although such measures were established to improve the quality of living for all inhabitants, nationals were generously provided with certain exclusive benefits (Abu Baker 1995). For example, education in public schools was free for nationals and certain non-national government employees. Public schools initially provided free food, clothing, books, and even allowances for children to encourage all parents to send their children to school. Nationals were awarded fellowships to study abroad to further improve the country's human capital supply, in line with the strategy to establish a knowledge-based economy. Non-Arabic speaking expatriates were given land and allowances to establish their own schools and other community facilities (Davidson 2005). Health care was also guaranteed for all, as the "the UAE Government's health policies aim at providing a range of facilities and at implementing programmes aimed at advancing the level of service and health education throughout the UAE" (Shihab, 2001). Another major consequence of the state's policies also provided Emiratis with land and building allowances—in the form of interest-free mortgages or loans—to construct their homes, especially among the newly educated populations.[10] The state's generous support encouraged the small society to grow and

---

[8] In a previous study with Moors et al., I have analyzed the differences in the discourses and media portrayals of the heavy reliance on domestic workers. Curiously, in the English media, the issue often focused on domestic workers' rights (or lack thereof) and their positions as victims, whereas the Arabic media focused on the negative impact of domestics on the family unit (Moors et al. 2009: 167). Women were singled out in such reports, both directly and indirectly, and burdened with the portrayal of being lacking and inadequate in their household roles and responsibilities.

[9] One of the other main concerns was the impact of domestic workers on the language of children and other types of cultural erosion that might arise from leaving children in the care of nannies (UAE MOWSA 1990).

[10] Most houses that are built are villas that vary in style and size according to the individual family's financial capacities; they often feature a garden surrounding the villa with high walls and greenery for privacy. Of course, not all nationals are able to own villas

provided young small nuclear families, especially the newlyweds, with more power and autonomy than the earlier, much stricter patriarchal extended family (Sabban 2012a). Therefore, the UAE state's accumulation of wealth did not only subtly play a role in transforming local families' collective wealth but also consequently helped to accelerate the reconfiguration of local households' structure, lifestyle practices, and cultural dependence on migrant domestic work in the contemporary period.

The greatest change of all for the newly formed UAE occurred as the population dramatically increased in size and changed in composition as a result of the major structural transformations that followed the economic boom and rapid urbanisation in the country. Prior to the UAE's formation, the whole population did not—as was established earlier[11]—exceed more than a hundred thousand people. These numbers began to grow suddenly in 1973 with the advent of oil and the establishment of the state, almost doubling to one hundred and eighty thousand (El Mallakh 1981). Furthermore, the population of the Emirates[12] during those early years still consisted mainly of inhabitants local to the region, who formed some 63 per cent of the populace whereas expatriates formed the remaining 37 per cent (Sabban 2012a). This demographic trend reversed completely within the following decade; between 1958 and 2000, the total population in the UAE quickly increased from 86,000 to 2,623,000, whereby expatriate populations accounted for 71% of the total UAE population. The local population, however, only represented 29% and has ever since been largely outnumbered by the expatriate population, even in the contemporary period. An independent think-tank organisation, the Gulf Labour Markets and Migration (GLMM) Population Program estimated that, in 2016, the expatriate population largely dominated the overall UAE population, representing 91% of the total population, whereas the local population has increasingly become a minority. Given the decreasing fertility rate in the UAE, the share of the local population against the total UAE population is projected to decrease in the long run. This new demographic trend certainly created an exponential market demand for domestic workers, and importing/recruiting agencies bloomed as newspapers carried advertisements daily. The employment of domestic workers as cooks, maids, and drivers was easy, cheap, and accessible (Sabban 2012a, 2012b). The cyclical nature of this upsurge ensured that the population would continue to increase and the need for domestic workers would remain firmly in place. As a result, almost all families—both national and non-national—employed domestic help in some capacity, depending on their level of income, ease, and accessibility (Sabban 2012a; 2012b).

Initially, given the historical ties and the long-term relationship between India and the coastal region of the Gulf and the UAE, most migrant domestic workers employed in the Emirates were from the South Asian region. In the late 1970s and early 1980s, for example, male Indian domestic workers were the most ubiquitous domestic help in many local UAE households (Moors et al. 2009). However, while some families would continue to employ male domestic workers from India, the market started changing very quickly, and soon domestic workers arrived from Indonesia,[13] Sri Lanka, and the Philippines. These three nationalities were treated with some hierarchy that dictated

---

due to their circumstances. Lower income families live in smaller houses with a small yard, in neighborhoods where houses were built by the government and provided to underprivileged nationals, among them widowed or divorced mothers unsupported by their husbands (Sabban 2012a). Non-nationals often reside in designated neighborhoods and/or working compounds that are owned by the companies that employ them. Construction workers and lower income workers also live in their own clusters known as "labor camps" (Khalaf 2006; Gardner 2011).

[11] See Table 4-1.

[12] Based on estimates from the 1960s.

[13] Those from Indonesia were particularly encouraged because of the country's Muslim status (see Silvey 2006; 2007)

the roles[14] that they would occupy and the salaries that were expected (Ghubash 1986; Khalifa 1986; Khalaf et al. 1987; Sabban 2012b). Domestic service—which is currently considered a common and essential feature of daily life—also encouraged the state to begin to ease the relevant domestic market regulations and, thereby, facilitating the importation of domestic workers, in order to ease the living of all inhabitants, particularly national families (Kapiszewski 1999; Shah 2009). The rate of dependency on domestic workers among nationals in particular reached 2.2 domestic workers per family by the mid-1990s (UAE MOWSA 1990; Sabban 2012a; 2012b), and more recently, the ratio of domestic workers per local family had increased to 3.5 in 2014 (Sabban 2012a). Thus, the growing dependence on migrant domestic work was not only a product of a state-led policy initiative but was also influenced by global social, economic, and political factors that triggered the influx of migrant domestic workers and their integration into local UAE households.

The Cost of Change: Consequences for Emirati Society

In the contemporary UAE period, the accumulation and distribution of oil wealth have certainly played a critical role for positioning the UAE at the centre of the world economy in terms of modernity and wealth (Sabban 2013; Hannieh 2011). It has also particularly functioned as a powerful force responsible for the shaping of the modern UAE family and society that exists today and, most importantly, the ensuing demand for migrant domestic work. The aspiration and determination of the country and its inhabitants to embrace global modernity in this era of globalisation thus cannot be underestimated. Dubai, in particular, is the most obvious embodiment of such ambitions because the city has embraced the task of moulding itself into a global brand[15] and initiating world-record megastructure projects, such as Palm Island. The global branding strategy of Dubai has ricocheted through the country and the wider region (Abdulla 2006; Krane 2009; Barret 2010) and has further shaped the UAE family and society, in a way, by embodying domestic service as part of a modernised attempt to symbolise and signal wealth and adaptation in a global context (Sabban 2012b; 2014a).

Although there are no official government data published on domestic worker populations in the UAE, recent estimates suggest that the current number of domestic workers has risen to approximately 800,000 (excluding those unregistered "illegal" or "unaccounted for" workers who remain in the country).[16] The heavy reliance on domestic workers is now de-rigueur among most local UAE families and, in the case of the many women, who opt to work and establish a presence in the public sphere, migrant domestic work is deemed to be a necessary tool to create a smooth, well-functioning family unit. Basically, local households in the UAE cannot function without support staff. The number of domestics per family has risen considerably to 3.5 per family, and domestic work has become much more professionalised with clearer roles for cleaning, cooking, child-care, elderly-care, driving, and gardening, among other duties (Sabban 2014a, 2014b). In a recent survey of 400 local families in the UAE, I found that 95% of families acknowledged their inability to survive without any form of migrant domestic help within their households (Sabban 2014a). Of course, not all Emirati families have migrant domestic workers, either through choice or by

---

[14] For example, household cooks—an institution in their own right in many large households—were often Indian, or in some cases Iranian, because of the expectations of their kitchen knowledge and local palates, whereas domestic workers from the Philippines were employed as household servants and nannies. Interestingly, domestic workers from the Philippines were also a sign of status for UAE families and women (Sabban, 2012b) because they were considered to be more modern and, therefore, more capable of helping the family in its shift to modernity.

[15] With projects like the tallest hotel (The Burj Khalifa) and the biggest mall in the region (The Dubai Mall).

[16] Multiple amnesties have been issued by the UAE government in attempts to resolve such issues over the decades, and no publicly available government data estimates are available (Fargues et.al 2015).

limitation of means. Less than 2 per cent of families are still striving to survive without domestic workers; however, these families are the exception to the general rule and are largely difficult to access for research purposes (Sabban 2014a). Additionally, Emirati families employ not all migrant domestic workers in the UAE; in fact, statistically speaking, a larger proportion of domestic workers are to be found in non-national households (Sabban 2012b). Many of the diverse expatriate families that now reside in the UAE hire domestic workers from their own community.[17]

Corporatisation of the UAE's Domestic Work Sector

After the passage of the UAE Federal Law No. 10 (2017), the state has increasingly institutionalised the domestic work sector by regulating and governing the recruitment and placement procedures of migrant domestic work in the UAE. The law stipulates the 19 different types of domestic workers operationally offered to local and expatriate households seeking domestic workers within their households or private facility premises. These diverse categories of domestic workers include housemaid, sailor, security guard, shepherd, jockey, tamer, falcon caretaker, worker, housekeeper, cook, nanny, gardener, private coach, private teacher, farmer, private nurse, private representative, private agricultural engineer, and family driver. These skill categorisations simply reflect the growing state attempt to professionalise domestic work. In governing and managing these newly developed categories, the UAE state has formed the Tadbeer Center, a multipurpose public-private-partnership (PPP) recruitment centre based in the UAE, which has recently become a symbol of 'corporate' approach in facilitating the recruitment and placement processes for domestic work. Governed and monitored by the UAE government, the Tadbeer centres are operationally monitored by the UAE state, as well as governed and managed by the private sector, strategically forming the private-public partnership (PPP) approach of the UAE government vis a vis the governing private sector.

As Tadbeer centres increasingly emerged in UAE society, Tadbeer centres thus operationally exist in Dubai and Abu Dhabi only, covering all the demand requests for domestic work across the UAE domestic work sector. The place of three Tadbeer centres in Dubai and nine Tadbeer centres in Abu Dhabi reflect the strategic and vital needs of local and expatriate families, as well as the high concentration of migrant domestic work' demand within the UAE, seeking migrant domestic workers for their households or private facility areas in the UAE. These centres, in fact, facilitate all various services, including recruitment, placement, upskilling training at all levels, counselling, dispute resolution process and certification process, workers' orientation process for both employers and workers. While these particular functions, especially dispute resolution, have been particularly governed by the local and origin states in the past, the UAE Federal Law No.10 now empowers the private sector to govern and corporatise the domestic work sector in order to effectively manage the labour interests of the local employers in the domestic labour market.

In addition, the Tadbeer centres have also become categorised and privatised, displaying the levels, nationality types, and capacities of domestic workers in various levels, skills, and pricing systems. In fact, in contrast to the narrow definition of domestic work prior to the passage of the Federal Law No. 10 in 2017, the Tadbeer centres under the new law have now reclassified

---

[17] The Indian community of the middle and upper middle class will hire Indian domestics, and the Filipino population will hire domestics from the Philippines. In the case of European expats, families will hire from a diverse range of backgrounds, whereas expatriate Arabs (Egyptians, Jordanians, Syrians, Lebanese, etc.) hire from all other available nationalities in the market, such as Filipino, Indonesian, Ethiopian, Bangladeshi, etc.

19categories of migrant domestic work, highlighting the various hierarchies and capital cost requirements for potential employers. The 'matching process' employed within the Tadbeer centres reflect the market demand and supply across the spectrum in the origin and destination countries, as well as the growing corporatism framed under the public-private partnership (PPP) between the state and the private sector in the domestic worker sector. To an extent, this new governance approach to migrant domestic work signifies the growing and, to an extent, evolving regulatory role of the state in controlling and managing the migrant domestic work flows within the country.

As domestic work sector becomes corporatised in the UAE, the culture of dependency among employers has also subtly evolving and deepening. When the deployment of Filipina domestic workers to the UAE, along with Indonesia and Ethiopia, was banned by the Philippine state in August 2014 and until now, the private sector (recruitment/placement agencies) tremendously suffered loss, while employers struggled to identify and meet their 'preferred'' care worker demand for their children, household, and other related demands. To respond to such regulatory blockage, UAE-based placement firms have opened multiple cleaning companies like "Supermaids" and "Dubai cleaners" readily available online, particularly in Dubai, offering highly individualised, part-time, and in some cases, seasonal cleaning services to the households, mostly expatriate households in the UAE. While local UAE households alternatively moved to prefer other nationalities, others, to a certain extent, have continued to use part-time domestic workers to perform mostly basic household functions, including cleaning, cooking, and childrearing for families.

On the other hand, expatriate families have increasingly relied on part-time cleaning workers who perform cleaning either daily or multiple times depending on the business requests or the actual needs of the employers. This new form of domestic work service transaction in the private market has, in fact, emerged in response to the ongoing blockade of migrant domestic work from the Philippines, Indonesia, and Ethiopia which simultaneously reinforces the 'ethnicised' preferences for certain domestic workers in the UAE labour market. Although most of their employer contracts and sponsors are now under the governing private sector, their critical functions mainly revolve around domestic work, thus symbolically reflecting the changing structure and functions of highly corporatised domestic work in the private sector.

Moreover, Filipinos, Indians, and more recently African domestic workers, providing various cleaning services to households, hotels, facilities, and other special events surrounding the hospitality and tourist sectors in the UAE, mostly dominate the domestic workers/cleaners. They have also become the new category of domestic work publicly visible in the UAE, operating in the public setting while other domestic workers, especially those who live-in domestic workers, have remained to an extent "invisible" in the public eye. While the ethnic preference for live-in domestic work on the basis of stereotypes has continued, the growing privatisation of invisibility of domestic work acting cleaners, reflect the visible market corporatism of the UAE domestic work sector.

The growing visibility/invisibility of migrant domestic work has also remained vital in understanding the changing and dynamic accommodation patterns of migrant domestic work in the UAE, particularly in Dubai. While live-in domestic workers reside within the local families, domestic work/cleaners, however, have become integrated in the public, whereby the employers often rent cheap accommodations for migrant domestic workers in various migrant towns in Dubai to accommodate their basic living accommodation needs. The glowingly colourful uniforms—often coded in blue, red, orange and green—signify the public categorisation and visible corporatised approach of private sector firms that accommodate and advertise migrant domestic work across the UAE. To a large extent, the strategic placement of migrant domestic work accommodation, combined with the color and skill coding reflected in uniform colors, reflect the converging push to the emerging visibility and complexity of the UAE's migrant domestic work sector.

The Cost of Change: Consequences for Emirati Society

In mainstream Emirati society, the local populations have found themselves in a paradoxical situation where, on the one hand,

> "...the basic structure of their tribal society has remained intact, even though for some families their changed economic circumstances have dramatically revolutionised many aspects of their lives. For others, access to modern housing, education and healthcare have made a great difference, but the basic pattern of their lives has not yet changed" (Heard-Bey 2001).

On the other hand, the combination of the transformation of the economy, the many functional developments that society has witnessed, the demographic imbalance due to migration, and government policies have facilitated transformations that have contributed to the change and reconfiguration of domestic life in the UAE. The conflicting position that was brought forth by modernity and globalisation has, ultimately, also resulted in a number of costs and consequences that have inevitably placed the traditional Emirati family in the UAE in the midst of a number of serious dilemmas in several respects:

Increased Domestic Work Dependence

Perhaps the most obvious and often decried outcome of the rise in migrant domestic services has been the greater dependence on domestic workers in contemporary UAE households. Emirati women, given the central role they are often deemed to play in the transference of tradition and identity to future generations, are subject to much of the burden of domestic responsibility for the real and perceived impact of domestic service. Young Emirati women are today reaping the fruits of increased government attention and appointments in positions as ministers and ambassadors[18] and in senior government posts. The more achievement women gain in public life, the higher their dependency on domestic help is in private. An entire generation of Emiratis has, in fact, been raised without the domestic skills that were once transferred through practice and observation of daily activities. The extended family structure that once allowed for domestic work to be shared amongst family members no longer directly serves as the main source of support or cultural/traditional knowledge transfer in the specific area of household chores and duties among UAE households.

Culture Clash and National Identity

---

[18] Certain behavior, such as travelling alone or working in mixed environments, was formerly considered unseemly for respectable Emirati women. In this area, there has also been a change in attitude among the wider local populace, particularly in recent years as the success of UAE women, particularly the younger generations, has become a huge source of pride for many families. The change has, however, been much more gradual as a friend of the author's who works in the diplomatic corps explained. The woman stated that, in choosing a career in public service that would require extensive travel and relocation, she took steps that were met with disapproval by her family, particularly her father. However, with perseverance, success, and the support of government initiatives for women to play a greater role in the public sphere, the woman observed that her father, who had initially rejected her first appointment in the diplomatic field, was now her biggest supporter and openly expressed his fatherly pride in seeing his daughter achieving such success. Needless to say, professional women today, married or single, have domestic workers who support them at home in order to continue in their public roles.

Emiratis are now grappling with the tension that constantly arises between tradition, heritage, and globalisation. Everything from the native Arabic language to local food and traditional dress, such as the *abaya* (a long thin black gown to cover the inner clothes) and *sheila* (a thin black head scarf) for women or the *kandora* (a long white dress) and *ghatra* (a white head cover with a black circle to keep it from moving) for men, is being observed much more loosely by the younger generations and is being negotiated as the society adapts and reinterprets global influences. Tension over national identity and personal behaviour is creating significant generation gaps (Khalaf 2005) as Emirati families adapt to changes. The serious issue of identity is becoming more apparent in society as a result (Sabban 2013; 2014a). In particular, an increasing concern among Emirati and other Gulf-based families centres on the influence of migrant domestic workers on local children's values, identity, and behaviours as they need to sustain the very family/population with the drop of fertility rate (Roumani 2005; Sabban, 2018).

Substantial Demographic Imbalance[19]

The UAE annually attracts millions of visitors and foreign workers, who substantially reinforce the demographic imbalance dilemma in the country. The inhabitants have recently reached an astonishing 10 million individuals according to Amin Al Amiri, Assistant Undersecretary, Public Health Policy and License Sector, Ministry of Health,[20] a startling population boom in so short a period. However, the massive influx of foreign migrant workers has created a dramatic demographic imbalance that has turned Emiratis into a minority. This has caused alarm among some members of the community, who fear that society and tradition is being irreparably lost through the increase in globalisation. These signs are worrying to those nationals who are open in spirit to the world but who are, through circumstance, surrounded by non-nationals in every capacity (Abdulla 2006; Sabban 2013; Malit et al. 2018) and who now have to face the sociocultural impacts that such exchanges have played on the development of the social fabric in mainstream UAE society.

Private and Public Human Rights Abuses

The preceding 20 years of this decade was fraught with private and public complaints of human rights abuses against domestic workers in the UAE. Research from the turn of the millennium studying from a legal and social framework, the status of female domestic work is rife with cases of abuse, both physical and psychological (Sabban 2002; Begum 2014). Fieldwork in discussion with 51 foreign female domestic workers in two time frames (1995 and 2001) in the UAE brought to light a number of difficulties faced by these women in the country. These range from emotional difficulties to language barriers; however, most pertinent to this conversation are the narratives on working conditions at the time. Isolation was found to be a primary cause of suffering for these women, who at the time were at not considered as part of the labour force. As these women were under total control of their sponsors, and had no legal rights, and were expected to remain socially separated, it created an ideal atmosphere of unreprimanded abuse. Wages and working hours were unregulated and a main concern.

---

[19] In the mid-1990s, the government began taking measures to regulate expat workers because the numbers were rising rapidly. One new regulation that affected domestic workers was to exclude the low-skilled earners from bringing any of their family members along (Sabban 2012b). This law also meant that, even in cases where the employer might allow them to do so, domestic workers were legally prohibited from forming their families in the country, which thus created a 'conditionality' based form of integration within mainstream UAE society (Malit et al. 2018). The introduction of a new government quota on the import of domestic workers by both nationals and non-nationals, along with a mandatory security deposit that was required for each domestic worker employed and that would be returned on termination, was also implemented in an attempt to steady the demographic imbalance (Sabban 2012b).

[20] See Cornwell (2015).

In terms of verbal abuse, the following was reported from a sample of the participants:

"They say Indian, knows nothing." Another respondent stated, "My employer is a nervous person. She always make us feel that we are her maids." A third respondent said, "They shout, they scream at me, they call me names, they make me feel as if I am like *kashra* or trash."A fourth foreign female domestic worker recalled, "They say you are an animal, a donkey, crazy, stupid (Sabban 2002, 28)."

Physical and sexual abuse was noted too, by several participants, and remains a problem, that at the very least, is being addressed today. On physical abuse, participants said:

"Once I hit my employer's car by accident. She started screaming at me. "Don't you see? Is it the first time you see a car? Why are you so stupid?" She was wearing a ring. She smacked my face. My face was red for a long time. I cannot forget this moment." A second foreign female domestic worker related, "Once we were in the kitchen. I was cooking, [and] she got angry with me, after we got in an argument. She hit me with a plate (ibid, 29)."

Sexual abuse and harassment were cited by the participants, and the data seemed to paint archetypes of the perpetrators. It was generally cited that 'elder men' or 'other male workers' in the household would be the reprobates of the attacks. A more recent report from the Human Rights Watch (2014) issued similar findings in addition to a number of recommendations to the United Arab Emirates government. Due to continuous findings of this nature in the still-young nation, local and international pressure begins to mount. In turn, the government takes local initiatives, discussed below, as well as international initiatives to repair their damaged image. This includes becoming signatories to Convention on the Elimination of All Forms of Discrimination Against Women and its Protocols, amongst others (Sabban Forthcoming). Other changes at a local level include a 2017's domestic workers rights bill (Kanso 2017). The issue was no longer solely of human rights abuses but of a flawed infrastructure and a damaged public image.

Triggered Change and Current Results

Domestic work in the UAE has been subject to a fair amount of scrutiny from a human rights standpoint as issues related to labour abuse, exploitation, and neglect have increasingly become more apparent in an economy where foreign migrant labour is the very means by which the transformation of UAE cities (mostly Dubai and Abu Dhabi) into global forces has been possible. As such, domestic work regulations have increased in the UAE to protect both the family and domestic workers from unethical and illegal practices committed by agencies. As a result, local families have also felt under pressure to address these issues too, and they are constantly being subjected to criticism by international labour and rights groups, both in social media and in public life. Laws and regulations are continually evolving to ensure that labour and human rights violations and exploitations are eradicated; however, the process is one that requires a considerable amount of organisation and regulation, which puts the country under increased pressure in terms of the protection of labour rights and treatment of domestic workers (Fernandez and De Regt 2014, see also Ishii, Chapter 5). Recently, for example, the UAE Ministry of Human Resources and Emiratization (UAE MOHRE) passed a new domestic law that guarantees labour rights (that is, living conditions, working conditions, salary, etc.) and increases workers' access to dispute resolution mechanisms in an attempt to bolster their access to legal justice in the UAE. The UAE MOHRE's Domestic Work Department has also created at least 30 Tadbeer offices—a centralised recruitment, placement, and domestic work training agency--across the country in order to systematically regulate the recruitment of migrant domestic work both here and abroad. Therefore, the labour and human rights issues embedded in the context of migrant domestic work narratives have not only triggered and impacted on the "branding consciousness" of the uae but have also constructively influenced local families to rethink the complex issues of labour and human rights, as well as their domestic legal responsibilities and rights to protect their image and avoid major repercussions for the country's global standing.

Conclusion

The UAE has certainly achieved unparalleled socioeconomic growth and development in recent decades, while simultaneously continuing to exhibit strong determination to set its sights firmly on the future, as codified under the UAE 2030 vision plan. In the age of mass globalisation, as the UAE continues to engage with modernity and globalising forces, local UAE families and society are dramatically evolving, posing more complex and critical threats to their local culture, national identity, and security. One critical consequence of globalisation on the UAE family is the inevitable and, to a large extent, long-term dependence on migrant domestic work. Although the fertility rate is declining in the UAE, the heavy dependency on migrant domestic workers continues to grow. Although some families view domestic work as an inevitable tool to embrace modernity and globalisation and as a signaling factor to convey wealth and social status, other UAE families view it as an imperative domestic support that is needed to create an efficient local household structure.

As local UAE families' dependency on migrant domestic work increases, the consequences and costs on local UAE families and society also deepen in the long run. Many of these sociocultural challenges are rooted in the rapid social transformation after the discovery of oil, which has created a unique environment where the presence of domestic help is one of the most contentious and apparent outcomes of this dramatic economic transformation. More importantly, it is noteworthy that migrant domestic service has deeply impacted on the fundamental nature, structure, and culture of the Emirati family, which is deemed to be the very core of this exceptionally private and traditional culture. The evolution of the family unit in the Emirates as a result of the reliance on domestic help has also resulted in a unique set of complex labour and human rights issues and challenges that are a constant part of the discourse in the public and private spheres in the mainstream UAE community. The causes and consequences of these challenges, and the concerns themselves, are not only complex and unpredictable, but as the current situation stands, it is not clear if there is a "one size fits all" solution to the sociocultural conflicts that subtly impact on the local household cultures, structures, and practices. The speed of the complex social, economic, and cultural change and the constant imposition of migration as a development strategy reflects not only the uniqueness of the UAE families' dilemma but also the achievements of the UAE's brilliant ability to move from living in the shadow of history to becoming a young, successful nation-state globally. The cost, however, of such economic transformation on local UAE families' structure, culture, and traditions has many complex and multiple repercussions that may come with an "invisible" tomorrow in the long run.

Moreover, given the dominance of domestic work sector in the UAE, the evolving reconfiguration of domestic work sector critically reflects the growing corporatised approach to domestic work sector in the UAE. It also displays the emerging social visibility of the 'invisible' labour sector, as we as the shifting responsibility from the state to the private sector in their attempt to control and govern the holistic dimensions of transnational migrant domestic work industry. Therefore, it is essential to conclude that the domestic work will remain high and market driven sector, as the governing state continues to devise institutional and policy reforms to govern and corporatise its sector in the long run.

References

Abdulla, Abdul Khaleq. 1984. *Political Dependency: The Case of the United Arab Emirates.* Unpublished Ph.D. Dissertation. Georgetown University.

Abdulla, Abdul Khaleq. 2006. "Dubai: An Arab City Going Global." *Journal of Social Affairs* 23 (92): 53–85.

Abu Baker, Albadr. 1995. *Political Economy of State Formation: The United Arab Emirates in Comparative Perspective.* Unpublished PhD. Dissertation. University of Michigan.

Al-Fahim, Mohammed. 2006. *From Rags to Riches: A Story of Abu Dhabi.* London: The London Center of Arab Studies.

Al Faris, Mohammed Faris. 2000. *Al Awdaa Al Iqtisadiya Fi Imarate al Sahil Al Emarate Al Yom 1862–1965 UAE.* Emirates Center for Strategic Studies and Research. Abu Dhabi, UAE. In Arabic.

Al Sayegh, Fatima. 2001. "Women and Economic Changes in the Arab Gulf: The Case of the United Arab Emirates." *Digest of Middle East Studies* 10 (2): 17–39.

Al Sharekh, Alanoud. 2007. *The Gulf Family: Kinship Policies and Modernity.* London: Saqi Books.

Al-Tarrah Ali. 2007. "Family in the Kinship State." In *The Gulf Family: Kinship Policies and Modernities*, edited by Al Sharekh, 119–124. London: Saqi Books.

Barret, Raymond. 2010. *Dubai Dreams: Inside the Kingdom of Bling.* London: Nicholas Brealey Publishing.

Begum, Rothna. 2014. "United Arab Emirates: Trapped, Exploited, Abused". *Human Rights Watch.* https://www.hrw.org/news/2014/10/22/united-arab-emirates-trapped-exploited-abused.

Cornwell, Alexander. 2015. "UAE Population Edging Closer to 10 Million." Gulf News, 1 October 2015. Accessed 31 October 2015. http://gulfnews.com/news/uae/society/uae-population-edging-closer-to-10m1.1579486.

Crabtree, Sara Ashencaen. 2007. "Culture, Gender and the Influence of Social Change amongst Emirati Families in the United Arab Emirates." *Journal of Comparative Family Studies* 38 (4): 575–592.

Davidson, Christopher. 2005. *The United Arab Emirates: A Study in Survival.* Boulder: Lynne Rienner Publishers.

El Haddad, Yahya. 2003. "Major Trends Affecting Families in the Gulf Countries." Paper presented at the Conference of the College of Arts and Science, Bahrain University. May 17, 2003. Manama, Bahrain.

El Mallakh, Ragaei. 1981. *The Economic Development of the United Arab Emirates*,.London: Croom Helm.

Enloe, Cynthia. 1989. *Bananas, Beaches and Bases: Making Feminist Sense of International Politics.* London: Pandora Press.

Embassy of the United Arab Emirates. 2011. "Cultural Division of the UAE Embassy Washington D.C." Accessed 31 October 2015. http://www.uaecd.org.

Fargues, Philippe, Nasrah Shah, , and Francoise De-Bel Air. 2015. "Addressing Irregular Migration in the Gulf States." GLMM Policy Brief 1/2015. http://cadmus.eui.eu/handle/1814/37518.

Faris, Abdul-Razak. 1994. "Development Pattern and Structural Changes in the Labor Market in UAE." Unpublished Paper. UAE University: Faculty of Economics and Administrative Sciences.

Fernandez, Bina, and Marina de Regt, eds. 2014. *Migrant Domestic Workers in the Middle East: The Home and the World.* New York: Palgrave Macmillan.

Joyakoday, R., A. Thronton, and W. Axinn. 2008. "Perspectives of International Family Change." In *International Family Change: Ideational Perspectives*, edited by R. Joyakoday, A. Thronton and W. Axinn (Eds.), pp. 1–18. New York: Lawrence Erlbaum Publishers.

Gardner. Andrew. 2011. "Gulf Migration and the Family." *Journal of Arabian Studies: Arabia, the Gulf and the Red Sea* 1 (1): 3–25.

Ghubash, Moza. 1986. *Foreign Migration and Development.* Unpublished Masters Thesis. Sociology Department, University of Cairo. In Arabic.

Gulf Labour Markets and Migration (GLMM). 2016. "GCC: Total population and percentage of nationals and foreign nations in GCC countries (national statistics, 2010–2016) with numbers)).

Halabi, Romina. 2008. "Contract Enslavement of Female Domestic Workers in Saudi Arabia and the United Arab Emirates." *Topical Research Digest: Human Rights and Welfare.* 43–58. https://www.du.edu/korbel/hrhw/researchdigest/slavery/index.html.

Hannieh, Adam. 2011. *Khaleeji Capital: Capitalism and Class in the Arab Gulf States.* New York: Palgrave Macmillan.

Harding, Sandra. 1990. "Feminism, Science and the Enti-Enlightenment Critiques." In *Feminism/Postmodernism*, edited by Linda J. Nicholson. New York: Routledge.

Harding, Sandra. 1991. *Whose Science? Whose Knowledge? Thinking from Women's Lives.* New York: Cornell University Press.

Heard-Bey, Frauke. 2001. "The Tribal Society of the UAE and its Traditional Economy." In *United Arab Emirates: a new perspective*, edited by Ibrahim Al Abed and Peter Hellyer, 98–116. London: Trident Press.

Heard-Bey, Frauke. 2004. *From Trucial States to United Arab Emirates*. Dubai: Motivate Publishing.

Kanso, Heba. 2017. "UAE On Track To Improve Conditions For Migrant Domestic Workers: Rights Organization". *Reuters*. https://www.reuters.com/article/us-emirates-migrant-workers/uae-on-track-to-improve-conditions-for-migrant-domestic-workers-rights-organization-idUSKBN18Z2DN.

Kapiszewski, Andrew. 1999. *Native Arab Population and Foreign Workers in the Gulf States*. Krakow: TAIWPN Universitas.

Kazim, Aqil. 2000. *The United Arab Emirates A.D. 600 to the Present*. Dubai, UAE. Gulf Book Centre.

Khalaf, Ahmad, Hussein Rifai, Bader Omar, and Hala Omran. 1987. *Foreign Nannies Phenomenon: Causes and Consequences*. Bahrain: Bureau of the Ministers of Work and Social Affairs in the Arab Gulf Countries. In Arabic.

Khalaf, Sulayman. 2005. "National Dress and the Construction of the Emirati Cultural Identity." *Journal of Human Sciences* 11 (Winter Issue): 230–267.

Khalaf, Sulayman. 2006. "The Evolution of Gulf City Type, Oil and Globalization." In *Globalization and the Gulf*, edited by J. Fox, N. Mourtada-Sabbah, and M. al-Mutawa, 244–265. London: Routledge.

Khalifa, Ibrahim. 1986. *Foreign Nannies in the Arab Gulf Household*. Riyadh: Arab Bureau of Education for the Gulf States.

Krane, Jim. 2009. *Dubai the Story of the World's Fastest City*. New York: St Martin Press.

Malit, Jr., Froilan, Mouawiya Alawad, and Kristian Alexander.. 2018. "Globalisation and The *Khadama* Dependency Syndrome: Effects, Determinants, and Implications for Future Domestic Work Demand on Local Families' Socioeconomic Status in the United Arab Emirates (UAE)." *Arabian Humanities.* Forthcoming.

Malit, Jr., Froilan, Jenny Morrison, and George Naufal. 2018. "Conditional Migrant Integration in the United Arab Emirates: Consequences on Foreign Workers' Welfare." In *Migration and the Crises of the Modern Nation State?* Vernon Press. Delaware, USA.

Malit, Jr. Froilan and S. Ghafoor. 2014. "Domestic Work Legislation in the Gulf Cooperation Council: A Comparative Policy Review." *International Gulf Organization Policy Review* (1) 1: 1-13.

Ministry of Economy. "Annual Economic Report 2016". Accessed 14 February 2018. http://www.economy.gov.ae/Publications/MOE%20Anual%20Repoert%20English%202016.pdf.

Mitchell, Juliet. 1973. *Women's Estate.* New York: Vintage.

Moors, Annelies, Ray Jureidini, Ferhunde Ozbay, and Rima Sabban. 2009. "Migrant Domestic Workers: A New Public Presence in the Middle East?" In *Publics, Politics and Participation: Locating the Public Sphere in the Middle East and North Africa*, edited by Seteney Shami, 151–175, New York: Social Science Research Council.

Oakley, Ann. 1974. *The Sociology of Housework.* New York: Pantheon Books.

Oakley, Ann. 1981. *Subject Women: Where Women Stand Today - Politically, Economically, Socially, Emotionally.* New York: Pantheon Books.

Roumani, Hala. 2005. "Maids in Arabia: The Impact of Maids as Carers on Children's Social and Emotional Development." *Journal of Early Childhood Research* 2 (3): 149--167.

Sabban, Rima. 1996. 'Broken Spaces; Bounded Realities: Foreign Female Domestic Workers in the UAE. PhD dissertation. American University of Washington.

Sabban, Rima. 2002. "Mirgrant Women in the United Arab Emirates: The Case Of Female Domestic Workers". *International Labor Office*. https://www.ilo.org/wcmsp5/groups/public/---ed_emp/documents/publication/wcms_117955.pdf.

Sabban, Rima. 2012a. *Maids Crossing: Domestic Workers in the UAE.* Saarbrucken, Germany: Lambert Academic Publishing.

Sabban, Rima. 2012b. "Dubai Transnational Domestics: Visibility of the Invisible?" *Journal of Social Affairs* 28: 112.

Sabban, Rima. 2013. *Al HadathaWalTataworWaTa'thirihoma Fi Al A'datWalTakalid Fi Al Mojtama't Al Khalijya*. Center for Research and Strategic Studies UAE. Abu Dhabi, UAE. In Arabic.

Sabban, Rima. 2014a. "UAE Family Under Global Transformation." Report Presented to the National Research Foundation as part of a fellowship grant, UAE.

Sabban, Rima. 2014b. "Domestic Workers Between Two Paradigms: Dependency and Self Sufficiency: An Examination of the Opposing Models of Japan and the UAE." *Journal of Kagawa University International Office* 5: 59–86.

Sabban, Rima. 2018. "United Arab Emirates and Oman," in Suad Joseph eds (2018) in *Arab Family Studies: Critical Reviews.* New York, Syracuse University Press.

Saif A. Ramahi. 1973. *Economics and Political Evolution in the Arab Gulf States*. New York: Carlton Press.

Scott, James C. 1990. *Domination and the Arts of Resistance: Hidden Transcripts.* New Haven: Yale University Press.

Shah, Nasra. 2009. "The Management of Irregular migration and Its Consequence for Development: Gulf Cooperation Council." ILO Working Paper. http://www.ilo.org/wcmsp5/groups/public/---asia/---ro-bangkok/documents/publication/wcms_105105.pdf.

Shihab, Mohamed. 2001. "Economic Development in the UAE." In *United Arab Emirates: a new perspective*, edited by Ibrahim Al Abed and Peter Hellyer, 249–259. London: Trident Press.

Silvey, Rachel. 2006. "Consuming the transnational family: Indonesian migrant domestic workers to Saudi Arabia." *Global Networks* (6)1: 23-40.

Silvey, Rachel. 2007. "Mobilising Piety: Gendered Morality and Indonesia-Saudi Transnational Migration." *Journal of Mobilities* (2)2: 219–229.

Smith, Joan and Immanuel Wallerstein. 1992. *Creating and Transforming Household: The Constraints of the World Economy.* Cambridge: University Press of Cambridge.

Soffan, Usra. 1980. *The Women of the United Arab Emirates*. London: Croom Helm.

Trask, B. S. 2010. *Globalisation and Families: Accelerated Systemic Social Change*. Springer. London, United Kingdom.

UAE Government Portal. "Population and demographic mix." Accessed February 14, 2018. https://government.ae/en/information-and-services/social-affairs/preserving-the-emirati-national-identity/population-and-demographic-mix.

UAE Ministry of Work and Social Affairs (MOWSA). 1990. *Impact of Nannies on the UAE Family*. Dubai, UAE. In Arabic.

UAE Government. 2018. "UAE Vision 2030." Accessed on February 14, 2018. https://www.government.ae/en/about-the-uae/uae-future.

UAE General Information Authority (GIA). 1994. "Population Growth and Composition in the UAE since 1900." Accessed on February 14, 2008. http://www.gia.gov.ly/ar.

Zahlan, Rosemarie Said. 1978. *The origins of the United Arab Emirates: a political and social history of the Trucial States.* Palgrave Mcmillan: London, United Kingdom.

September 2020
Volume: 17, **No**: 5, pp. 669 – 679
ISSN: 1741-8984
e-ISSN: 1741-8992
www.migrationletters.com

MIGRATION
LETTERS

First Submitted: 12 April 2019 Accepted: 7 May 2020
DOI: https://doi.org/10.33182/ml.v17i5.754

Recruitment Strategies Used by Mexican Sex Traffickers

Simón Pedro Izcara Palacios[1]

Abstract

This article, based on a qualitative methodology that includes in-depth interviews with 43 Mexican sex traffickers, analyses the strategies used by sex traffickers to recruit women from Mexico and Central America demanded by the US illegal sex industry. We conclude that trafficking is a demand-led industry. Traffickers recruit vulnerable women from Mexico and Central America who fit with US procurers' requirements. Foreign girls smuggled into the United States should be young (in many cases underage girls), beautiful, slim and healthy. Mexican sex traffickers' job is to entice with salaries in US dollars impoverished Latin American girls who do not want to migrate or enter prostitution. Maintaining trafficked women captive against their will is more time consuming and less profitable than wining women's will with a salary.

Keywords: *Sex traffickers; Migrant women; Mexico; United States.*

Introduction

In the United States most recent research has been concentrated in the study of domestic minor sex trafficking, while sex trafficking of migrant women has been neglected. On the other hand, while the focus of attention has been on the victims of human trafficking, little research has focused on the facilitators of trafficking. Accordingly, most of our knowledge regarding sex trafficking relies on victim's description of interactions between themselves and sex traffickers, not from the standpoint of third parties (Serie et al., 2018; Hannem & Bruckert, 2017: 825). However, it is not possible to connect all the pieces of the puzzle if sex trade facilitators' voice is missing.

In US literature, the figure of the sex trafficker is mostly imagined as a man of colour, (Roe Sepowitz, 2019; Reid, 2016; Raphael & Myers Powell, 2010). Much of the research on this topic has focused on male traffickers. However, there is a common understanding that women are valuable recruiters in sex trafficking due to their easier access to other women, as it is easier for women than for men to develop trusting relationships with other women (Miccio Fonseca, 2017: 28). The role of women in sex trafficking recruitment appears prominent (Constantinou, 2019: 11; Broad, 2015: 1061; Brayley et al., 2011: 137). However, female participation in trafficking is initiated differently from their male counterpart. A woman becomes a sex trafficker from being victimised. Women were victims before becoming offenders, while men usually had prior criminal records. As a result, female traffickers are depicted having subservient low-level roles or acting under duress, under fear of violent reprisal at the hands of a male trafficker (Miccio Fonseca, 2017; Broad, 2015). By contrast, only a few studies portray male traffickers coerced into trafficking (Raphael & Myers Powell, 2010).

[1] Simón Pedro Izcara Palacios, Professor of Sociology at the Department of Sociology (UAMCEH), Tamaulipas University, Mexico. E-mail: sizcara@uat.edu.mx.

Academic research on sex traffickers focuses principally on the recruitment strategies used by them. Most studies analyse the methods and techniques used by sex traffickers to persuade, entrap, or entice the victims to coerce them into prostitution. These studies conclude that traffickers entice young girls through the pretense of love (Montiel Torres, 2015 & 2018; García, 2014), psychological manipulation (Brayley et al., 2011: 138; Reid, 2016: 499), financial debt (Constantinou, 2019: 17; Roe Sepowitz, 2019), drug addiction or physical might (Acharya, 2013, Acharya & Salas Stevanato, 2005), to the point that traffickers leave women feeling that they have few alternatives to prostitution (Kennedy et al., 2007). Other studies examine what is called "techniques of neutralisation" used to minimise trafficker's agency and responsibility by evoking socially acceptable justifications in order to defend their behaviour (Antonopoulos & Winterdyk, 2005; Copley, 2014; Montiel Torres, 2015 & 2018). Still other studies explore the connections between the recruitment process and sex trafficker's control of their victims (Bouché & Shady, 2017).

Research on sex traffickers follow a double narrative: a narrative of oppression and a narrative that questions conventional stereotypes about sex trafficking. These narratives can be differentiated by their methodological approach; by their focus; by the way sex traffickers' narratives are framed, and by their conceptualisation of sex procurement and sex trafficking.

Firstly, the methodological approach used to study sex traffickers frequently influences the results. Studies realised *ex situ,* based on social service providers or law enforcement official testimonials (Brayley et al., 2011; Reid, 2016), on post-arrest testimonials by traffickers in punishment institutions (Shively et al., 2017; Serie et al., 2018; Langhorn, 2018; Roe Sepowitz, 2019) or by victims in rescue institutions (Kennedy et al., 2007), tend to follow a narrative of oppression. By contrast, studies realised *in situ*, based on testimonials from active sex trade facilitators or active women in sex work are more prone to challenge conventional narrative of offenders' trickery, brutality and coercion (Zhang, 2011; Marcus et al., 2014; Hannem & Bruckert, 2017). Interviewing individuals confined in law enforcement or rescue institutions is easier and safer than interviewing them *in situ*. However, drawing conclusions from retrospective accounts *ex situ* does not allow researchers to independently verify data (Marcus et al., 2014: 226)

Secondly, the narrative of oppression focuses on individual actors: on predatory traffickers who lure innocent girls into prostitution to control, exploit and brutalise them in a manner that renders them akin to enslavement (Kennedy et al., 2007; Farley, 2018: 101). Prostitution is believed to be a form of slavery since the prostituted girl lacks choice, and both the enslaved and the prostituted girl are potentially subject to the arbitrary will of another person (Farley, 2018: 102). This literature concentrates on the victimisation of trafficked girls, and frames sex trafficking as a form of violence against innocent victims of merciless organised criminal syndicates (Terwilliger et al., 2017; Langhorn, 2018). Therefore, this narrative demand increased use of anti-trafficking laws. By contrast, the narrative that questions conventional stereotypes focus on structural factors and complex social processes that put women into precarious situations and make them vulnerable to trafficking. This narrative challenge the treatment of prostitute-pimp relation as being largely based on entrapment, exploitation and violence (Marcus et al., 2014; Zhang, 2011), and contests the organised crime-human trafficking dyad (Zhang, 2011; Constantinou, 2019). As a result, this narrative expresses some concerns about anti-trafficking laws, as the excuse of saving innocent women becomes a justification to tighten borders (Agustín, 2020: 223).

Thirdly, the first approach always discredits third parties' narratives, framed as techniques of neutralisation. It is assumed that traffickers are aware that their behaviour is deviant. Therefore, traffickers' narrative is interpreted as evidence of justification of their behaviour to preserve a respectable identity (Antonopoulos & Winterdyk, 2005; Copley, 2014; Montiel Torres, 2015 & 2018). On the contrary, the second approach does not impute motives to traffickers' accounts of their own realities, quite the opposite; it gives credit to sex trade facilitators' voice, as it frames procurers' narratives as the verbalised evidence of their internal identity negotiations (Hannem & Bruckert, 2017: 834). Agustín (2007: 69; 2020: 224) points out that sex traffickers are ordinary people who form part of migrant's own networks.

Finally, the line dividing sex procurement from sex trafficking is difficult to draw. Anti-trafficking law is underpinned in opaque concepts lacking uniform understandings, such as "abuse of a position of vulnerability" or "consent". If there is consent sex procurement cannot be framed as sex trafficking. However, anti-trafficking law underlines that women's consent is invalid if a position of vulnerability is abused. Both narratives agree about one idea: the difference between sex procurement and sex trafficking is constructed rather than essential. According to the narrative of oppression, women cannot consent to prostitution because it is detrimental to their dignity. Therefore, the concept of voluntary prostitution is fictional: sex procurement and sex trafficking are indistinguishable. Sex procurement is understood as sex trafficking because procurers always exploit victim's vulnerabilities (Farley, 2018: 103). On the contrary, the second approach questions the dominant discourses of sex trafficking, because it understands that sex trafficking victims are compelled into the sex trade by a complex set of life crises (Hannem & Bruckert, 2017: 826). Moreover, relationships between women and sex traffickers are understood in many cases as instrumental for both (Marcus et al., 2014: 243). Therefore, sex trafficking is mainly understood as sex procurement. According to the second narrative, in most cases, sex procurement cannot be understood as sex trafficking because procurers do not use force or coercion. According to Agustín (2007: 30) "most migrants who work on the sex industry knew from early on that their work would have a sexual component".

Empirical studies published by Mexican scholars tend to follow a narrative of oppression, as they portray women as vulnerable and innocent preys who helplessly wait for their rescue. The focus of this literature is domestic sex trafficking since it is understood that Mexican traffickers obtain higher economic gains exploiting their victims in Mexico. Also, it is believed that surveillance in airports and frontiers disincentives international sex trafficking (Acharya, 2013: 238, Acharya & Salas Stevanato, 2005: 517). Studies focusing on traffickers' discourse implicitly discredit them, as third parties' narratives are framed as techniques to minimise/neutralise their responsibility (Montiel Torres, 2015 & 2018; Ruenes, 2018). Trafficking is presented as a family business, and the trafficker is depicted as a figure that preys on vulnerable women. The trafficker binds needy young girls to him by offering love and attention and isolating them (Montiel Torres, 2015 & 2018; García, 2014; Vargas Urías, 2016; Ruenes, 2018).

The objective of this article is to analyse the strategies used by Mexican sex traffickers to recruit women from Mexico and Central America demanded by the US illegal sex industry. The article proceeds as follows. First, the methodology is outlined and the sample is described. Next, the strategies used by sex traffickers to recruit women from Mexico and Central America are examined.

Materials and Methods

Due to the nature of this study, a qualitative methodology was used. The technique used to collect discursive data was in-depth interviewing. Interviews were guided by an interview protocol that consisted of open-ended questions related to recruitment strategies utilised by the interviewees. Interviews were conducted in an environment that was comfortable for the participants. In some cases, interviewees were interviewed at their homes, while others were interviewed in places where human smugglers gather. During the Easter Festivity many traffickers gather in specific points during several days to thank God for being alive. Most of them reverence Jesus Christ death and resurrection, and many worships the Holy Death. Therefore, Easter was the best period to interview them. Each interview varied in length from one hour to well over two hours. With the participants' consent we audio recorded each interview; recordings were transcribed, and all personal identifiers were removed.

Contact with interviewees was made via social networks and snowballing in a few different Mexican States: Tamaulipas, Nuevo Leon, Coahuila, San Luis Potosí, Veracruz, Mexico City, Chiapas, and Tabasco. Tamaulipas, Nuevo Leon, and Coahuila were selected because are Border States with Texas, which is the main entry point of Central America women to the United States. On the other hand, Chiapas is the main entry point into Mexico of Central American women seeking migrant smugglers to help them reach the United States. Mexico City and Tabasco were selected because they are nodal points from which sex traffickers' networks spread across the country. Finally, the two main transit points of migrant-smuggling networks that operate along the eastern sector of the US-Mexico border were selected: San Luis Potosí and Veracruz.

Five strategies were used to attempt to corroborate the veracity of the stories collected: i.) Respondents were instructed not to provide names or details that would reveal the identity of the persons mentioned in the stories. ii) Respondents received no financial compensation for participating in this study. iii) Interviews were conducted with a guide that included dozens of questions, some of which we modified several times during the course of the investigation to exclude items that generated little heuristic richness and to include other more relevant aspects that surfaced in connection to the empirical reality. iv) Some sensitive questions were asked multiple times in varying ways to check the consistency of responses. v) In three cases we prepared a second guide, different for each respondent, to address in a second encounter inconsistent issues or discussions that were left unfinished during the first verbal interaction.

Forty-three sex traffickers were interviewed between November 2012 and December 2017. Interviewees performed a leading role in the sex trafficking network they belonged to; none of them had ancillary positions. All but one of them were men, and all had considerable experience in the business of sex trafficking, as they had spent between 3 and 17 years in this trade. Respondents had on average 5 years of schooling, and their low level of education was the result of needing to work from childhood to sustain the family financially. The age when they started working fluctuated from 6 to 22.

Texas, California, and Florida were the states where most Mexican sex traffickers operated. However, they also brought women to Louisiana, New York, Illinois, Colorado, Oklahoma, South Carolina, New Mexico, and Missouri (see table 1).

All study procedures received approval from the Ethics Committee of Tamaulipas University research group "Migration, development and human rights". Informed oral consent was obtained from the respondents, and participants were provided with verbal information about the study purpose in simple language. Interviewees were informed about the voluntary nature of their participation in the study and were told that the information they shared would be handled confidentially and processed anonymously. Participants were assured that individual names would not be collected or used in any study findings. To ensure the anonymous and confidential nature of the data collected each respondent was assigned a code. Accordingly, the names of the participants in this study are pseudonyms. We also informed each participant of their right to withdraw from the interview at any point in time. Even no money was paid, many traffickers accepted to be interviewed, probably because we were able to build trust with them. Interviews were conducted within the span of 5 years. During this time, some traffickers knew other colleagues who participated in this study. Therefore, they could realise that the information they gave us was confidential and was not used against them. As interviewees did not consider themselves criminals, this research gave them the opportunity to get out their side of the story.

Table 1: States in the US where Mexican sex traffickers operated

State	n	%	State	n	%
Texas	30	69.8	Colorado	1	2.3
California	9	20.9	Oklahoma	1	2.3
Florida	3	7.0	South Carolina	1	2.3
Louisiana	2	4.7	New Mexico	1	2.3
New York	1	2.3	Missouri	1	2.3
Illinois	1	2.3	Total	43	100

Source: Compiled by the author from data recorded in the interviews.
Percentages sum up more than 100 because some sex traffickers transported women to several states.

Results

Commercial sex markets in the US are comprised of foreign girls smuggled into the country, as well as American women and legal permanent residents. The former are demanded because they are the most vulnerable and the most willing to fulfill clients' caprices (Izcara Palacios, 2017a: 35). However, recruiting foreign women to be employed in the US sex industry is not an easy task because most women who want to migrate do not want to work in prostitution. Accordingly, Mexican sex traffickers usually try to recruit women involved in prostitution in Mexico or Central America. Frequently, the owners of places such as bars, cantinas or brothels work as recruiters for sex traffickers (Izcara Palacios, 2018). The owners of these places generally have an agreement with a trafficker, who pays a fee for every woman he recruits (Izcara Palacios, 2017a: 37). The fee usually ranges from one thousand to three thousand Mexican pesos (from 50 to 150 USD) per woman. When a trafficker that does not have an agreement with the owner tries to recruit a woman, the former is rejected by the latter. In some cases, traffickers do not have to make an effort to recruit women because are the owners of these places the ones who convince the girls. However, in most cases traffickers are the ones who must convince them. In both cases the fees payed to the owners of bars, cantinas or brothels in Mexico are similar. According to interviewees, if a woman does not want to work in the US the owner of the place does not force her, and traffickers are not allowed to take girls by force from these places.

Women working in prostitution in their country of origin are not eager to migrate to the US; therefore, sex traffickers have many difficulties trying to convince them. As Alejandro (2012) pointed out: "It isn't an easy job to recruit them, I have to battle to convince them to go; some have family, others are doing well in Mexico and don't want to go. I am battling in searching them and in convincing them to go (...) It is not easy to convince them to go, and I have people who help me recommending the women with me". Accordingly, interviewees used active recruiting techniques, a reason for engaging in prostitution being fabricated. Some respondents pointed out that when women said that they did not want to migrate to the US to work in prostitution, they tried to change her mind charming them with stories of fast money and exciting lifestyle. As Sergio pointed out: "I have *labia* (glibness) to convince them." Traffickers scrutinise women's economic needs and vulnerabilities and present themselves as the solution to all their problems. This was reflected in expressions such as: "I speak them nicely …. I tell them that there they are going to do better. I have my secrets to convince them" (Melchor, 2014); "I *las envuelvo* (wrap them) according to the needs they have" (Natalio, 2014) or "I try to convince them on the economic side. In this way I hit them[2], I speak of money and it is when they accept to go" (Pascual, 2014).

Sex trafficking is a demand-led industry. Mexican traffickers recruit only those women who comply with the standard set up by US procurers. Interviewees were salaried workers. They usually worked for a middleman between them and US procurers, who was called "patron" (the boss). In some cases the boss was a US procurer, while in other cases their boss was a former trafficker, like them; but after acquiring experience in this business, he became the leader of a sex trafficking network, and recruited other traffickers. None of the bosses mentioned by the respondents appeared to be members of drug cartels, as interviewees expressed very negative opinions about these organisations. According to interviewees Mexican drug cartels extort sex traffickers, but the former does not smuggle women into the United States (Izcara Palacios, 2017b: 21).

US sex industry only accepts women who fit with a specific profile: they must be young, beautiful, slim, and healthy. Mexican traffickers cannot bring any women, and many women who want to work in prostitution do not meet the requirements demanded by US procurers. Only a fraction of women with experience in prostitution fit the profile demanded by sex traffickers. According to interviewees US clients are very picky, and only the most beautiful and well-formed women satisfy their demands. As Natalio (2014) explained: "Those who want to go cannot go, because not all persons are eligible to be accepted there; the girls that I take are special girls for demanding men, very demanding". As can be seen from Table 2, age was the most important requirement, girls should be young. In prostitution, as the age of the women increases, the number of clients decreases due to client preference (Acharya, 2010: 32; Izcara Palacios, 2018: 7). Almost all (95.3 %) the traffickers interviewed had instructions to recruit women of a certain age range. On average this range fluctuated from a minimum of 15.8 to a maximum of 26.5 years old. Women who passed the maximum age limit were not transported to the US even if they were beautiful, because if sex traffickers did so, they were not paid for that. As Rogelio (2015) explained: "age is compulsory because after a certain age a woman cannot perform this job; well, she is able to do this job, but men who pay prefer young (girls), because of this the age is a requirement". Likewise, Paulino (2014) pointed out: "The boss doesn't like them if they are more than 20 years old because he doesn't make the same (money) with a 20-year-old girl than with a younger girl". Sex traffickers also must recruit well-formed, slim, and beautiful women. As Melchor (2014) pointed out: "There (in the US) they ask me to bring women almost perfect (…) This is a very delicate job and requires an almost perfect selection because the better the women are the most valuable they are". Being slim and having a shaped and curvaceous body was more valued that being beautiful. Three-fifths

---

[2] The interviewee used metaphorically the Spanish expression "Por ahí les doy el golpe".

(58.1 %) of the interviewees commented that women should be slim, while only two-fifths (39.5 %) mentioned that women should be beautiful. Eight respondents said that they only were requested to comply with the size; women should be small or medium sizes; on the contrary, women of large size were never accepted. Some interviewees said that if women were not beautiful, they did not carry them; while six of them pointed out that the age was the only basic requirement, as even ugly or fat women could be fixed with make-up or with a diet (see table 2).

A characteristic more important than beauty was women's desire to work in prostitution. According to almost half (46.5 %) of the interviewees trafficked women should wish to perform sex work, or if they did not like this job they should be in need, eager and happy to do a job that pays well. Four traffickers pointed out that at least women should be ambitious and tempted by the easy money. Respondents said that maintaining women against their will was not good for business because to force them was time consuming, and women retained by force did not give a good service, or did not perform a work well done, as clients who paid demanded. Accordingly, Malarek (2005: 236) quotes a conversation recorded by the FBI, where a pimp resident in California pointed out that the merchandise (women trafficked from Ukraine against their will) easily could escape.

One-third (32.6 %) of the interviewees pointed out that having a good temper, and being loving, gentle and friendly to clients was a compulsory requirement. Two interviewees said that women should have some communication skills, as they should be cheerful and talkative to attract the clients. One-fourth (25.6 %) of the respondents said that having experience in prostitution was an important or compulsory requirement. On the contrary, six interviewees (13.9 %) indicated that not having experience in prostitution or being a virgin was a desirable thing. Only one of the respondents did not make any selection (see table 2).

Table 2: Requirements that sex traffickers have to comply when recruiting women

	n	%
The age is the most important requirement, girls must be young	41	95.3
Should have a curvaceous body and must be slim	25	58.1
Must have a desire to work in prostitution	20	46.5
Should be beautiful	17	39.5
Should have a good temper, should be loving, gentle and friendly to clients	14	32.6
Having experience in prostitution is an important/compulsory requirement	11	25.6
The most important thing is the size	8	18.6
Shouldn't be minors, must be over 18 years old	8	18.6
Must be healthy	8	18.6
Not having experience in prostitution is desirable	6	13.9
If they are ugly or fat they can be fixed with make-up or with a diet	6	13.9
Should like easy money and be ambitious	4	9.3
Must be single and shouldn't have children	4	9.3
Should have communication skills	2	4.6
Should like to party	1	2.3
Doesn't make any selection	1	2.3
Total	43	100

Source: Compiled by the author from data recorded in the interviews.
Percentages sum up more than 100 because most sex traffickers had to comply with more than one requirement.

To fill the quotas of women that US sex industry demands, sex trafficking networks in Mexico have turned their eyes on Central American women. Central Americans are preferred by US procurers because they are more profitable as they stay longer in the US than Mexicans. This was reflected in comments such as: "In the case of women, Central American women are preferred over Mexican; but only in prostitution" (Valerio, 2017) or "Women from Central America are more preferred than Mexicans in prostitution jobs" (Vicente, 2017). On the other hand, interviewees commented that Mexican women were more reticent to migrate. Francisco (2013) affirmed: "Mexican women go and continue going; but they are going less for fear to organised crime; they think that something can happen to them or if they can't come back; sometimes they put a lot of excuses and they don't want to go". According to respondents, Central Americans were more in need than Mexican women; therefore, it was easier to entice them to work in prostitution. As Paulino (2014) explained: "With women coming from other countries there is not much to talk about, because they are looking to pass to the other side. You invite them and they say yes because that is what they want. Because of this, I choose them from Central America to carry them. So, there is no problem". Women from Central America in transit through Mexico desire so much to go to the US that sex traffickers do not have to make a great effort to convince them. According to some interviewees, in the case of Central Americans, the most difficult task was not to convince them but to find girls who complied with the standards set up by US sex industry. As Paulino (2014) pointed out: "I am battling choosing them, not searching for them". Sex traffickers approach Central American girls who meet the above criteria and try to entice them speaking about the high salaries paid by the sex industry. As can be seen from table 3 three-fourths (76.7 %) of sex trafficking networks studied recruited women from Central America; while, only two-thirds (67.4 %) carried Mexican women.

Table 3: Place of origin of the women transported by sex trafficking networks

	n	%
Only from México	10	23.3
Only from Central America	12	27.9
Mexico and Central America	13	30.2
Mexico, Central America and other Latin America countries	6	13.9
Central America and other Latin America countries	2	4.6
Sex trafficking networks that transport women from Central America	33	76.7
Sex trafficking networks that transport women from Mexico	29	67.4
Total	43	100

Source: Compiled by the author from data recorded in the interviews.

Conclusion

The recruitment of women from Mexico and Central America to be employed in the US illegal sex industry is a time consuming endeavour because most women who want to migrate do not want to work in prostitution, and women working in prostitution in their country of origin are not eager to migrate to the US. To change women's mind traffickers, do whatever necessary to win them over. They scrutinise women's economic needs and vulnerabilities and present themselves as the solution to all their problems. The lack of a promising future in their country of origin creates the necessary conditions and facilitates the ease with which traffickers recruit women. However, sex trafficking depends principally on the demand from US sex industry. The pull of demand was stronger than the push of poverty, although both were at play.

According to interviewees some women (especially migrant women from Central America) are willing to work in prostitution in the US; however, most women do not want to. Women trafficked to the US do not choose to be recruited by sex traffickers, the former are chosen by the latter. Mexican traffickers are not allowed to recruit any women they find. If trafficked girls do not comply with the standard set up by US procurers, traffickers will not receive any payment. Therefore, Mexican traffickers only recruit migrant women who are very young (in many cases underage girls), beautiful, slim, and healthy, and are gentle to clients. As women who fit this profile usually do not want to migrate or enter prostitution, sex traffickers' job is to entice with comparatively high salaries vulnerable Latin American girls. Central American women are more vulnerable than Mexicans; as a result, the former are more frequently trafficked than the latter.

On the other hand, Mexican traffickers declare they do not use force or coercion to recruit migrant women, and relationships between the former and the latter are not violent. As a result, interviewees did not consider themselves as engaging in a criminal activity.

Acknowledgements

Funding for this research was provided by the National Council of Science and Technology (SEP/CONACYT), Research Project N° CB-2013-01 220663 "Trata y prostitución en México".

References

Acharya, A. K. & Stevanato, A. (2005) "Violencia y tráfico de mujeres en México: una perspectiva de género". Revista Estudios Feministas. 13(3): 507-524.

Acharya, A. K. (2013). "Mujeres invisibles y victimización sexual en México: El caso de la trata de mujeres en Monterrey". Estudios sociales, 21(42): 233-258.

Acharya, A. K. (2010). "Feminisation of migration and trafficking of women in Mexico". Revista de Cercetare şi Intervenţie Socială, 30: 19-38

Agustín, L. (2007). Sex at the margins. Migration, Labour Markets and the Rescue Industry. New York: Zed Books.

Agustín, L. (2020). Snake Oil. Journal of Human Trafficking, 6(2), 221-225.

Akee, R., Basu, A. K., Bedi, A., & Chau, N. H. (2014). "Transnational trafficking, law enforcement, and victim protection: A middleman trafficker's perspective". The Journal of Law and Economics, 57(2): 349-386.

Antonopoulos, G. A., Winterdyk, J. A., & John, A. (2005). "Techniques of neutralising the trafficking of women". European Journal of Crime, Criminal Law, and Criminal Justice, 13: 136-147.

Bouché, V., & Shady, S. (2017). "A pimp's game: a rational choice approach to understanding the decisions of sex traffickers". Women & Criminal Justice, 27(2): 91-108.

Brayley, H., Cockbain, E., & Laycock, G. (2011). "The value of crime scripting: Deconstructing internal child sex trafficking". Policing: A Journal of Policy and Practice, 5(2): 132-143.

Broad, R. (2015). "'A vile and violent thing': Female traffickers and the criminal justice response". British journal of criminology, 55(6): 1058-1075.

Constantinou, A. G. (2019). "The roles and actions of sex traffickers in Cyprus: an overview". Trends in Organized Crime, 1-26. https://doi.org/10.1007/s12117-019-09369-4

Copley, L. (2014). "Neutralising their involvement: Sex traffickers' discourse techniques". Feminist Criminology, 9(1): 45-58.

Farley, M. (2018). "Risks of prostitution: When the person is the product. Journal of the Association for Consumer Research". 3(1): 97-108.

García, D.E. (2014). "La violencia en las migraciones: el caso de la trata de mujeres. Modus operandi en las formas de engaño y enganche". Dilemata, (16): 121-142.

Hannem, S. & Bruckert, C. (2017). "I'm Not a Pimp, but I Play One on TV": The Moral Career and Identity Negotiations of Third Parties in the Sex Industry. Deviant behavior, 38(7): 824-836.

Izcara Palacios, S.P. (2017a). "Prostitution and Migrant Smuggling Networks Operating between Central America, Mexico, and the United States". Latin American Perspectives, 44(6): 31-49.

Izcara Palacios, S.P. (2017b). "Migrant smuggling on Mexico's gulf route: The actors involved. Latin American Perspectives, 44(6): 16-30.

Izcara Palacios, S.P. (2018). "Prostitución de menores en locales registrados en México". Revista Internacional de Sociología, 76(1), e087. https://doi.org/10.3989/ris.2018.76.1.16.23

Kennedy, M. A., Klein, C., Bristowe, J. T., Cooper, B. S., & Yuille, J. C. (2007). "Routes of recruitment: Pimps' techniques and other circumstances that lead to street prostitution". Journal of Aggression, Maltreatment & Trauma, 15(2): 1-19.

Langhorn, M. (2018). "Human trafficking and sexual servitude: Organised crime's involvement in Australia". Salus Journal, 6(1): 1-25.

Malarek, V. (2005). Las Natashas tristes. Esclavas sexuales del siglo XXI. Madrid: Kailas Editorial.

Marcus, A., Horning, A., Curtis, R., Sanson, J., & Thompson, E. (2014). "Conflict and agency among sex workers and pimps: A closer look at domestic minor sex trafficking". The ANNALS of the American Academy of Political and Social Science, 653(1): 225-246.

Miccio Fonseca, L. C. (2017). "Juvenile female sex traffickers". Aggression and violent behavior, 35: 26-32.

Montiel Torres, O. (2015). "La estructura básica de la explotación sexual. Propuesta de modelo teórico". Revista de Estudios en Antropología Sexual, 1(6): 83-101.

Montiel Torres, O. (2018). "El ciclo vital de las mujeres en situación de prostitución y el sistema proxeneta". Nueva antropología, 31(88): 31-51.

Raphael, J., & Myers Powell, B. (2010). From victims to victimisers: Interviews with 25 ex-pimps in Chicago. Chicago: Schiller DuCanto & Fleck Family Law Center of DePaul University College of Law.

Reid, J. A. (2016). "Entrapment and enmeshment schemes used by sex traffickers". Sexual Abuse, 28(6): 491-511.

Roe Sepowitz, D. (2019). "A six-year analysis of sex traffickers of minors: exploring characteristics and sex trafficking patterns". Journal of Human Behavior in the Social Environment, 29(5): 608-629.

Ruenes, M. (2018). "Víctimas y victimarios. Un acercamiento a los procesos y las lógicas que configuran la trata de personas". El Cotidiano, 34(209): 77-84.

Serie, C. M., Krumeich, A., van Dijke, A., de Ruiter, E., Terpstra, L., & de Ruiter, C. (2018). "Sex traffickers' views: a qualitative study into their perceptions of the victim–offender relationship". Journal of human trafficking, 4(2): 169-184.

Shively, M.; Smith, K.; Jalbert, S. y Drucker, O. (2017). Human Trafficking Organisations and Facilitators: A Detailed Profile and Interviews with Convicted Traffickers in the United States. NCJRS. https://www.ncjrs.gov/App/Publications/abstract.aspx?ID=273351

Terwilliger, G. Z., Frank, M. J., & Merkl, T. A. (2017). "Human Trafficking and Organized Crime: Combating Trafficking Perpetrated by Gangs, Enterprises, and Criminal Organisations". United States Attorneys' Buletin, 65.

Troshynski, E. I., & Blank, J. K. (2008). "Sex trafficking: an exploratory study interviewing traffickers". Trends in Organized Crime, 11(1): 30-41.

Vargas Urías, M. A. (2016). "Una aproximación conceptual a la participación masculina en la trata de personas con fines de explotación sexual dentro de los procesos migratorios del contexto mexicano". Sociológica, 31(89): 131-162

Annex: Interviews quoted in the manuscript:

ALEJANDRO	Sex trafficker from Tamaulipas interviewed in 2012
FRANCISCO	Sex trafficker from Tamaulipas interviewed in 2013
MELCHOR	Sex trafficker from the State of Mexico interviewed in 2014
NATALIO	Sex trafficker from Chiapas interviewed in 2014
PAULINO	Sex trafficker from Tamaulipas interviewed in 2014
PASCUAL	Sex trafficker from Tamaulipas interviewed in 2014
ROGELIO	Sex trafficker from Chiapas interviewed in 2015
SERGIO	Sex trafficker from Tabasco interviewed in 2016
VALERIO	Sex trafficker from Nuevo Leon interviewed in 2017
VICENTE	Sex trafficker from California interviewed in 2017
All names are pseudonyms.	

September 2020
Volume: 17, **No**: 5, pp. 681 – 693
ISSN: 1741-8984
e-ISSN: 1741-8992
www.migrationletters.com

MIGRATION
LETTERS

First Submitted: 19 May 2020 Accepted: 9 August 2020
DOI: https://doi.org/10.33182/ml.v17i5.1002

What Money Can't Buy: Educational Aspirations and International Migration in Ecuador

Paúl Arias-Medina[1] and María-José Rivera[2]

Abstract

This article studies how educational aspirations of children are shaped in Biblián, Ecuador, a traditional sending country. Data sources were a multi-level survey and semi-structured interviews that were analysed using logistic regression and thematic analysis, respectively. Several theoretical relationships are confirmed: the household socioeconomic status, caregiver's educational aspirations and age are the most important variables that predict the educational aspirations of children. Child migratory dreams and the absence of the father or the mother only predict the educational aspiration of getting a high school degree, but do not predict the aspiration of a graduate degree. Thematic analysis suggests that, besides seeing education as a means to have higher incomes, mothers perceive it as a sign of social status and assign it an intrinsic value.

Keywords: *Education; aspirations; expectations, migration; mixed methods.*

Introduction

The link between education and migration becomes extremely complex because of the direct and indirect relations with different analysis levels (individual, familial and structural conditions), intergenerational relationships, and cognitive dimensions. Effects of migration on educational variables are often mixed. For instance, despite evidence that shows that the financial benefits of migration might allow children to continue their education, there is also an adverse effect by reducing the motivation to educational attainment (Kandel & Kao, 2001). Such motivation is reinforced through communication. In both, migrant and non-migrant households, the parent-child relationship is the channel which serves to transmit the family cultural values and norms to children. Furthermore, the figure of parents as role models has been reported in different researches (Chiapa, Garrido & Prina, 2012; Beaman et al., 2012; Krishnan and Krutikova, 2013).

The theory of relative deprivation and the migration network theory state that interpersonal contexts contour the motivations to migrate. First, the principle of relative deprivation has been confirmed by empirical works in rural contexts (Czaika & Vothknecht, 2014; Izcara-Palacios, 2011; Kafle et al., 2020), such as Biblián. Second, the theory of migration networks provides a proper framework to understand the inter-subjective nature of the relationship between migration and society[3]. In consequence, the nexus between migration and education involves topics of age, gender,

---

[1] Paúl Arias-Medina, VLIR-UC Project of International Migration and Local Development, and Faculty of Psychology, University of Cuenca, Ecuador. E-mail: paul.arias@ucuenca.edu.ec.
[2] María-José Rivera, VLIR-UC Project of International Migration and Local Development, and Faculty of Psychology, University of Cuenca, Ecuador. E-mail: mjose.riverau@ucuenca.edu.ec.
[3] Pedone (2005) has found that migration networks and chains explain intergenerational relationships mediated by migration in the familial sphere. This author studies the case of Ecuador and evidences a consolidated migration culture supported by the fact that

parental roles, bargaining power and 'brain gain', as Antman (2013) synthesizes. It seems that in Ecuador, familial transnationalism (Herrera, 2004), social remittances (Mata-Codesal, 2013), and stereotypes and social imaginaries in the origin country (Herrera, 2005; Pedone, 2005, Villavicencio et al., 2011) reveal a broader, and also thorough, spectrum of migration-related factors that may shape left-behind children's education in Ecuador.

Aspirations and expectations[4] lean on *habitus*; the experience affected by class socialisation, actions and observation differs across ethnic groups or minorities (Bohon et al., 2006). In the context of international migration, Latino parents that have suffered discrimination or lack of opportunities translate into scepticism about the value of education. The longer they are exposed to the American life, the lower their aspirations become (Goldenberg et al., 2001). In other cases, migration is widely accepted as a plausible option to have a better life. Consequently, the event of migration of a family member might affect the aspiration of children by lowering it because migration is portrayed as an effective manner to achieve economic goals (Kandel & Kao, 2001; McKenzie et al., 2013; Meza & Pederzini, 2009; McKenzie & Rapoport, 2011). The rationale might be put in this words: 'If it is better to live in New York than in Biblián and holding a degree is indifferent for an undocumented migrant, then why should one invest time in studying?'. Nonetheless, some evidence (Parella, 2007) demonstrate that children may also experience a sense of pride knowing that their parents are making a sacrifice for them, following the suggestions of Carling (2014) regarding how migrants are seen by their families. The parents' response might be even more important than the children's because of the realistic assumption that parents face less asymmetry of information and because children's answers and intentions tend to be more volatile (Alexander & Cook, 1979). Such parental aspirations, influenced by their socioeconomic status and economic situation of the neighbours, determine their investment behaviour towards their children (Mookherjee et al., 2010). A valuable insight regarding the value of education among Latino migrants is that parents do not see education just as a way to achieve economic goals, but as personal fulfilment or moral development resource (Goldenberg et al., 2001). This is especially important since the parental nurture effect is one of the primary drivers of intergenerational human capital transfer (Holmlund et al., 2011) and might not be compensated by increased income (Shea, 2000).

This paper aims to contribute to the understanding of the nexus education-migration by studying the educational aspirations of children in a traditional sending country like Ecuador. Indeed, it is during 1999 - 2003 that massive outflows of working age people are recorded, predominantly to the USA, Spain and Italy. For instance, according to official statistics there was a variation of 140.1 % between the emigration rates of 1998 and 1999 and it is estimated that 685 857 Ecuadorians left the country during this period, most of them were from the Southern region of Ecuador, mainly from the Provinces of Azuay and Cañar (Ramirez & Ramirez, 2005: 70). The Ecuadorian National Institute of Statistics and Census, INEC (2019) pointed out the USA as the

---

decisions on migration involve many generations and their current power relationships. Similarly, ethnographic works have pointed out how feelings, emotions and perceptions fund the sociological myth of the 'successful migrant' in the origin communities (Herrera, et al., 2018; Levitt & Schiller, 2004). In the same vein, transnational theory emerges supported by many authors such as Levitt & Schiller (2004) and Parella & Speroni (2018). Indeed, contemporary literature on migration has looked again to the household and family. However, some authors have found that these relations are permeated by tensions (Herrera, 2013) and reproduction of gender inequality (Herrera 2013; Rivas, 2011; Zapata, 2016).

[4] Aspirations and expectations are two related but different concepts. Aspirations reflect hopes and dreams that might be detached from reality. For instance, low aspirations have always been identified as an internal constraint that impedes the individual to escape poverty, reinforcing a so-called poverty trap (Dalton et al., 2016). Expectations are more closely linked to the socioeconomic conditions. Expectations are related to the liabilities that children might face while trying to achieve a specific educational level. Contrary to aspirations, expectations should reflect real struggles and obstacles that might impede a wish to materialise.

first destination for Ecuadoreans since 1997, and that 528,486 of them left to this country by 2019. Furthermore, since many migrants go irregularly to the USA, a significant sub-record is calculated. It is important to note that being irregular means constant uncertainty, higher danger, risk of deportation, and less probability of visits to the origin country. Indeed, several cases of deportation, journeys of unaccompanied minors and smuggling and drug trafficking are usually reported in the area[5].

This paper studies the case of Biblián, a town of the Province of Cañar. Biblián was chosen because of the following reason: In 2001, while the called 'migratory stampede', its emigration rate was 11.31 % –the third-highest rate in the country– and the poverty rate, measured by unsatisfied basic needs, rose to 67.48 % (Ramirez & Ramirez, 2005). During the last census in 2010, its population was 20,817 inhabitants and its migrant population was 1,891 and, in consequence, the proportion of migrants relative to the total population was the highest in Ecuador (INEC, 2010). Unfortunately, there is no updated statistics regarding emigration from Biblián. However, the local government (GAD Cañar, 2016) highlights remittances as financial sources and social impacts of migration in its official plan for 2015-2019.

In order to meet the research objectives, we used a quantitative strategy to identify which variables predict the educational aspiration and a qualitative research to describe how parents might influence children aspirations in international migration-related contexts.

Methods

Biblián is a small parish located in the Ecuadorian Andean region where international migration is prevalent. We used an explanatory sequential design: the quantitative study was followed by a qualitative one purpose of which was to describe the mechanisms of influence from parents to children regarding their educational aspirations, in migrant households. In the quantitative stage, the data was collected between May and June 2015 by the VLIR-IUC Migration and Local Development Project of the University of Cuenca through a survey called Problems, Expectations and Aspirations of Children (PEACH). A randomized cluster sample was applied to select the schools and the surveys were applied in 9 educational institutions[6] of Biblián.

The PEACH was applied for students, caregivers and teachers and included questions related to household sociodemographic characteristics, academic performance (only for teachers), expectations, and aspirations. For the qualitative stage, a sample of seven mothers who participated in the first stage of the study was selected. The selection criterion was that the partner (husband) was still living abroad. The gathering of data, as well as the analysis and presentation of results, was done following the Ministry of Education of Ecuador and American Psychological Association requirements.

The variables collected for the quantitative stage were defined as follows:

Educational Expectations. Measured by the question: "Considering the following scale, where 0 represents impossibility, and 10 represents certainty, what probability do you think you have to

---

[5] Unluckily, there is no systematization of this panorama. An interesting –although rather anecdotal– work is offered by Ramirez & Lagomarsino (2014). However, many press reports (originally in Spanish) might depict this situations: *Deportation of Ecuadorian citizens from the U.S., Two Ecuadorian teenagers deported trying to reach the US, Authorities warn that 'coyotes' force migrants to take drugs to the US.*

[6] Ecuador's general educational levels are two: General Basic Education (from 5 to 14 years-old children) and General High school (similar to US high school, from 14 to 18 years-old children), although each institution usually manage both.

reach the education level you want?" The main caregiver responded to a similar question: "Considering the following scale, where 0 represents impossibility and 10 represents certainty, what probability do you think [name of the child] has to reach the education level [name of the child] wants?"

Educational Aspirations. Captured by the question: "What is the highest educational level you wish to achieve?" The question includes six levels: 1= Basic education (10 years of elementary school), 2= high school diploma, 3= profession (such as carpentry, plumbing), 4= technologist (computer sciences, electrician, mechanistic), 5= graduate degree and 6= postgraduate degree. Parents responded to a variation of the same question: "If there were not economic problems and the other aspects of your life would go by normally, what is the highest educational level you wish [name of the child] could complete?"

Academic Self-efficacy. Built using five questions from the student's questionnaire: 1) "I learn fast the content of all the subjects", 2) "I like reading", 3) "I like math", 4) "I always get good grades in math", 5) "I always get good grades in literature". All the questions have a 5-point Likert scale that ranges from "always" to "never" (α=.736).

Academic Disengagement. Information of the student's behaviour in the classroom provided by their teachers captured by three questions: 1) "Would you consider that [name of the child] has emotional difficulties", 2) "Would you consider that [name of the child] has focusing difficulties", and 3) "Would you consider that [name of the child] has conduct difficulties". All questions have a 4-point Likert scale that ranges from "no" to "severe difficulties" (α= .774).

Socio-economic Status of the Household. Index built using Principal Components Analysis. The literature about the construction of socio-economic status indices suggests a wide range of variables that might be included. For this paper, the following variables were considered: 1) whether the household has bathrooms or latrine, 2) availability of electricity service, 3) whether the household has water from pipe water inside the house, piped water outside the house, waterhole, or stream water, 4) availability of sewerage system, 5) availability of garbage collection service, 6) availability of at least one own computer, 7) whether there are books, encyclopaedias and a place for the student to study in the house, and 8) the possession of a cell phone.

Educational Performance. The average grade obtained by the student at the end of the year. The educational grading system in Ecuador evaluates the students over 10 points and classified such score into 4 categories: 1) grades ranging from 1.00 to 4.99 indicate failure to achieve the required knowledge, 2) grades ranging from 5.00 to 6.99 indicate proximity to reach the required knowledge, 3) grades ranging from 7.00 to 8.99 indicate that the required knowledge was achieved, and 4) grades ranging from 9.00 to 10.00 indicate full grasp of the required knowledge.

Age. Considering that aspirations and expectations might vary across age groups, we created an ordinal categorical variable with three levels: 1) childhood: children from 8 to 11 years old, 2) adolescence: students from 12 to 16 years old, and 3) late adolescence: students from 17 to 21 years old.

Migratory Dream. Measured by the question "Do you think it would be good to live and work in another country?" A similar question was asked to parents regarding their children. The responses were coded 1=Yes and 0=No.

Caregiver involvement in educational activities. Caregivers were asked whether or not they take their time to help their children with their homework.

Caregiver education level. The highest educational level they reached. Only two categories were found and coded 0=Elementary school and 1=High school. Nobody in the sample of caregivers reported getting a graduate degree.

Siblings. Number of children living in the household including stepbrothers and stepsisters.

Household with migrants. We identified as a household of migrants those that have at least one parent living abroad; we considered both biological parents and stepparents.

Regarding the data analysis, a sequential explanatory mixed methods design was used in order to estimate and understand educational aspirations and its relation to the international migration phenomenon. After obtaining descriptive statistics, we ran four logit regression model. In Model 1 and 3, the dependent binary variable indicates whether the students wish to get a graduate degree or higher, while in Model 2 and 4, the binary variable indicates whether the student wishes to get at least a high school degree. The issue of endogeneity in migration research has been assessed by using instrumental variables or panel data. Given the cross-sectional nature of the available dataset used in this paper, we rely on a second best strategy that is including several variables to control for other effects.

For the qualitative stage, in-depth interviews were analysed by the method of thematic analysis, following the strategy of finding common topics and ideas to provide insights into the role of parents on children's aspirations and how they react towards the possibility of children becoming migrants. The themes were determined by using an analysis matrix and group research workshops to guarantee credibility and dependability. Trustworthiness of the qualitative study was carried out by triangulation with theory and the quantitative stage results, which regression analysis demonstrated that the most significant variable to predict educational aspirations of children was the caregiver's aspiration. Pseudonyms were used to present the results.

Results

This section provides evidence regarding the extent to which migration shapes migrant's children educational aspirations and the meanings and nuances which explain this relation in the case of Biblián, Ecuador. Correspondingly, the quantitative results, obtained from the PEACH (children, parents and teachers) are described below and followed by the qualitative data from interviews applied to some mothers, heads of migrant households.

Estimating educational aspirations and its relation to international migration

The descriptive statistics (Table 1-2) state that 48.62 % of the children live with both parents, while the migration of only the mother is rare (0.52%). Whereas most of caregivers express that it might not be good for their children to live and work abroad (53.93 %), children themselves answered positively to this question (60.75 %). It was found that children and caregivers have high aspirations and expectations, regardless of their sociodemographic characteristics.

However, the results show that aspirations and expectations of caregivers and children are slightly higher in households without migrants.

Table 1. Descriptive statistics of categorical variables

Variable		Frequency	Percentage
Sex	Male	762	49.93
	Female	764	50.07
Age category	Childhood	488	31.98
	Adolescence	821	53.8
	Late Adolescence	217	14.22
Children migratory dreams	Yes	921	60.75
	No	595	39.25
Caregiver migratory dreams	Yes	287	46.47
	No	336	53.93
Child performance	9.00 to 10.00 (full grasp)	319	22.74
	7.00 to 8.99 (required)	1042	74.27
	5.00 to 6.99 (proximity)	33	2.35
	1.00 to 4.99 (failure)	9	9
Household composition	Both parents living with the child	742	48.62
	Both parents are international migrants	207	13.56
	Mother at home, father abroad	291	19.07
	Father at home, mother abroad	8	.52
	Other (widows, divorced parents, etc.)	278	18.22
Socioeconomic Status (Quintiles)	1	304	20.03
	2	308	20.29
	3	320	21.08
	4	285	18.77
	5	301	19.83
Caregiver involvement in homework	Yes	393	85.62
	No	66	14.38
Educational level of the caregiver	School	440	76.52
	High school	135	23.48
Communication *	Yes	428	88.43
	No	56	11.57

* At least one parent maintains contact with the child

Table 2. Descriptive statistics of numerical variables

Variable	Obs.	Median	Mean	Standard deviation	Min	Max
Academic self-efficacy	1517	20	19.47	3.11	6	25
Academic Disengagement	1353	4	5.41	1.95	4	15
Age of the child	1526	13	13.14	2.82	8	21
Children aspiration	1524	5	4.80	1.15	1	6
Children expectation	1518	8	7.62	2.23	1	10
Caregiver aspiration	605	4	4.04	1.12	1	5
Caregiver expectation	626	8	7.59	2.33	0	10

Most children from Biblián declared that learning is their main motivation to study. The bivariate analysis does not find evidence of the association of this variable with the migration history of the household (χ^2 =1.78, df= 4, p=.78). Similarly, while studying the attitude towards school with the migratory history of the household, no relation was found (χ^2 =3.35, df=4, p=.5). More surprisingly, there is no association between the aspiration and the migration history of the household (χ^2=8.9,

$df=5$, $p=.11$). By comparing the median values and distributions of the educational aspirations this study failed to find strong evidence that it is associated with the migration history in the household ($z= 1.91$, $p=.056$; $\chi^2=1.11$, $df=1$, $p=.29$). Furthermore, the comparison controlling by age category found similar results for children ($z= 1.67$, $p=.09$; $\chi^2 = .72$, $df=1$, $p=.39$), adolescents ($z=.60$, $p=.54$; $\chi^2=.59$, $df=1$, $p=.44$), and late adolescents ($z=.61$, $p=.54$; $\chi^2=.59$, $df=1$, $p=.44$).

Nonetheless, this study found a significant relationship between the migration history in the household and the question of whether or not the children think it would be good to live and work in another country ($\chi^2 =30.43$, $df=1$, $p<.01$). This dependence persists in all but the late adolescent's group ($\chi^2 =2.48$, $df=1$, $p=.11$). Additionally, there is an association between age category and whether the children think it would be good to live and work in another country ($\chi^2 =14.61$, $df=2$, $p<.01$).

The association between sex and the migratory dream is only significant among children; interestingly, girls are more prone to answer 'yes' to this question (60.4 %) than boys (47.2 %) ($p<.01$). Although this association is not statistically significant for adolescents ($p=.433$) and late adolescents ($p=.476$).

The results of the proposed logistic regression models are presented in Table 3 in the form of odd ratios. Children who replied affirmative to the question about the migratory dream have higher probabilities of aspiring to obtain at least a graduate degree. The variable which indicates whether the child belongs to a household with migrants is significant only to predict the aspiration to get a graduate degree, but its effect disappears when the dependent variable accounts for the aspiration of getting at least a high school degree.

For Models 3 and 4 that include the full set of covariates, there was no sign of strong multicollinearity (mean Variance Inflation Factor was 1.24 for both models); good model specification (in both models the linear predicted value is significant ($p<0.01$) and the linear predicted value squared is not), and adequate goodness of fit (In both models, the Hosmer and Lemeshow's goodness-of-fit test yields a non-significant p-value).

For Model 1, the variables sex, educational performance, age, expectations of children, academic self-efficacy, academic disengagement, child migratory dream are significant. In Model 2, the educational performance, age, academic self-efficacy, and child migratory dream are predictors of children's aspirations. In Model 3 where a set of household variables are introduced, only the socio-economic status, the caregiver aspiration, and whether there's at least one migrant at home are significant. Regarding the initial set of variables, just age, children's expectations and children's migratory dream remain significant. After introducing the set of covariates related to household characteristics (Model 4), sex, educational performance, age category, socio-economic status and caregiver aspiration are predictors of educational aspirations.

Understanding the educational aspirations in migrant households

The respondents were seven women, whose age was between 28 and 46 years old and 4 of them accomplished the primary education while the others reached the secondary level of education. All of them were married and their husbands were in the USA and have from 1 to 2 school-age children. Two main nodes were identified by the thematic analysis: value of education and parent-child transmission channel.

Table 3. Logistic regression results

Variable	Model 1	Model 2	Model 3	Model 4
Sex	.47 (.07)***	.90(.19)	.68(.23)	3.39 (2.08)**
Performance (group)				
Required	.44 (.10)***	.3246 (.12)***	.62 (.28)	.33(.2)*
Proximity	.24 (.11)***	.3284 (.22)	.68 (.78)	
Failure	.17 (.15)**			
Age (group)				
Adolescence	1.61 (.2730)***	2.02 (.47)***	3.38 (1.45)***	4.76 (2.70)***
Late adolescence	2.45 (.6175)***	3.91 (1.59)***	2.86 (1.72)*	4.49 (6.51)
Children Expectation	1.12 (.0384)***	1.08 (.05)	1.16 (.10)*	.90 (.13)
Academic Self-efficacy	1.08 (.0277)***	1.07 (.04)*	1.03 (.07)	.99 (.08)
Academic Disengagement	.917 (.0313)**	.93 (.04)	.91 (.09)	.84 (.10)
Child Migratory dream	1.68 (.2394)***	1.73 (.36)***	2.09 (.75)**	.87 (.51)
Siblings			1.50 (.71)	2.08 (1.22)
SES			1.31(.15)**	1.39(.21)**
Caregiver aspiration			1.84 (.25)***	1.62 (.29)***
Caregiver expectation			1.03 (.08)	.99 (.14)
Caregiver migratory dream			.90 (.32)	1.33 (.64)
Parent involvement school			2.06 (1.01)	2.72 (2.11)
Caregiver education level			1.11 (.46)	1.82 (1.09)
Household with at least one migrant			.50 (.18)*	.67 (.30)
Cons	1.10 (.77)	4.97 (4.96)	.01 (.03)**	1.04 (2.54)
pseudo R2	.09	.07	.222	.3156
Obs	1219	1212	260	256

***p< .01
** p< .05
* p< .1

The Value of Education

The literature review on migrant households suggested that parents tend to assign values to education: as an instrumental means to obtain better jobs and higher income and as an intrinsic value or, in other words, being educated independently of the financial benefits it could report. The qualitative results state that the second meaning is stronger than the first one in these mothers. Being asked about a scenario where her son migrates, Sonia says: "Maybe to study… maybe… but not to work" and she continues, "for me studying is the most important thing, I want them to study, the three of them [referring to their children] to be professionals, any profession, but professionals". Parents from Biblián seem to give education an intrinsic value, as a mother replied, "of course money is quite important, but about that… As my sister always says, dummy[7], only has money and knows nothing about other things. Money is not the only important thing, as I say, it is quite important considering these days and our needs, but the most important thing is the study" (Ramona). Rocío shares a similar thought and illustrates it by the phrase "if you are not a high school graduate, you are practically nobody".

Education has also a perceived instrumental value for parents. Juana reported that she advises her daughter to finish high school because it is important "for everything". In the same interview, regarding the possibility of her daughter's migration, she says that there are jobs in Biblián as well

---

[7] In Spanish the mother said *indio bruto*, which is a pejorative way of saying dummy indigenous.

and that if her child studies she will be better than her. Similarly, Rosario says: "I did not finish high school, [I have] nothing, I milk cows, sometimes enduring rain, sun, one goes. If she gets the high school diploma, she can get a job". Another mother, Ana, shares the optimism regarding the instrumental benefits of education by saying: "I think studying is important to [achieve] a more bearable lifestyle, [...] because right now, without studies, you are worthless".

Parent-child transmission channel

According to the bibliographical review, the longer the exposure in the host country, the less optimistic migrants become, because of the hard conditions they have to endure. Consequently, in Biblián, migration is not an opportunity that parents consider for their children. This is depicted when Eloisa tells: "[my husband] is already nine years there [USA] and he also says no, this is not a place to work, if one day is possible that you would come to know the place, but not to work, only to know because he is there and he says it's hard. Parents are also aware of the dangers involved in the illegal trip to the USA, especially for girls.

However, even in a scenario of no dangers, the interviewed caregivers are still reluctant to consider the idea of their children migrating. Juana reveals the advice given to her daughter, "the father talks to her saying 'darling, [it is] hard here, there [in Biblián] you may go to [your] family and your family offers you a cup of coffee... at least a soup, but daughter, here [USA] if you don't work there's nothing'".

Discussion and Conclusion

Clearly, both parents and children have high aspirations and expectations regardless of the migratory history of the household. However, the multivariate analysis reveals that the effect of expectations of the caregivers disappears after controlling for other variables. The influence of the significant variables after the logistic regression results is also reported in other research (Gil-Flores et al., 2011; Archer, et al., 2014). This study found strong evidence of the influence of the caregivers as providers of social-emotional influences on the educational aspirations of children of Biblián, as suggested in Expectancy-Value Theory and showed in past research (Eccle, 2009; Kirk et al., 2011). The migratory dream of children also positively predicts aspiration in three of the suggested models. The bivariate analysis showed a significant association between this variable and the migratory history in the household.

Guo et al. (2015) and Rojewski & Yang (1997) discussed the importance of socioeconomic status on aspirations and found significant associations between them. By contrast, according to Nauta et al. (1998) and Rottinghaus et al. (2002), self-efficacy is not a predictor of aspirations which fades with the inclusions of the second block of variables. In both, Model 3 and 4, the effect of expectations disappears and the caregiver aspirations remain as strongly significant.

While the results suggest that gender is relevant only in two of the four proposed models, past research has revealed that girls are more ambitious in their educational aspirations than boys (Schoon & Polek, 2011; Rothon et al., 2011). Interestingly, the ambivalence of the results might be explained by the strong migration culture of Biblián which may have contributed to destabilise gender roles. However, it is noteworthy that the qualitative instrument was not developed to deepen into gender issues.

The dummy variable, which indicates whether the child belongs to a household of migrants is only significant to predict the aspiration to obtain at least a graduate degree. Belonging to a household with at least one migrant parent lowers this probability, according to Model 3, but the variable is not significant in Model 4. Research on Mexican migrants revealed that having a migrant father does not affect the aspiration, but having a migrant mother does (Dreby & Stutz, 2012). In both migrant and non-migrant households, expectations of students are significant only to predict their aspiration to get a graduate or a higher degree, but not to predict their aspiration to finish high school; similar results are observed regarding academic self-efficacy. This is not surprising given the fact that several students were already in high school. Thus, finishing high school might not be a very difficult task.

The qualitative results offered a deeper understanding of the quantitative analysis concerning the relevance of the caregivers' influence, which was found significant for predicting the educational aspirations of children in Biblián. The direct contributions from the qualitative stage were the meanings of the value of education and the parent-child transmission channel. Regarding the role of parental educational aspirations from families with migrants, as in other research among Latino families (Goldenberg et al., 2001), the qualitative results suggest that mothers value education beyond its instrumental value. Mothers interviewed seem to concede value to education for its own sake. However, education might be also perceived as a sign of social and economic status by mothers of migrant households, even as a fact to disincentive their children's migration.

The parent-child transmission channel of transnational parenthood is mainly related to migration by communicating (Kandel & Kao, 2001) the difficulties that the migrant father experience in the destination country. This is not surprising since irregular migration sets a particular negative condition in the USA. This kind of social remittances (Mata-Codesal, 2013) may nuance the stereotypes and social imaginaries in the origin country (Herrera 2005; Pedone, 2005, Villavicencio, Tenorio & Orellana, 2011). Nonetheless, the results do not provide enough evidence to describe in a broad way how familial transnationalism (Herrera, 2004) is shaping the left-behind children's education in Biblián. Moreover, a further study from the children's voices is needed to give detail on the meanings of transnational parenthood and communication.

Despite the fact that the qualitative results are based on respondent mothers' perceptions and cannot predict how education and migration relate to each other, they corroborate the complexity and tensions (Antman, 2013; Herrera, 2013) that permeate this relation. For instance, in accordance to the quantitative analysis, the interviews did not indicate a clear reproduction of gender inequality as Herrera (2013) and Zapata (2016) stated. Additionally, while Kandel & Kao (2001) suggest that children's migration dream discourages their educational aspirations, the quantitative results corroborate that aspirations and expectations of caregivers and children are only slightly higher in households without migrants. The interviews analysis supported this result by stressing that money cannot buy the status education itself provides, so the children were not just another 'dummy' with money.

The role of international migration for educational aspirations of children of Biblián is influenced by several factors. This paper shows that the educational aspirations of parents are a strong predictor of their children's aspirations in both migrant and non-migrant households. Household-related variables, including their migration history, have a stronger effect than individual ones when predicting the educational aspirations of children. Aspirations and expectations of caregivers and children, are slightly higher in households without migrants. Education has a value that transcends the material benefits that it might report, but rather it has a moral value.

Acknowledgements

Principalmente, agradecemos a la gente de Biblián por compartirnos su tiempo y experiencias. [Most important, we are grateful to the people of Biblián for opening to us and sharing their time and experiences]. We acknowledge Evelyn Sinchi, Juan Diego Sacoto, Yessenia Peralta and Alejandra Herrera for their field work help and the VLIR-UC Project of International Migration and Local Development, a cooperation between the University of Cuenca and the IOB of the University of Antwerp.

References

Alexander, K. L., and Cook M. A. (1979). "The Motivational Relevance of Educational Plans: Questioning the Conventional Wisdom". Social Psychology Quarterly. 42 (3): 202–13.

Antman, F. M. (2013). "The impact of migration on family left behind". In: International handbook on the economics of migration. Edward Elgar Publishing.

Archer, L., DeWitt, J. and Wong, B. (2014). "Spheres of Influence: What Shapes Young People's Aspirations at Age 12/13 and What Are the Implications for Education Policy?". Journal of Education Policy. 29 (1): 58-85 https://doi.org/10.1080/02680939.2013.790079.

Beaman, L., Duflo, E., Pande, R. and Topalova, P. (2012). "Female Leadership Raises Aspirations and Educational Attainment for Girls: A Policy Experiment in India". Science 335 (6068): 582–86. https://doi.org/10.1126/science.1212382.

Bohon, S. A., Kirkpatrick Johnson, M. and Gorman, B. K. (2006). "College Aspirations and Expectations among Latino Adolescents in the United States". Social Problems 53 (2): 207–25. https://doi.org/10.1525/sp.2006.53.2.207.

Carling, J. (2014). "Scripting remittances: making sense of money transfers in transnational relationships". International Migration Review, 48: S218-S262.

Chiapa, C., Garrido, J. L. and Prina, S. (2012). "The Effect of Social Programs and Exposure to Professionals on the Educational Aspirations of the Poor". Economics of Education Review 31 (5): 778–98. https://doi.org/10.1016/j.econedurev.2012.05.006.

Czaika, M., and Vothknecht, M. (2014). "Migration and aspirations–are migrants trapped on a hedonic treadmill?". IZA Journal of migration, 3 (1), 1.

Dalton, P. S., Ghosal, S. and Mani, A. (2016). "Poverty and Aspirations Failure". Economic Journal 126 (590): 165–88. https://doi.org/10.1111/ecoj.12210.

Dreby, J., and Stutz, L. (2012). "Making something of the Sacrifice: Gender, Migration and Mexican Children's Educational Aspirations". Global Networks. 12: 71-90. https://doi.org/10.1111/j.1471-0374.2011.00337.x.

Eccles, J. (2009). "Who am I and What am I Going to Do with My Life? Personal and Collective Identities as Motivators of Action". Educational Psychologist. 44 (2): 78-89. https://doi.org/10.1080/00461520902832368.

GAD Cañar. (2016). Plan de Desarrollo y Ordenamiento Territorial de la Provincia del Cañar 2015 -2019

Gil-Flores, J., Padilla-Carmona, M. T. and Suárez-Ortega, M. (2011). "Influence of Gender, Educational Attainment and Family Environment on the Educational Aspirations of Secondary School Students". Educational Review. 63 (3): 345-363. https://doi.org/10.1080/00131911.2011.571763.

Goldenberg, C., Gallimore, R. and Garnier, H. (2001). "Cause or Effect? A Longitudinal Study of Immigrant Latino Parents' Aspirations and Expectations, and Their Children's School Performance". American Educational Research Journal. 38 (3): 547–82. https://doi.org/10.3102/00028312038003547.

Guo, J., Marsh, H. W., Parker, P., Morin, A. and Yeung, A. S. (2015). "Expectancy-Value in Mathematics, Gender and Socioeconomic Background as Predictors of Achievement and Aspirations: A Multi-Cohort Study". Learning and Individual Differences. 37: 161-168. https://doi.org/10.1016/j.lindif.2015.01.008.

Herrera, G. (2004). "Género, familia y migración en el Ecuador: lo viejo y lo Nuevo". In: Fuller, N. Jerarquías en jaque. Estudios de género en el área andina. Lima: CLACSO-PUCP. 383-403.

Herrera, G. (2005). "Mujeres ecuatorianas en las cadenas globales del cuidado". In: Herrera, Carrillo y Torres. La migración ecuatoriana. Transnacionalismo, redes e identidades. Quito: FLACSO- Plan Nacional Migración y Desarrollo. 281-303.

Herrera, G. (2013). Lejos de tus pupilas. Familias transnacionales, cuidados y desigualdad social en Ecuador. FLACSO Sede Ecuador y ONU Mujeres.

Herrera, G., Lafleur, J. M., and Yépez del Castillo, I. (2018). "Introducción: Migraciones andinas, desarrollo y transformación social". Migraciones internacionales en Bolivia y Ecuador: crisis global, Estado y desarrollo, 1-22. FLACSO Ecuador

Holmlund H., Lindahl, M. and Plug, E. (2011). "The Causal Effect of Parents' Schooling on Children's Schooling: A Comparison of Estimation Methods". Journal of Economic Literature 49 (3): 615–51.

INEC. (2010). Censo de población y vivienda (CPV-2010) URL: https://www.ecuadorencifras.gob.ec/informacion-censal-cantonal/

INEC. (2019). Registro Estadístico de Entradas y Salidas Internacionales Año 2018. Excel file. URL: https://www.ecuadorencifras.gob.ec/entradas-y-salidas-internacionales/

Izcara-Palacios, S. (2011). "La etiología de la migración internacional: privación relativa y demanda laboral (el ejemplo tamaulipeco)". Migraciones. Publicación del Instituto Universitario de Estudios sobre Migraciones. (29): 11-29.

Kafle, K., Benfica, R. and Winters, P. (2020), Does relative deprivation induce migration? Evidence from Sub-Saharan Africa. American Journal of Agricultural Economics. 102: 999-1019. https://doi.org/10.1002/ajae.12007

Kandel, W., and Kao, G. (2001). "The Impact of Temporary Labor Migration on Mexican Children's Educationul Aspirations and Pefomance". International Migration Review. 35 (4): 1205–31. https://doi.org/10.1016/j.childyouth.2008.07.020.

Kirk, C. M., Lewis-Moss, R. K., Nilsen, C. and Colvin, D. Q. (2011). "The Role of Parent Expectations on Adolescent Educational Aspirations". Educational Studies. 37(1), 89–99. https://doi.org/10.1080/03055691003728965.

Krishnan, P., and Krutikova, S. (2013). "Non-Cognitive Skill Formation in Poor Neighbourhoods of Urban India". Labour Economics. 24: 68–85. https://doi.org/10.1016/j.labeco.2013.06.004.

Levitt, P., and Schiller, N. G. (2004). "Perspectivas internacionales sobre migración: conceptuar la simultaneidad". Migración y desarrollo, 3: 60-91.

Mata-Codesal, D. (2013). "Linking social and financial remittances in the realms of financial know-how and education in rural Ecuador". Migration Letters, 10 (1): 23-32.

McKenzie, D., and Rapoport, H. (2011). "Can Migration Reduce Educational Attainment? Evidence from Mexico". Journal of Population Economics 24 (4): 1331–58. https://doi.org/10.1007/s00148-010-0316-x.

McKenzie, D., Gibson, J. and Stillman, S. (2013). "A Land of Milk and Honey with Streets Paved with Gold: Do Emigrants Have over-Optimistic Expectations about Incomes Abroad?". Journal of Development Economics 102: 116–27. https://doi.org/10.1016/j.jdeveco.2012.01.001.

Meza, L., and Pederzini, C. (2009). "Migración Internacional y Escolaridad Como Medios Alternativos de Movilidad Social: El Caso de México". Estudios Económicos. 163-206.

Mookherjee, D, Napel, S. and Ray, D. (2010). "Aspirations, Segregation, and Occupational Choice". Journal of the European Economic Association 8 (1): 139–68. https://doi.org/10.1017/CBO9781107415324.004.

Nauta, M. M., Epperson, D. L. and Kahn, J. H. (1998). "A Multiple-Groups Analysis of Predictors of Higher Level Career Aspirations among Women in Mathematics, Science, and Engineering Majors". Journal of Counselling Psychology. 45 (4), 483–496. https://doi.org/10.1037/0022-0167.45.4.483.

Parella, S. (2007). "Los vínculos afectivos y de cuidado en las familias transnacionales: Migrantes ecuatorianos y peruanos en España". Migraciones internacionales, 4 (2): 151-188.

Parella, S., and Speroni, T. (2018). "Las perspectivas transnacionales para el análisis de la PS en contextos migratorios". Autoctonía. Revista de Ciencias Sociales e Historia, 2 (1): 37-56.

Pedone, C. (2005). "Tú, siempre jalas a los tuyos. Cadenas y redes migratorias". La migración ecuatorian. Transnacionalismo, redes e identidades, 105-143.

Ramirez and Lagomarsino (2014) "Los coyotes del Pacífico". In: Ramírez, J. Con o sin pasaporte. Análisis socio antropológico sobre la migración ecuatoriana. IAEN.

Ramírez, J., and Ramírez, F. (2005). La estampida migratoria ecuatoriana: Crisis, redes transnacionales y repertorios de acción migratoria.

Rivas, A. (2011). "Más allá de las remesas: el costo social de la migración en los niños de la región del Austro en Ecuador". In: Calfat G. and Roldan, D. Migración internacional y remesas: Contribuciones al debate de su relación con el desarrollo. 290-323.

Rojewski, J. W., and Yang, B. (1997). "Longitudinal Analysis of Select Influences on Adolescents' Occupational Aspirations". Journal of Vocational Behavior. 51 (3): 375-410 https://doi.org/10.1006/jvbe.1996.1561.

Rothon, C., Arephin, M. Klineberg, E., Cattell, V. and Stansfeld, S. (2011). "Structural and Socio-Psychological Influences on Adolescents' Educational Aspirations and Subsequent Academic Achievement". Social Psychology of Education. 14 (2): 209–231. https://doi.org/10.1007/s11218-010-9140-0.

Rottinghaus, P. J., Lindley, L., Green, M. A. and Borgen, F. H. (2002). "Educational Aspirations: The Contribution of Personality, Self-Efficacy, and Interests". Journal of Vocational Behavior. 61 (1): 1-19. https://doi.org/10.1006/jvbe.2001.1843.

Schoon, I., and Polek, E. (2011). "Teenage Career Aspirations and Adult Career Attainment: The Role of Gender, Social Background and General Cognitive Ability". International Journal of Behavioral Development. 35 (3): 210–217 https://doi.org/10.1177/0165025411398183.

Shea, J. (2000). "Does Parents' Money Matter?". Journal of Public Economics. 77 (2): 155-184. https://doi.org/10.1016/S0047-2727 (99)00087-0.

Villavicencio, F., Orellana, A., and Tenorio, P. (2012). "Prejuicios y estereotipos negativos que perciben los niños de emigrantes de sus compañeros de escuela". Maskana, 3 (1): 1-11. https://doi.org/10.18537/mskn.03.01.01

Zapata, A. (2016). "Madres y padres en contextos transnacionales: el cuidado desde el género y la familia". Desacatos, (52): 14-31.

September 2020
Volume: 17, **No**: 5, pp. 695 – 704
ISSN: 1741-8984
e-ISSN: 1741-8992
www.migrationletters.com

MIGRATION
LETTERS

First Submitted: 6 June 2019 Accepted: 16 January 2020
DOI: https://doi.org/10.33182/ml.v17i5.803

How Can Migrants' Language Proficiency Be Measured? A Discussion of Opportunities and Challenges When Studying the Impact of Language Skills on Social Position

Isabell Diekmann[1] and Joanna Jadwiga Fröhlich[2]

Abstract

Language proficiency is crucial for migrants' social position in the labour market and therefore plays a key role in the (re-)production of social inequalities in modern societies. There are different ways of capturing language skills in quantitative studies. However, it is important to question the extent to which existing language measures mirror migrants' realities and relevant linguistic everyday life practices. In our paper, we contribute to this question by disentangling various measures of language proficiency. We use a large sample of migrants in Germany (GSOEP) that contains numerous language measures. We conduct detailed quantitative analyses on how various language variables influence migrants' social position, by which we mean migrants' socioeconomic status (as measured by ISEI). The ISEI is mainly based on occupation, but also on education and income. Our findings indicate that especially the self-assessed German speaking proficiency is an important and parsimonious predictor for migrants' social position in Germany.

Keywords: Migration; social inequalities; language proficiency; social position; language measures.

Introduction

Language(s) play an exceptional role in being part of a world characterized by increasing mobility and global migration, increasing virtual as well as physical connections and the tertiarization of labour. Whilst a few selected languages, such as English, can be described as "key to integration" into what has become a global labour market, most labour markets are still national ones in which a demand for workers with skills in the host countries' language(s) dominates. In the context of migrants' labour market integration, disadvantages based on language are a well-known and often discussed burden for non-native speakers and their descendants in Germany as well as several other countries, such as the Netherlands, Spain, the UK and the US (Aldashev et al., 2009; Chiswick and Miller, 2010; Dustmann and Fabbri, 2003; Euwals et al., 2007; Kalter, 2006; Markova, 2008). The language of the country of immigration, often understood as human capital, plays an important role (among others) for migrants' positioning in the labour market (Esser, 2006; Henkelmann, 2012). Besides, language (proficiency) cannot only be seen as human capital and therefore as a resource or an instrument of inclusion and exclusion for immigrants, but also as a "unifying element" within the host society, which is especially important for otherwise highly heterogeneous societies such as the US (Zolberg and Woon, 1999). In this case, foreign languages can be perceived as threatening

---

[1] Isabell Diekmann, Bielefeld University and University of Osnabrück, Germany. E-mail: isabell.diekmann@uni-bielefeld.de.
[2] Joanna Jadwiga Fröhlich, Bielefeld University, Germany. E-mail: joanna.froehlich@uni-bielefeld.de.
Acknowledgements: The authors would like to thank Thomas Faist, Inka Stock, Maximilian Wächter, and Anica Waldendorf for their useful criticism on our paper as well as support with the visualization of our findings. This work was supported by the German Research Foundation (DFG) [FA 284/7-1].

by the host society, and therefore represent a crucial barrier to integration for immigrants due to obvious linguistic differences between migrants and non-migrants. Language proficiency is decisive for various dimensions of integration (e.g. cultural, social, labour market). An evaluation of the effectiveness of language courses as a part of political integration programs is therefore important, but also methodologically challenging in the context of measuring language proficiency (Rother, 2010).

We study the impact of language on migrants' social position in the labour market because good language skills promote a good placement in the labour market and can therefore be seen as highly important for integration in the receiving countries (Verwiebe et al., 2014). By social position we mean the International Socio-Economic Index of Occupational Status (ISEI). Existing empirical social research draws on a broad spectrum of language proficiency measures. Potential language proficiency measures include objective language tests, language assessments conducted by interviewers and, as is more common in sociological studies, self-assessed language skills (van Niejenhuis et al., 2015). Many migration researchers lack access to objective measures and diagnostic testing procedures but instead use survey data mainly with information on self-assessed language proficiency. However, it is rarely discussed which of these measures is best suited to capture language proficiency in statistical analyses. Therefore, we want to discuss which potential subjective language measures are most promising and parsimonious when it comes to research on social positions.

In our paper we contribute to this field by analyzing different measures of language proficiency and their impact on migrants' social position in the labour market. Certainly, one's social position in the labour market is not solely influenced by language skills. Numerous different factors such as personal traits (e.g. self-confidence, self-esteem, personality [Big Five]), the household setting, and macro-structural factors (e.g. employment rates, immigration and labour policies, and national and regional labour market conditions) might play an important role for social positions and labour market integration. For now, we focus on different measures of language proficiency and a minimum set of characteristics on the individual level (e.g. sex, age, education) in order to find a parsimonious measure that can be integrated in more complex models in the future.

For our analyses, we use a relatively new data set from a longitudinal study in Germany (GSOEP) that has made strong efforts to cover many migration related variables to study social inequalities in Germany. We discuss a variety of well-established as well as less established indicators of language proficiency, such as (self-assessed) speaking, writing, and reading skills in the language of both the country of destination (before and after migrating) and the country of origin, third languages, or language usage with family, friends and at work, to cover the variety of potential operationalizations of language. Operationalizing language proficiency is a difficult process because what is considered to be a good operationalization of language proficiency may change over time and requires permanent development and adaptation to current social conditions (Duchêne et al., 2018). With our paper, we attempt to raise awareness for the different possibilities to measure language proficiency and we would like to share and discuss our ideas on potential advantages and disadvantages of these measures based on our own empirical work. Beyond that we also argue that a dynamic concept of language proficiency measures is crucial for the study of migrants' social position in the labour market.

After a short introduction into the GSOEP data as well as the methods that we use in our paper we present our empirical findings, for which we calculated several regression models with different language variables. In the conclusion, we discuss further implications of our findings for studies of social inequalities and migration.

Data and Methods

For our analyses, we run several linear regression models. We use a large-scale panel survey, the German Socio-Economic Panel (GSOEP); more precisely the IAB-SOEP Migration Sample, a subsample covering 4,964 participants in 2,723 households (Kroh et al., 2015). Data from the first wave (survey year 2013) of this particular subsample is used. These data have the great advantage of providing many different ways of measuring different dimensions of language proficiency: German language proficiency before migrating and today (differentiated between reading, writing and speaking skills), attended German classes, speaking German with family, friends and at work, and speaking a third language[3]. The GSOEP Migration Sample also provides information on the language of the participants' (or parents') country of origin. In the sense of the Common Underlying Proficiency (CUP) model, linguistic skills are transferable, which means a high level of proficiency in the first language may serve as a good basis to learn additional languages (Cummins, 2000; van Niejenhuis et al., 2015). Because of potential interdependencies we also include country of origin language skills in our analyses. All of these language measures are independent variables in the following linear regression models. Participants were asked questions about their language proficiency only once when they started to participate in the panel survey.

The International Socio-Economic Index of Occupational Status serves as the dependent variable (Ganzeboom et al., 1992). It is based on the International Standard Classification of Occupations (ISCO-08) and takes into account information on occupation, education and income. The ISEI is internationally comparable and has a metric scale level, which allows extensive stratification analyses and is not restricted to only a few categories. It varies between 10 (subsistence farmers, fishers, hunters and gatherers) and 89 (medical doctors).

Table 1 shows the independent variables. In every model, we controlled not only for age, gender, and education, but also for parents' education and the migration specific variable "country of origin". Each model also contained one of the previously mentioned independent language variables. After calculating separate models, all language variables were integrated into an overall model. Some of the language variables had to be removed from further analysis and the overall model due to multicollinearity. Following the principle of *listwise deletion*, all cases with at least one missing value for one of these variables were eliminated. After doing so, a total of 1,675 valid observations remained for analysis.

Language Measures for Migrants' Social Position: Empirical Findings

To study the role of language for migrants' social position in Germany, different potential language measures are examined in the following. In the first step, separate models, each of which included only one language variable besides the control variables[4], were calculated (figure 1).

---

[3] Due to too few observations in the categories "other language spoken with family/with friends/at work" we had to exclude them from the statistical analysis. Nonetheless, the findings indicate a strong effect: those who speak another language at work have a much higher ISEI value. This group of very high-skilled workers who speak another language at work needs further investigation.

[4] In the separate models, we controlled for various common variables. The findings show that high education on behalf of both the participants and their parents leads to a higher social position in the labor market in Germany. Having parents with a university degree compared to parents with vocational training or parents with neither a university degree nor vocational training also increases the social

Table 1: Independent variables used in the regression models based on GSOEP data

Variable	Descriptives[1]	
Attended German classes	No = 573	Yes = 1102
German reading proficiency before migration[2]	Mean: 2.16	Standard deviation: 1.35
German speaking proficiency before migration[2]	Mean: 2.06	Standard deviation: 1.26
German writing proficiency before migration[2]	Mean: 2.03	Standard deviation: 1.27
Actual German reading proficiency[2]	Mean: 4.01	Standard deviation: 0.89
Actual German speaking proficiency[2]	Mean: 4.01	Standard deviation: 0.82
Actual German writing proficiency[2]	Mean: 3.75	Standard deviation: 1.02
Language of country of origin reading proficiency[2]	Mean: 4.73	Standard deviation: 0.63
Language of country of origin speaking proficiency[2]	Mean: 4.78	Standard deviation: 0.52
Language of country of origin writing proficiency[2]	Mean: 4.68	Standard deviation: 0.71
Language spoken with family	German = 391	
	Language of country of origin = 786	
	Both = 498	
Language spoken with friends	German = 580	
	Language of country of origin = 429	
	Both = 666	
Language spoken at work	German = 1365	
	Language of country of origin = 83	
	Both = 227	
Third language	No = 828	Yes = 847
Gender	Men = 845	Women = 830
Age[3]	Mean: 41.31	Standard deviation: 9.48
Education[4]	Mean: 10.66	Standard deviation: 1.43
Country of origin	Non-EU-citizens = 1054	
	EU-citizens = 621	
Education of mother	No vocational training or university = 882	
	Vocational training = 580	
	University = 213	
Education of father	No vocational training or university = 588	
	Vocational training = 817	
	University = 270	

[1] Nominal and ordinal variables with frequencies; metric variables with mean and standard deviation; [2] 1 = not at all; 2 = badly; 3 = okay; 4 = well; 5 = very well; [3] metric (in years); [4] metric (in years; 7 = no degree to 18 = university degree)

The language variables show many significant correlations. In the separate models, all German speaking, reading and writing skills (before migrating and today) have a significant effect (p < 0.001). The ISEI increases significantly if migrants perform well in speaking, reading and writing German, whereby these effects are noticeably stronger for today's language proficiency compared

position in the labor market. These findings indicate that there is an enormous gap between university degree and non-university education when it comes to social positions and the intergenerational transfer of cultural capital. Even under control of education, age, and language proficiency, women have a significantly lower ISEI than men. In contrast to gender, the country of origin is insignificant in every model. As the only exception within the included control variables, being born in another EU country or outside of the EU seems to be a rather irrelevant factor for explaining migrants' social position in Germany.

to German language skills before migration. In contrast to German language skills, language skills in the language of the country of origin (of the participants or their parents) are less important for explaining social positions and social inequalities: language of country of origin reading skills are not significant at all; language of country of origin speaking and writing skills slightly improve migrants' ISEI ($p<0.05$). Having attended a German course is even more irrelevant, since we do not find any significant effects regarding this variable. Given that this is the only variable measuring language using objective criteria, these results might lead to the assumption that actual German skills are more important for migrants' social position than how these language skills were obtained and also more important than certificates that demonstrate language proficiency.

Figure 1: Regression coeffecients in separate models; black indicates a significant effect and gray indicates an insignificant effect; own calculations based on GSOEP data

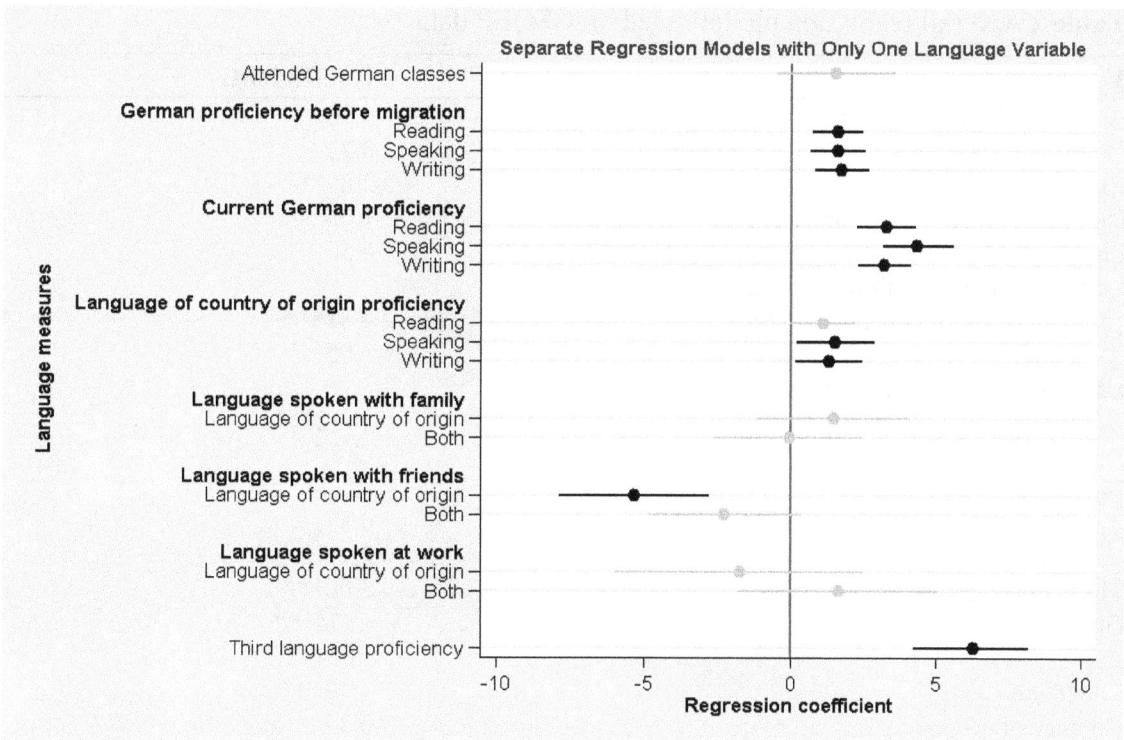

Speaking an additional foreign language, however, strongly increases the social position in the labor market of the country of destination. Speaking a third language, meaning a language other than the one of the country of origin and the immigration country, is considered to be an advantage because of the aforementioned potential interdependency effects. Third languages seem to be a resource on the labor market, although we would need to investigate which language is beneficial for a good position in the labor market in more depth.

In the separate model, the language spoken with the family does not have a significant effect on the social position. Although this variable ("language usage at home" and "language spoken with family") is often used to measure language proficiency and educational achievement, there is no evidence that this variable explains the social position of migrants. The same can be said about speaking German at work, as we cannot observe any significant effects for this variable in the respective separate model. While there seems to be little evidence for the hypothesis that speaking German with family members or at work improves one's social position, the situation is different for the role of language spoken with friends. Speaking German with friends (compared to speaking the language of the country of origin with friends) significantly improves migrants' social position. This strong effect is in line with findings from social network analysis, indicating that ethnically and linguistically more heterogeneous networks influence the probability of having a good social position (e.g. better integration (Esser, 2009), lower probability of poverty (Heizmann and Böhnke, 2016), and shorter unemployment duration (Lancee and Hartung, 2012)).

Finally, all aforementioned language and control variables are included in an overall model. Table 2 displays the results from this overall model, in which explained variance (R^2) increases from between 26 and 30 per cent (depending on the respective separate model) to now 35 per cent.

Table 2: Overall regression model based on GSOEP data

Variable	Coefficients
Attended German classes	0.70
German reading proficiency before migration	0.72
Current German speaking proficiency	2.89***
Current German writing proficiency	1.05
Language of country of origin speaking proficiency	0.56
Language spoken with family	
Language of country of origin	4.83***
Both	1.05
Language spoken with friends	
Language of country of origin	-4.32***
Both	-2.37
Language spoken at work	
Language of country of origin	0.53
Both	2.47
Third language	5.00***
Gender	-5.74***
Age	-0.14**
Education	1.49***
Country of origin	0.34
Education of mother	
Vocational training	1.55
University	5.75**
Education of father	
Vocational training	0.18
University	6.79***
R2	0.35

Notes: ***: p =< 0.001; ***: p =< 0.01; ***: p =< 0.05

In this overall model only three language variables that have shown significant correlations in the separate models remain significant and improve the social position: the ability to speak at least one other foreign language, current German speaking skills and German language spoken with friends. Since these three variables do not only have a significant but also a quite strong effect on migrants' social position, all of them seem to be important language measures. Obvious discrepancies emerged regarding language usage in the family. These results are again not in line with our expectations, since speaking German with family members decreases the ISEI significantly. Strikingly, in the overall model language usage in the family finally becomes significant, but unexpectedly, speaking German with family members has a negative effect on one's social position.

However, there are also some variables that were significant in the separate models, but whose effects disappear in the overall model. German speaking skills before migrating and country of origin speaking skills, for instance, no longer influence the social position when other language measures are controlled for. These results lead to the assumption that speaking the language of the country of origin well and having learnt German before migrating to Germany are not as important for the current social position as actual German speaking skills today. In addition, German speaking skills seem to be more important for migrants' social position than their writing skills. These findings are in line with previous research on this topic in the UK (Dustmann and Fabbri, 2003).

In essence, these results suggest that the different language measures provided in the GSOEP Migration Sample have a varied impact on migrants' social position. There are some important insights that can be derived from our analyses. Firstly, self-perceived German speaking skills and third language skills are crucial for migrants' social position in the German labour market. However, in the future, a deeper analysis of what "third language" means is necessary. It would be interesting to shed light on the languages hidden behind the so-called third language and to take a closer look at which languages are perceived as being a resource or as posing an advantage (for example English) and which are perhaps stigmatized and lead to disadvantages. Our findings indicate that the perception of actual German speaking skills is generally related to education – the higher the level of education, the higher the evaluation of one's abilities. But, the group with the highest level of education – people with a doctoral degree – has, on average, a lower self-perceived level of spoken German than those with a master's degree. This indicates that positions which require highly-qualified employees are not necessarily related to German speaking abilities and English is probably more important for success.[5] Secondly, a very good and at the same time parsimonious variable to study the social position of migrants seems to be self-assessed German speaking skills. Actual German speaking skills seem to depict one's language proficiency better than, for instance, the objective measure of having attended a German class or not.

Descriptive analyses support our findings: 32.46 per cent of the participants who have not attended any German course say that they speak German very well. For those who attended a German course, 29.13 per cent rate their German speaking skills as very good. In addition, descriptive analyses with our data shows that migrants with better German speaking abilities also have a higher social position in the labour market beyond ISEI (such as Erikson Goldthorpe Portocarero [EGP]) and are unemployed less often.[6] Thirdly, language usage in the family seems

---

[5] Mean values of German speaking proficiency by education: primary education 3.6 (78 observations), lower secondary education 3.7 (308 observations), upper secondary education 4.0 (566 observations), post-secondary education 4.1 (277 observations), short-cycle tertiary education 4.2 (10 observations), bachelor or equivalent 4.2 (359 observations), master or equivalent 4.8 (51 observations), doctoral or equivalent 4.4 (26 observations).

[6] Mean values of German speaking skills by EGP value 2013: higher managerial and professional workers 4.6 (124 observations), lower managerial and professional worker 4.4 (224 observations), routine clerical work 4.3 (166 observations), routine service and sales

to be interesting because speaking German with family members decreases the ISEI. A reason for this might be the vagueness of the concept "family". The question arises of what is meant by family in general and for migrants in particular. This question is also important for "language usage at home", a concept often used in research projects on children and education. "Home" might be interpreted differently by transnational families. Taking into account that parents' education is controlled for, another explanation might be that the language of the country of origin is perceived as an important resource that should be maintained or that additional language skills and bilingual language arrangements, in general, are positive for one's social position.

Discussion and Conclusion

The goal of the present study was to investigate the role of language for migrants' social position. We examined the quality of different language measures for research on migrants' social position. In line with previous research, our findings indicate that German language proficiency is crucial for migrants' social position in the labour market in Germany. Disentangling various language measures, we are able to show that self-assessed German speaking proficiency is a good and parsimonious indicator and also a rather direct method of measuring language proficiency. Therefore, we argue that direct measures seem to be better indicators than indirect ones, such as the information on attended German courses.

After a long period of manual workers coming to Germany in the aftermath of World War II, the tertiarization of labour occured. Discussions prophesied a strong decrease of immigration to Germany due to the change in demand for employees with good linguistic and professional qualifications in the tertiary sector (Verwiebe, 2004). This prophecy turned out to be incorrect and nowadays Germany is still a favoured destination for both high-skilled and low-skilled immigrants. Our analyses show that most respondents assess their German language proficiency to be good or very good and the migrants for which this is the case achieve a significantly higher position in the German labor market (as indicated by the ISEI).

A surprising finding of our analysis is that language usage in the family is significant in the overall model and has a negative effect on the ISEI. This finding can be discussed in the light of transnational family studies which argue that it is necessary to consider that multi-locally organized and multilingual families may have a different interpretation of "family" and "language within the family" than assumed by the researchers. These linguistic practices in transnational families are – similar to the language proficiencies – very dynamic and dependent on the familial composition and therefore vary over time. An understanding of this concept as a time-constant variable might therefore make this a rather problematic indicator of individuals' language proficiency.

Some limitations of our study can be derived when it comes to the link between language proficiency and one's social position. The GSOEP provides manifold language measures and therefore offers an excellent starting point for our analyses. Nevertheless, it should be noted that most measures are based on self-assessment and objective measures, such as language tests, were not included in the analyses except for whether a German language course was taken or not. This

---

work 4.2 (196 observations), small self-employed with employees 3.9 (38 observations), small self-employed without employee 3.7 (43 observations), skilled manual worker 3.9 (330 observations), semi- and unskilled manual workers 3.7 (515 observations), agricultural labour 3.5 (34 observations), self-employed farmers 4.5 (2 observations). Distribution of German speaking abilities by actual (un-)employment registration: registered unemployed (not at all 0.0% / poor 8.7% / fairly 36.2% / good 37.7% / very good 17.4%; in total 69 observations) and not registered unemployed (not at all 0.1% / poor 3.5% / fairly 21.2% / good 44.5% / very good 30.8%; in total 1,606 observations).

makes it difficult to draw a direct conclusion about the objective assessment of language proficiency and social position (for a similar discussion on methodological challenges in studying objective assessment see also Rother, 2010). The data presented in this study used a variety of language measures, but some important aspects are not covered by the data, for example, the importance of foreign accents and the knowledge of regional German dialects for the ISEI. These linguistic aspects require further consideration in social inequality studies. Moreover, a cross national perspective on this question would be highly interesting because it could be assumed that the role of language for migrants' social position in the labour market in Germany differs from, for instance, the US, where Spanish has a market share that is not comparable to any immigrant language in Germany or Europe overall (Zolberg and Woon, 1999). This might lead to an easier entry into the labour market for Spanish speaking immigrants in the US, compared, for instance, to Turkish speaking immigrants in Germany. In addition, taking a closer look at the role of third languages, which showed a strong significant effect on the ISEI in our analyses, could be a promising approach for future research. Which language is a valuable resource in the labour market? Which language can be transferred into a valuable skill in the labour market and under which circumstances (e.g. English as the global lingua franca)? Or is the knowledge of three or more languages a general indicator of intelligence and personal potential, which then influences education and success in the labour market?

An important methodological aspect refers to the dynamics of language proficiencies. In line with Levitt (2001) and Portes et al. (2002), we call for more longitudinal designs for migrants' inequality studies that constantly collect data on language proficiency in order to trace the linguistic development. Language proficiency changes over the course of time and also depends on the duration of stay (Spörlein and Kristen, 2018). In light of this, when measuring the influence of language proficiency on social status, it is particularly important to know the current language proficiency, rather than the language proficiency several years ago. Therefore, future longitudinal panel data studies need to investigate the complex nexus between time, language and social position.

Beyond that, future studies also need to reflect on the selectivity of the sample. Geographically highly mobile respondents cannot be included and permanent residents of the host country become part of the survey because it is easier to (re-)contact them over time. This creates a bias against the mobile population in the country and may also lead to a loss of important transnational aspects (Horvath, 2012). Longitudinal studies need to reflect and address this challenge by having more flexible or innovative forms of data collection that can cover high spatial mobility, for instance, stronger use of internet surveys, which offer the possibility to participate over a long period of time regardless of physical mobility or presence in the respective country.

In a nutshell, we believe that our study contributes towards the vital ongoing scientific discussion and reflection of measures in social sciences in general, and in the very dynamic field of migration studies in particular.

References

Aldashev, A., Gernandt, J. and Thomsen, S. L. (2009). "Language usage, participation, employment and earnings. Evidence for foreigners in West-Germany with multiple sources of selection". *Labour Economics,* 16: 330–341. http://dx.doi.org/10.2139/ssrn.1307646

Chiswick, B. R. and Miller, P. W. (2010). "Occupational language requirements and the value of English in the US labor market". *Journal of Population Economics,* 23 (1): 353-372. https://doi.org/10.1007/s00148-008-0230-7

Cummins, J. (2000). *Language, power and pedagogy: Bilingual children in the crossfire.* Tonawanda, New York: Multilingual Matters. https://doi.org/10.1080/15235882.2001.10162800

Duchêne, A., Humbert, P. N. and Coray, R. (2018). "How to ask questions on language? Ideological struggles in the making of a state survey". *International Journal of the Sociology of Language*, 25: 45–72. https://doi.org/10.1515/ijsl-2018-0014

Dustmann, C. and Fabbri, F. (2003). "Language proficiency and labour market performance of migrants in the UK". *The Economic Journal*, 113: 695–717. https://doi.org/10.1111/1468-0297.t01-1-00151

Esser, H. (2006). *Migration, language and integration*. Programme on Intercultural Conflicts and Societal Integration (AKI). Social Science Research Center Berlin.

Esser, H. (2009). "Pluralisierung oder Assimilation? Effekte der multiplen Inklusion auf die Integration von Migranten". *Zeitschrift für Soziologie*, 38 (5): 358–378. https://doi.org/10.1515/zfsoz-2009-0502

Euwals, R., Dagevos, J., Gijsberts, M. and Roodenburg, H. (2007). "The labour market position of Turkish immigrants in Germany and the Netherlands: Reason for migration, naturalisational and language proficiency". IZA Discussion Paper 2683.

Ganzeboom, H. B. G., de Graaf, P. M. and Treiman, D. J. (1992). "A standard international socio-economic index of occupational status". *Social Science Research*, 21 (1): 1–56. https://doi.org/10.1016/0049-089X(92)90017-B

Glick Schiller, N., Çaglar, A. and Guldbrandsen, T. C. (2006). "Beyond the ethnic lens: Locality, globality, and born-again incorporation". *American Ethnologist*, 33: 612–633. https://doi.org/10.1525/ae.2006.33.4.612

Guarnizo, L. E. and Smith, M. P. (1998). "The locations of transnationalism". In M. P. Smith and L. E. Guarnizo (eds.) *Transnationalism from Below*, New Brunswick, NJ: Transaction.

Heizmann, B. and Böhnke, P. (2016). "Migrant poverty and social capital: the impact of intra- and interethnic contacts". *Research in Social Stratification and Mobility*, 46: 73–85. https://doi.org/10.1016/j.rssm.2016.08.006

Henkelmann, Y. (2012). *Migration, Sprache und kulturelles Kapital*. Wiesbaden: Springer VS.

Kalter, F. (2006). "Auf der Suche nach einer Erklärung für die spezifischen Arbeitsmarktnachteile Jugendlicher türkischer Herkunft". *Zeitschrift für Soziologie*, 35 (2): 144–160. https://doi.org/10.1515/zfsoz-2006-0204

Kroh, M., Kühne, S., Goebel, J. and Preu, F. (2015). "The 2013 IAB-SOEP Migration Sample (M1): Sampling design and weighting adjustment". SOEP Survey Papers 271: Series C. Berlin: DIW/SOEP.

Lancee, B. and Hartung, A. (2012). "Turkish migrants and native Germans compared: the effect of inter-ethnic and intra-ethnic friendships on the transition from unemployment to work". *International Migration*, 50 (1): 39–54. https://doi.org/10.1111/j.1468-2435.2011.00736.x

Levitt, P. (2001). "Transnational migration: Taking stock and future directions". *Global Networks*, 1: 195–216. https://doi.org/10.1111/1471-0374.00013

Markova, E. (2008). "The determinants of labour market earnings for Bulgarian migrants: Some micro-level evidence from Madrid, Spain". *Migration Letters*, 2: 177–178. https://doi.org/10.33182/ml.v5i2.52

Portes, A., Guarnizo, L. E. and Haller, W. J. (2002). "Transnational entrepreneurs: an alternative form of immigrant economic adaptation". *American Sociological Review*, 67 (2): 278–298. https://doi.org/10.2307/3088896

Rother, N. (2010). "The German Integration Panel: how to measure the influence of integration courses on migrants integration". *Migration Letters*, 1: 43–55. https://doi.org/10.33182/ml.v7i1.179

Spörlein, C. and Kristen, C. (2018). "Educational Selectivity and Language Acquisition among Recently Arrived Immigrants". *International Migration Review*. https://doi.org/10.1177/0197918318798343

van Niejenhuis, C., van der Werf, M. P. C. and Otten, S. (2015). "Predictors of immigrants' second-language proficiency: a Dutch study of immigrants with a low level of societal participation and second-language proficiency". *International Journal of the Sociology of Language*, 236: 75–100. https://doi.org/10.1515/ijsl-2015-0022

Verwiebe, R. (2004). *Transnationale Mobilität innerhalb Europas: Eine Studie zu den sozialstrukturellen Effekten der Europäisierung*. Berlin: edition sigma.

Verwiebe, R., Teitzer, R. and Wiesböck, L. (2014). "New forms of intra-European migration, labour market dynamics and social inequality in Europe". *Migration Letters*, 2: 125–136. https://doi.org/10.33182/ml.v11i2.234

Zolberg, A. R. and Woon, L. L. (1999). "Why Islam is like Spanish: Cultural incorporation in Europe and the United States". *Politics & Society*, 27 (1): 5–39. https://doi.org/10.1177/0032329299027001002

September 2020
Volume: 17, **No**: 5, pp. 705 – 718
ISSN: 1741-8984
e-ISSN: 1741-8992
www.migrationletters.com

MIGRATION
LETTERS

First Submitted: 15th June 2020 Accepted: 16th September 2020
DOI: https://doi.org/10.33182/ml.v17i5.1048

The COVID-19, Migration and Livelihood in India: Challenges and Policy Issues

R.B. Bhagat[1], Reshmi R.S.[2], Harihar Sahoo[3], Archana K. Roy[4], and Dipti Govil[5]

Abstract

The worldwide spread of COVID-19 first reported from Wuhan in China is attributed to migration and mobility of people. In this article, we present how our understanding of migration and livelihood could be helpful in designing a mitigating strategy of economic and social impact of COVID-19 in India. We conclude that there are many challenges migrants face during the spread of COVID-19 resulting from nationwide lockdown. Many internal migrants faced problems such as lack of food, basic amenities, lack of health care, economic stress, lack of transportation facilities to return to their native places and lack of psychological support. On the other hand, COVID-19 has also brought into sharp focus the emigrants from India and the major migration corridors India shares with the world as well. There is a huge uncertainty about how long this crisis will last. This article further provides some immediate measures and long term strategies to be adopted by the government such as improving public distribution system, strengthening public health system, integration of migrants with development, decentralisation as a strategy to provide health services, and providing support to return migrants to reintegrate them, and also strengthen the database on migration and migrant households.

Keywords: *Covid 19; Migration; Livelihood; Challenges; India*

Introduction

The epidemics of the past was hardly concerned with migration and livelihood during the colonial India, although major Indian cities like Kolkata (Calcutta), Mumbai (Bombay), Chennai (Madras) and many other urban places hugely suffered from influenza, smallpox, plague, malaria and cholera (Davis, 1951; Banthia and Dyson, 1999; Hill, 2011). Mumbai experienced a deadly plague in 1896 and also an influenza in 1918. Hill observed that epidemic of influenza arrived in Mumbai in September 1918 which swept through north and east India. He found that excess mortality due to influenza was negatively related with out-migration at district level analysis, but offered no explanation (Hill, 2011). Compared to the epidemics, the famine was seen not only causing mortality but also migration in the past (Maharatna, 2014). In 1994, a major epidemic of plague

---

1 Professor and Head, Department of Migration and Urban Studies, International Institute for Population Sciences, Mumbai. E. Mail: rbbhagat@iips.net
2 Assistant Professor, Department of Migration and Urban Studies, International Institute for Population Sciences, Mumbai. E. Mail: reshmi@iips.net
3 Assistant Professor, Department of Development Studies, International Institute for Population Sciences, Mumbai. E. Mail: harihar@iips.net
4 Professor, Department of Migration and Urban Studies, International Institute for Population Sciences, Mumbai. E. Mail: royarchana@iips.net
5 Assistant Professor, Department of Population Policies and Programmes, International Institute for Population Sciences, Mumbai. E. Mail: dgovil@iips.net

broke out in western India with epicentre in Surat. There was a huge exodus of migrant population from the industrial city of Surat.

When migrants flee from the city, they not only lose their livelihood but they may carry the infections to their native places (BBC, 2020). In the period of epidemic of HIV/AIDS which broke during the 1980s in various parts of the world, migrants were greatly stigmatised as a carrier of the disease and considered to be a population at risk. This has obliterated the great contribution of migrants in economic growth, innovation, skill development and entrepreneurship in building cities and the nation. On the other hand, policies and programmes of urban development and planning in India hardly launched any specific programmes for the migrants as they were not considered as a part of the urban community. Failure to recognise migrants as a stakeholder in urban development is one of the biggest mistakes in achieving urban sustainability and realising the goals of sustainable development in India. It is to be realised that migrants are not a victimiser, nor a victim, but they are vulnerable. They are engaged in many 3D jobs (dirty, dangerous and demeaning) which the urban natives hate to do. Access to social security programmes, access to health care and other entitlements are grossly denied to many of these migrant workers due to lack of their inclusion in urban society. Several of them also lose their political rights as being away at the time of election from their home constituency and are not able to vote.

Many migrants suffer from the double burden of being poor and migrants. Many programmes meant for the poor do not reach them due to lack of identity and residential proofs. The lack of fulfilment of the economic, social and political rights of migrants is a serious issue even though they are formal citizens, their substantive citizenship rights are not fulfilled. The Working Group on Migration (2017) set up by the Ministry of Housing and Urban Poverty Alleviation has examined the plight of the migrant workers in the country and submitted its report to Central Government in 2017. However, action on the report is still awaited. In the meantime, the sudden eruption of migration crisis resulting from the out-break of COVID-19 again reminds us of the urgency of the matter. This paper presents how our understanding of migration and livelihood could be helpful in designing a mitigating strategy of economic and social impact of COVID-19.

Migration and Livelihood

Migration is a livelihood strategy adopted by millions of people in India. Most of the migration for work and employment is directed towards the urban centres. About half of the urban population are migrants and one-fifth of them are inter-state migrants (see Fig. 1). Rural to urban migrants are mainly concentrated in 53 million-plus urban agglomerations (with one million and more) that comprises 140 million out of 377 million urban population of the country equivalent to 43 per cent of total urban population as per 2011 Census. Out of 53 million-plus cities, eight of them are mega-cities with a population of 5 million and more. These eight cities reported about 55 per cent COVID cases of India, although constitute only 7 per cent of India's population. The relevant information on these eight cities has been provided in Table 1. As on 10th June 2020, the respective districts of eight mega cities reported more than half of the coronavirus positive cases (https://www.covid19india.org/). The incidence of COVID-19 shows that these metropolitan areas are the centres from where the disease has been spreading to the near as well as far off places.

Migrant workers constitute the backbone of Indian economy. Out of 482 million workers in India, about 194 million are permanent and semi-permanent migrant workers (Fig. 2). In addition, there are about 15 million short-term migrant workers of temporary and circulatory nature. The inter-state share in labour migration is about one-third for permanent/semi-permanent migration and about two-fifth for short-term temporary and circulatory migration. In general, in-migration rates were high in high-income states such as Delhi, Goa, Haryana, Punjab, Maharashtra, Gujarat and Karnataka, whereas low-income states such as Bihar, Uttar Pradesh, Jharkhand, Rajasthan and Odisha reported relatively higher rates of out-migration (Fig. 3). Some of the in-migrating states such as Maharashtra, Gujarat and Delhi are badly affected by the incidence of COVID-19. There are conspicuous corridors of migration flows within the country – Bihar to Delhi, Bihar to Haryana and Punjab, Uttar Pradesh to Maharashtra, Odisha to Gujarat, Odisha to Andhra Pradesh and Rajasthan to Gujarat (Bhagat and Keshri 2020). The inter-state migration flow is presented in Fig. 4.

Figure 1. Migration Intensity and Share of Inter-State Migrants in Rural and Urban Areas, India, 2011

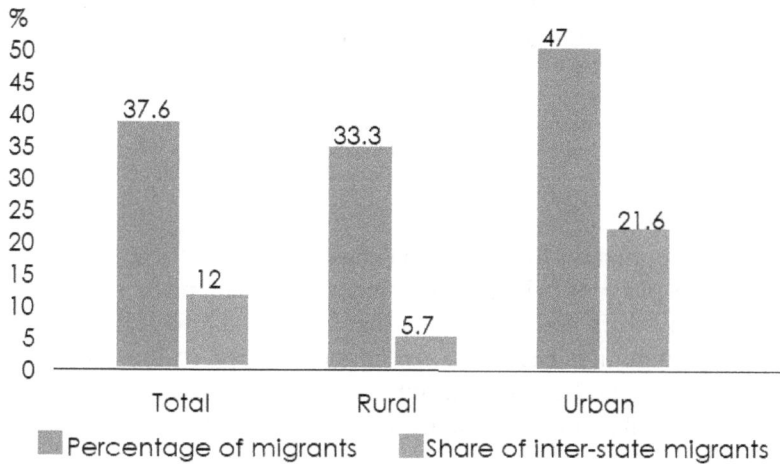

Source: D2 Migration Table, Census of India 2011

Table 1. Migration Intensity, Share of Inter-Sate Migrants, India, 2011and Covid-19 Cases in Mega Cities, 2020

Urban Agglome-ration (UA)	Population (2011)	Percentage of migrants to total population	% Share of inter-state migrants to total migrants	Number of COVID cases in the respective districts as on 10th June 2020 (Total Cases in India 279,721)
Delhi	16,349,831	43.1	87.8	31,309
Greater Mumbai	18,394,912	54.9	46	65,163*
Kolkata	14,057,911	40.8	18.2	3,018
Chennai	8,653,521	51	11.8	25,937
Bruhat Banglore	8,520,435	52.3	35.1	564
Hyderabad	7,677,018	64.3	7.1	2,371
Ahmedabad	6,357,693	48.7	24.1	14,962
Pune	5,057,709	64.8	22.3	10,073
Urban India	**377106125**	**47.0**	**21.6**	**Share of Covid 19 cases in these metro cities to total cases of India is 55 %**

Source: D3 (Appendix) Migration Table, Census of India 2011; https://www.covid19india.org/accessed on 10th June, 2020)
Note : * indicates total cases in Greater Mumbai Urban agglomeration, ie, Mumbai and Thane districts

Figure 2. Stock of Migrant Workers (in million), India, 2011

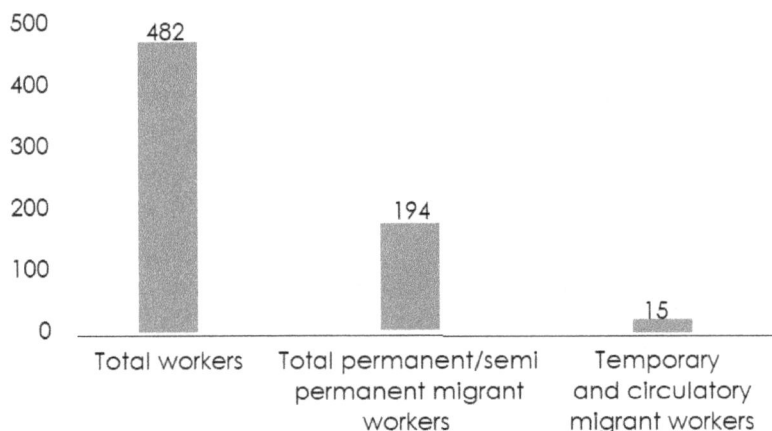

Note: Total workers and total permanent/semi-permanent migrant workers are based on B1 Economic Table and D6 Migration Table of Census of India 2011. It includes both main and marginal workers. Temporary and circulatory migration is the short-term migration based on NSS 64th Round. Based on the rate of NSS 64th Round for the year 2007-08 it is projected for the census year 2011 (see also Keshri and Bhagat 2012).

When workers do not get any option for livelihood and employment and there is an expectation of economic improvement in the place of origin, labour migration takes place (Lall, Selod and Shalizi, 2006). In many cases, they work and stay in an urban area for a long time while in other cases, short term or temporary migration become a livelihood strategy of the rural poor. The National Commission for Enterprises in the Unorganised Sector (NCEUS) reports around 92 per cent of India's workforce with informal employment are substantially drawn from migrant labour (NCEUS, 2007). About 30 per cent of migrant workers are working as casual workers, are therefore quite vulnerable to the vagaries of the labour market and lack social protection. Only 35 per cent of migrant workers are employed as regular/salaried workers (NSSO, 2010).

Impact of COVID-19 on Migrant Workers

The spread of Coronavirus from the epicentre of Wuhan in China to worldwide is linked to migration and mobility of people (Sirkeci and Yucesahin, 2020). The medical professionals largely believe that the control of this infectious disease is possible through immobility and confinement like lockdown and social distancing. Moreover, in a globalised world, the lockdown is likely to bring an unprecedented breakdown of our economic and social system. Migrants are most vulnerable to urban disasters and epidemics. The first case of COVID-19 surfaced in India on 30th January, 2020, and following the out-break the lockdown in the entire country was announced on 24th March for a period of 21 days. Borders were sealed, transportation was ceased, factories, shops, restaurants and all type of the economic activities were shut, barring only the essential services. This proved to be a nightmare for hundreds of thousands of migrant workers, who lost their livelihoods overnight and became homeless. The immediate challenges faced by these migrant workers were related to food, shelter, loss of wages, fear of getting infected and anxiety. As a result, thousands of them started fleeing from various cities to their native places. Many migrants lost their lives either due to hardship on the way to their destination, hunger, accident or comorbidity and some even committed suicide. A telephonic survey of more than 3000 migrants from north-central India by Jan Sahas (2020) shows that majority of the workers were the daily wage earners and at the time of lockdown, 42 per cent were left with no ration, one third was stuck at destinations city with no access to food, water and money, 94 per cent did not have worker's identity card (Jan Sahas, 2020). Sudden lockdown also stranded many migrants in different cities of the country. Those who were travelling were stuck up at stations or state or district borders. Many were forced to walk hundreds of miles on foot to reach their home villages finding no public transport. Those who reached their native villages, were seen as potential carriers of the infection and were ill-treated by the police and locals (India Today, 2020). This is one of the biggest streams of mass return migration in the country. The very effort to stave off the pandemic turned into one of greatest human tragedy in India's recent history.

Figure 3. State wise Net Migration Rates (NMR %) (0-4 year duration), 2011

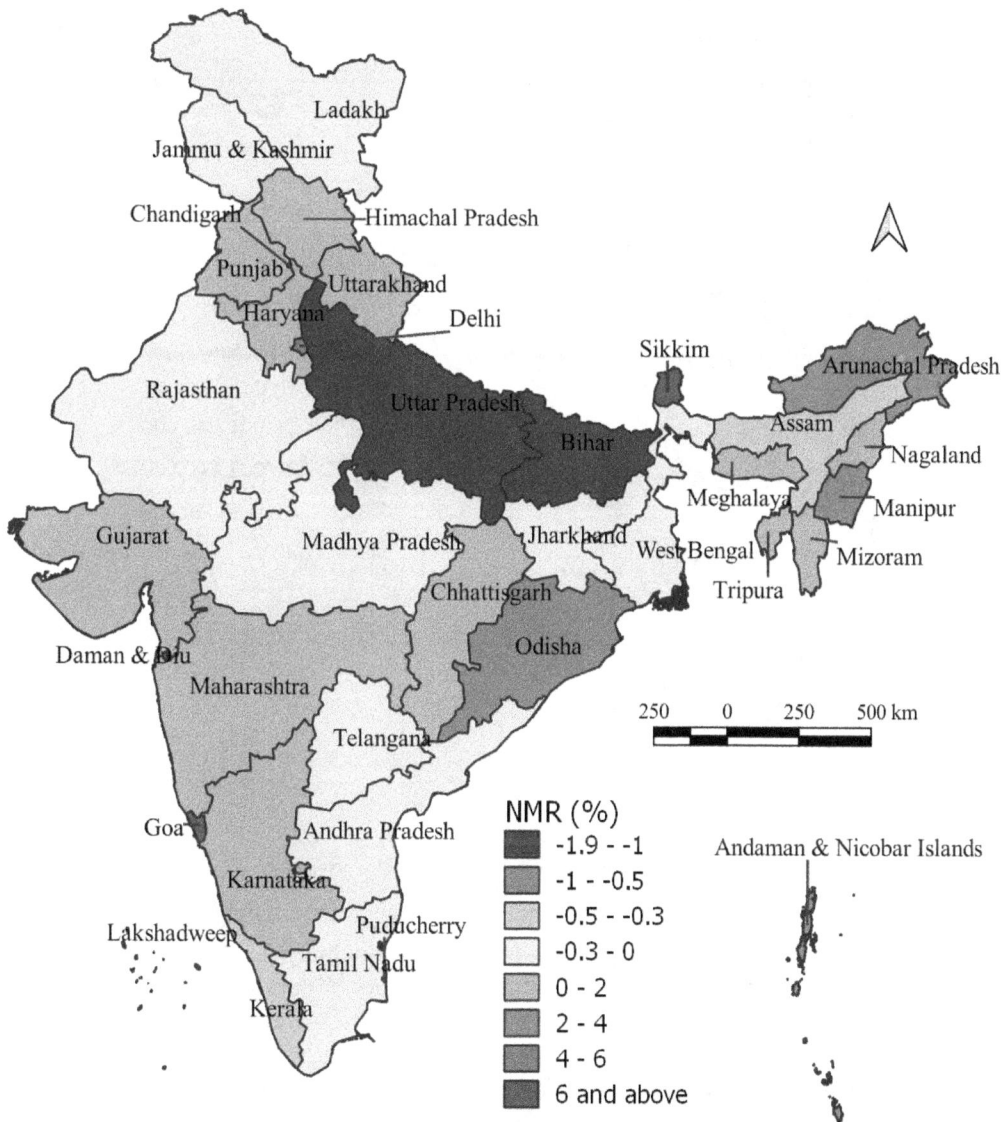

Source: Census of India 2011, D-2 Migration Table (www.censusindia.gov.in).

Figure 4. Net migration Flows between States, duration 0-4 years, 2011

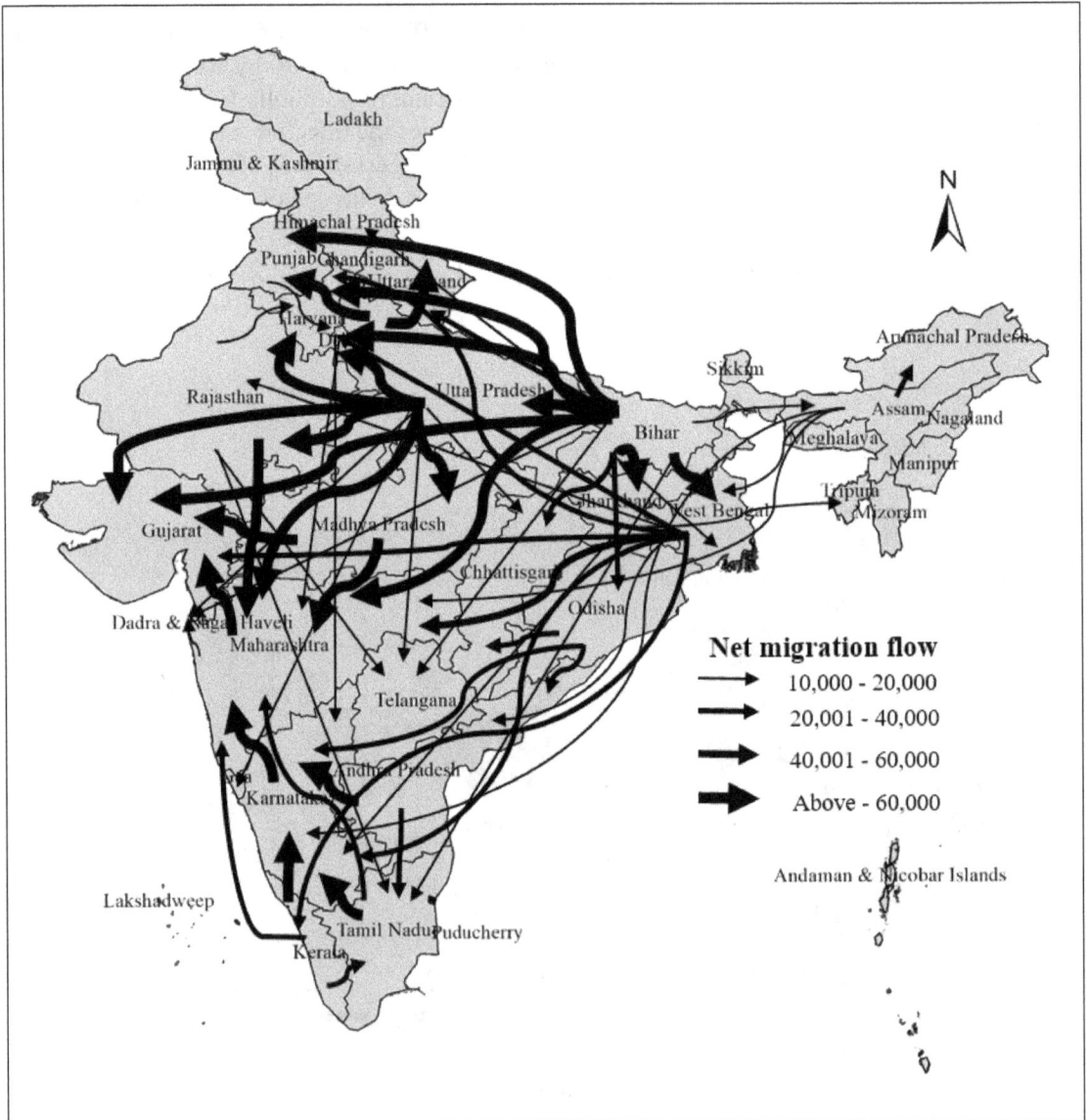

Source: Calculated from Census of India 2011, D-2 Migration Table (www.censusindia.gov.in).

Coronavirus out-break led to a loss of livelihood for those who either work on short-term contracts or those who are without any job contracts. This includes several jobs in different industries. For example, in the tourism industry, guide, employees of parking contractors, cleaners, waiters in restaurants, suppliers of vegetables and flowers to the hotels and so on. A similar scenario would likely to prevail in other industries (like manufacturing and non-manufacturing) mainly because of the falling demand. Manufacturing industries such as cement, plastics, rubber, food products and textiles would reduce substantial jobs. Transportation sector is also badly affected. This will lead to the cut down of the job market (especially those who are employed) and also make hardship for job creation. Besides, this will also have an effect on pay-cuts and late increments.

India is likely to face the job crisis because of the COVID 19. Migrant workers and workers in the informal sector are likely to be badly hit (ILO 2020).

The most vulnerable section would be those migrant workers who are employed in the informal sector, those who do not have either security of employment or any social protection. In urban areas, average wage earnings per day by casual labour engaged in works other than public works ranged between INR 314 to INR 335 (less than $5) among males and nearly INR 186 to INR 201 (less than $3) among females during 2017-18 (Ministry of Statistics and Programme Implementation, 2019). A large number of migrant workers and workers in the informal sector just have been surviving on subsistence wages. The Coronavirus out-break and subsequent lockdown are going to affect them badly, leading to their further impoverishment due to loss of livelihood. It may also affect their food and nutritional intake, access to health care and education of children hugely.

Immigrants and Refugees

The COVID-19 could be devastating for immigrants and refugees in both developed as well as developing countries. In less developed countries, having inadequate sanitation and infrastructural facilities can cause huge strains on public health systems which can impact hundreds of millions of people, especially immigrants, refugees, internal migrants and displaced populations. On the other hand, the official data on refugee and asylum seekers in India are small i.e., 2,07,808 as per UNHCR (http://popstats.unhcr.org/en/persons_of_concern). Luckily, India has a small immigrant population, i.e., about 6 million as per the 2011 Census.

Immigrants and the refugee population are often left out of epidemic preparedness planning and reaching out these marginalised population is a challenge. In some of the middle-east countries such as Iraq, Lebanon, Syria, where the public health system is very weak due to the continuous war and political neglect, it is difficult to control the spread of Coronavirus. This is because of the large number of refugees and displaced persons having dismal conditions such as no fixed place to live, authorities might not know how to contact them or have the capacity to coordinate a response. Sometimes, there is strong anti-refugee sentiment among national authorities. There is also scarce culturally and linguistically accessible information about COVID-19 and how to protect oneself and others, which further increases the risks to refugees and migrants as well as host populations (WHO, 2020).

In the United States of America and European countries, many of the migrant workers are subjected to adverse conditions with little to no safety equipment, no social distancing and no additional support or pay (Tharoor, 2020). Britain's National Health Service reported more than 13 per cent of the workforce is a non-British nationality. The first four doctors in Britain to die of COVID-19, the disease caused by the Coronavirus, while treating patients, were all from an immigrant background (Tharoor, 2020). However, xenophobic rhetoric about how migrants and refugees are potential carriers of the deadly virus pose a health threat (Zargar, 2020). On the United States-Mexico border, there are growing fears over the devastating consequences of a potential out-break of the virus in makeshift camps where thousands of migrants have been encamped for months, awaiting entry into the US.

With regard to South Asian Countries, the government of Thailand temporarily banned cross-border travel between Thailand and neighbouring countries. The Myanmar and Cambodian embassies in Thailand are urging migrant workers to not return home in order to avoid spreading the virus. However, the efforts were failed due to the number of migrant workers trying to exit

Thailand as they have the concern that staying back without work would lead to a shortage of food (Rogovin, 2020). While some of the countries like Libya, it has been reported that Coronavirus out-break could be 'catastrophic' for migrants. The International Organization for Migration (IOM) – a UN Agency, has warned that an out-break of the Coronavirus in Libya could be "truly catastrophic" for the internally displaced people (IDP) and close to 700,000 refugees and migrants in the war-torn country (Ghani, 2020). With the limited financial resources, overcrowded and unsanitary conditions in detention centres, non-accessibility of information about the virus and how to protect it and limited access to healthcare services gives an additional challenge during the out-break of COVID-19.

Various countries and organisations have responded on the impact of COVID-19 on migrants and the ways to provide support to migrants. For instance, Portugal has temporarily given all migrants and asylum seekers full citizenship rights, granting them full access to the country's healthcare as the out-break of the novel Coronavirus escalates in the country (The Week 2020). The Govt. of Malaysia has advised the illegal migrants or foreigners without travelling documents, including the Rohingyas to come forward for COVID-19 screening test (Daud, 2020). Migrants in Thailand are entitled to COVID-19 screening and treatment regardless of legal status, with documented workers covered by the Migrant Health Insurance Scheme or the Social Security Fund. Those who are registered under the Social Security Fund are also entitled to benefits for loss of income due to the government order to suspend employment in certain sectors.

Emigrants and Return Migrants

India is a leading country of origin of international migrants with about 17 million emigrants according to the latest estimates released by the United Nations (2019). India also continues to be the top remittance (USD 78.6 billion) recipient country as well (World Migration Report 2020). Every year a large number of people from India go abroad for overseas employment purposes. Some of the major destination countries of Indian emigrants are United States of America, Malaysia, Saudi Arabia, U.A.E, United Kingdom, South Africa, Canada, Singapore, Kuwait, Oman, Qatar, Thailand, and New Zealand. Although a number of skilled/semi-skilled workers, students and highly skilled professionals move to countries such as USA, UK, Canada, Australia etc., where labour and employment laws are well defined, and emigrants' interests are well protected under the local law, a considerable proportion of the emigrants from India are less educated and less or semi-skilled workers migrating to Gulf countries. Kerala tops the emigration rate among major Indian states followed by Punjab, Tamil Nadu, and Andhra Pradesh (including Telangana) (Bhagat *et al.*, 2013). These are the states badly hit by COVID-19. In some of the Gulf countries, many Indian migrants are locked down in a crowded neighbourhood, raising fears that it will become a coronavirus hotbed while some other countries have asked the migrant workers to stay home, and stopped paying them. The lockdown imposed in many of the Gulf countries has dramatically slowed their economies. This loss will affect not only the workers but also the respective state economies (The Indian Express, 2020).

Response of the Central and State Governments

The spread of the Coronavirus Disease 2019 (COVID-19), and subsequent nationwide lockdown to control its further outbreak brought turmoil in the lives of millions who are primarily involved in the informal sector. To mitigate the effect of the lockdown on the vulnerable groups, Government of India on 26th March 2020, announced a INR 1.70-lakh-crore package under the

Pradhan Mantri Gareeb Kalyan Yojana. It has within its ambit health workers, farmers, agricultural labourers, economically vulnerable categories, especially women, elderly, and unorganised-sector workers, Jan Dhan account holders and Ujjwala beneficiaries. The scheme entails an additional 5 kg of wheat or rice and 1 kg of preferred pulses every month to 80 crore beneficiaries for the next three months. Government of India also gave an order to the state governments to use Building and Construction Workers Welfare Fund of INR 52000 crores to provide relief to Construction Workers through direct benefit transfer (DBT) (DHNS, 2020; Government of India, 2020a). The PM Cares Fund also allocated 1000 crore to the state governments to meet the expenses of food, travel and shelter of migrant workers. The Reserve Bank of India (RBI) also joined later with a sharp cut of interest rate along with a series of unconventional measures to lend to besieged businesses (Bloomberg Quint, 2020).

However, the fear of loss of livelihood sparked into the mass exodus of millions of these migrant labourers in some parts of the country, who started on a long 'barefoot' journey with their families, in the absence of the transportation facilities, to their native places (Bindra and Sharma, 2020). Looking at the gravity of the situation, many states, i.e. Delhi, Uttar Pradesh, Rajasthan, Bihar, and Karnataka arranged special busses to drop these workers and their families to either state borders or to their districts (Bhora, 2020; NDTV, 2020; Press Trust of India, 2020a; Press Trust of India, 2020b). This massive migration led to the chaotic situation on national highways, bus stops and railway stations and raised misunderstandings between states. As this was the violation of and a threat to the benefits of lockdown and was risky for them and for people in the villages, Government of India gave a strict order to seal all inter-state and district borders on 29th March 2020 and asked states to issue necessary orders to district authorities to ensure adequate arrangements of temporary shelters (especially near highways) with adequate amenities and basic requirements, provision of food, clothing and health measure for the poor and needy people including migrants labourer, stranded due to lockdown measures in their respective areas (Press Trust of India, 2020c; Government of India, 2020b). The government classified the migrant workers as follows for a suitable action:

1. Migrant workers who are still in the cities of local residence, if they are found to be forming any congregation in bus station/railway stations or any other place of the city. Authorities should record the details of such people and follow them up for 14 days and risk screening should be done by district health authorities.
2. Migrant workers who are on their way and are yet to reach their destination city/village, for them the quarantine centre were to be set-up with proper amenities and basic requirement. Thermal screening will be carried out with appropriate actions for suspected or confirmed cases. They will be encouraged to be in contact with their families
3. Migrant workers who have reached their destination will be identified by the district administration and Integrated Disease Surveillance Program (IDSP) will follow them up at their residence.

As mentioned earlier, there are more than 200 million migrant workers in India. The inter-state migrants working in the informal sector and those who are temporary and circular migrants are hugely affected. The relief provided by the government and non-governmental organisation may bring some relief to the migrants, but looking into the huge migrant population, the amount of help is highly inadequate.

Challenges and Future Strategy

There is huge uncertainty about how long this crisis will last and what damage it would do to the economy and livelihood of people. Given its size and spread, management of migrants under lockdown and afterwards represents a massive logistic challenge. Some of these challenges need to be addressed instantly and some are in the long run:

The immediate challenges related to migrants are:

a. to provide food and basic amenities at camps/shelters by maintaining better hygiene and sanitation (soap/ water/ toilet/ waste management) to all of them;
b. to provide the basic income support to migrants and their left behind families who are not registered to the social schemes and depend on daily wages for survival
c. to provide basic health care and preventive kits (like masks, sanitisers, and gloves etc.);
d. to quickly appraise their conditions and do the screening of the possibly infected persons and quarantine them separately;
e. to maintain the social distancing for the migrants to check the spread of infection;
f. to provide counselling and psychological support to the migrants under the distress
g. to transfer migrants safely to their hometown:
There were incidences of mass gathering of migrant labourers, violating the norm of social distancing, in Mumbai, Surat and Delhi after the end of the first phase of lockdown, reflects their desperation to go back to their families in villages. The frequent extension of lockdown has created mental agony among them. A large number have managed to return by the end of May. Hence, there is a challenge to rehabilitate them in their villages and respective native places.

h. to deal with likely economic stress in the destination areas:
With the severe disruption in economic activities, the question arises whether reverse migrants will come back to work in towns or stay in their villages. If they don't return, how to deal with likely economic stress in the destination areas is a challenge. In the origin villages, where resources are scarce and opportunities are limited, it would be a challenge for the state government to meet the basic requirements of the people.

Governments need to address the challenges facing internal migrants by including them in health services and cash transfer and other social programs and protecting them from discriminati on (World Bank, 2020). Some of the strategies which are already adopted by the central and state government of India and various organisations, and some of the suggested strategies are as follows:

1. Several state governments are running relief/shelter camps in different states. There is no definite estimate available at the moment but not less than 10 million migrant workers are stranded. While their families at the place of origin are being supported through various measures under *Pradhan Mantri Gareeb Kalyan Yojana* announced on 26th March 2020, the stranded migrant workers have hardly got anything except food in the camps. It is suggested that each stranded migrant worker in cities should be given INR 6000 (less than $100) (i.e., the minimum rate of Mahatma Gandhi National Rural Employment Guarantee Scheme (MGNREGS) INR 202 (less than $3) per day X 30 days) by the Central Government in addition to the financial support by the State Government per month for at

least three months. It would be advisable to give monetary support in cash to the stranded migrant workers in camps, designated shelters and other places in cities.

2. The government issued the guideline for the movement of the migrant labourers on 19th April, 2020 which allows the movement of intra-state migrant labourers to carry economic activities outside the coronavirus hotspot zones. Following the prevention and screening guidelines for the intra-state transfer of the labour is a big challenge of both the state and central government. Further, in order to avoid stigma by the co-villagers, awareness may be provided to villagers with the help of NGOs, Self-Help Groups, health workers and functionaries of the local bodies.

3. There is an urgent need for the development of an authentic database for the stranded migrants at the destination, in highway camps and return migrants in villages. Data on volume and characteristics of the migrants (in camps, home quarantine) is needed to transfer the benefits of social welfare schemes at present and for future management needs.

Apart from these immediate measures, some of the following long term strategies may be adopted:

1. Food grain and pulses need to be supplied on a weekly basis to meet the food and nutritional needs of migrant workers and their families. The government should use the Public Distribution System (PDS) infrastructure and distribute the food grain lying as a buffer stock to the tune of 60 million metric tonnes with Food Corporation of India. It should also mobilise local bodies to ensure the supply of daily needs arising from the Coronavirus disruption.

2. Migrants cannot be neglected as a stakeholder in development for a long time. Integration of migrants with development is the need of the hour. The government should seriously look into the recommendations UNESCO-UNICEF and the Working Group on Migration and implement them at the earliest (Bhagat, 2012; Working Group on Migration, 2017).

3. The public health system, particularly at the primary and secondary care, needs to be strengthened, investment should be increased, drug supply and equipment need to be made available at massive scale, and most importantly human resources of the public health system need to be augmented a spectacular level.

4. India is a vast country with a population of about 1.3 billion. The approach of one size fits is not likely to work. There is a need to accept decentralisation as a basic strategy of providing health services. Apart from decentralisation, a convergence of various services related to food and nutritional programmes, water and sanitation programmes, employment and livelihood programmes must be made effective. It is high time to establish synergy and coordination between the central and state government. Other agencies need to be mobilised to fight COVID 19 by reveiving help from village Panchayat and Self Help Groups, and other stakeholders of society like NGOs and corporates.

5. Starting of health insurance scheme for internal migrants may be helpful for the state government as well as migrants at the destination, especially during any epidemic or pandemic. For instance, in Kerala, a health insurance scheme known as *Awaz Health Insurance Scheme*, is offered to support migrants. This scheme is also helpful to provide valid documents to migrants and helps the government to have a record of migrants.

6. There may be a large number of international migrants who might lose jobs due to COVID-19 pandemic and forced to return. Therefore, there is a requirement for the government to help those return migrants by providing them guidance, training and financial support to those who wish to set up business in order to reintegrate them in the place of origin successfully. For example, in Kerala, there is a scheme by Norka Department for Return Migrants which offers return migrants, who wish to set up a business in Kerala, a capital subsidy and interest subsidy for their investment.

7. There is a need to strengthen the database on migration and migrant households through Census, National Sample Survey (NSS), National Family Health Survey (NFHS) and Migration Surveys. The available data are very old and also not available on time. As migration has affected the households in almost all dimensions in both rural and urban areas, an effective inclusion of migrants in our official statistics and access will help to formulate robust and inclusive policy and programmes in the country.

Acknowledgement

Authors are thankful to K.S. James, P.M. Kulkarni and Tony Champion for their helpful suggestions and comments. We are also thankful to Gulshan Kumar, for his help in drawing the maps.

References

Banthia, Jayant and Dyson, Tim (1999) "Smallpox in Nineteenth Century India", *Population and Development Review*, Vol 25, No. 4. pp. 649-680.

BBC (2020) https://www.bbc.com/news/world-asia-india-52086274 access on 6th April 2020.

Bhagat, R. B. and Keshri, K. (2020). "Internal Migration in India", In Martin Bell, Aude Bernard, Charles-Edward, and Yu Zhu (Eds.) *Internal Migration in the Countries of Asia: A cross-national comparison*, Springer International Publishing, Chennai.

Bhagat, R.B. (2012) 'Summary Report', *Compendium on Workshop Report on Internal Migration in India*, Vol. 1, UNESCO and UNICEF, Delhi.

Bhagat, R.B., Keshri, K and Imtiyaz Ali (2013) Emigration and flow of remittances in India, *Migration and Development*, Vol. 2, No. 1, 2013, pp. 93-105.

Bindra J and Sharma NC (2020) Coronavirus: Govt. tells SC one-third of migrant workers could be infected. LiveMint, 1st April, 2020. Available at https://www.livemint.com/news/india/covid-19-govt-tells-sc-one-third-of-migrant-workers-could-be-infected-11585643185390.html, accessed on 5th April 2020.

BloombergQuint (2020) Covid-19: Supreme Court Seeks Report from Government On Steps To Prevent Migration Of Workers. 30th March 2020. Available at https://www.bloombergquint.com/law-and-policy/covid-19-fear-and-panic-bigger-problem-than-coronavirus-says-sc-seeks-report-from-govt-on-steps-taken-to-prevent-migration-of-workers, accessed on 5th April 2020.

Bohra S. (2020) Jaipur mirrors Delhi scenes as '30,000-40,000' migrants crowd bus stands to get back home. The Print, 29th March 2020. Available at https://theprint.in/india/jaipur-mirrors-delhi-scenes-as-30000-40000-migrants-crowd-bus-stands-to-get-back-home/390935/, accessed at 5th April 2020.

Daud, N (2020) COVID-19: Malaysia's illegal migrants urged to come forward for health Screening, https://www.malaysiaworldnews.com/2020/03/22/covid-19-malaysias-illegal-migrants-urged-to-come-forward-for-health-sceening/

Davis, K. (1951) *The Population of India and Pakistan,* Princeton University Press, Princeton.

DHNS (2020) A poorly thought-out package for the poor. Deccan Herald, 27th March, 2020. Available at https://www.deccanherald.com/opinion/first-edit/a-poorly-thought-out-package-for-the-poor-818067.html, accessed on 5th April 2020.

Ghani, F (2020) Libya: Coronavirus out-break could be 'catastrophic' for migrants https://www.aljazeera.com/news/2020/04/covid-19-outbreak-libya-catastrophic-migrants-200403101356223.html

Government of India (2020a) Pradhan Mantri Garib Kalyan Package. Press Information Bureau, 26th March 2020. Available at https://www.mohfw.gov.in/pdf/MoFPMGaribKalyanYojanaPackage.pdf, accessed on 5th April 2020.

Government of India (2020b) Order - No 40-3/2020-DM-I(A), Ministry of Home Affairs, New Delhi, 29th March 2020. Available at https://labourcommissioner.assam.gov.in/sites/default/files/swf_utility_folder/departments/coi_labour_uneecopscloud_com_oid_14/this_comm/mha_order_restricting_movement_of_migrants_and_strict_enforement_of_lockdown_measures_-_29.03.2020.pdf.pdf.pdf, accessed on 5th April 2020.

Government of India (2020c) Advisory for quarantine of migrant workers. Available at https://www.mohfw.gov.in/pdf/Advisoryforquarantineofmigrantworkers.pdf, accessed on 5th April 2020.

Government of India (2020d). Psychological Issues among Migrants during COVID-19. Available at https://www.mohfw.gov.in/pdf/RevisedPsychosocialissuesofmigrantsCOVID19.pdf, accessed on 5th April 2020.

Hill, Kenneth (2011) "Influenza in India 1918: excess mortality reassessed", *Genus* , Vol. 67, No. 2, pp. 9-29.

India Today (2020) https://www.indiatoday.in/india/story/coronavirus-migrants-sprayed-with-disinfectants-on-road-in-up-bareily-dm-assures-action-1661371-2020-03-30.

International Labour Organization (2020) ILO Monitor 2nd edition: COVID-19 and the world of work, Available at: https://www.ilo.org/global/topics/coronavirus/impacts-and-responses.

International Organization for Migration (2019) World Migration Report 2020, IOM, Geneva.

International Organization for Migration (2020) COVID-19: Guidance for employers and business to enhance migrant worker protection during the current health crisis. https://iris.iom.int/covid-19-crisis-response.

IOM (2020) IOM strategic preparedness and response plan—coronavirus disease 2019 https://www.iom.int/sites/default/files/country_appeal/file/iom_covid19_appeal_2020_final_0.pdf.

Jan Sahas, (2020) Voices of the Invisible Citizens: A Rapid Assessment on the Impact of COVID-19 Lockdown on Internal Migrant Workers. April, New Delhi.

Kehsri, Kunal and Bhagat, R.B. (2012) "Temporary and Seasonal Migration: Regional Pattern, Characteristics and Associated Factors", *Economic and Political Weekly*, Vo. 47, No. 4 (28th January), pp. 74-81.

Kulkarni S (2020) 6.6 lakh migrant workers in more than 21,000 camps: Centre Sagar. Deccan Herald, 31st March 2020. Available at https://www.deccanherald.com/national/66-lakh-migrant-workers-in-more-than-21000-camps-centre-819809.html, accessed on 5th April, 2020.

Lall, V., Selod, H, and Shalizi, Z., (2006), "Migration in Developing Countries: A Survey of Theoretical Predictions and Empirical Findings", World Bank Policy Research Working Paper no.3915, Working Paper Series, 1st May, 2006.

Maharatna, Arup (2014) Food Scarcity and Migration *Social Research* , Vol. 81, No. 2, pp. 277-298.

Ministry of Housing and Urban Poverty Alleviation (2017) *Report of the Working Group on Migration, Govt of India*, New Delhi.

Ministry of Statistics and Programme Implementation (2019), *Annual Report Periodic Labour Force Survey (PLFS), 2017-18*, National Statistical Office, Government of India, New Delhi.

NCEUS (2007) *Report on Conditions of Work and Promotion of Livelihoods in the Unorganised Sector*, National Commission for Enterprises in the Unorganised Sector, Govt. of India, New Delhi.

NDTV (2020) Bleach Sprayed On Migrants in UP Over COVID-19, Kerala Uses Soap Water (30th March, 2020). Available at https://www.ndtv.com/india-news/coronavirus-india-lockdown-disinfectant-sprayed-on-migrants-on-return-to-up-shows-shocking-video-2202916, accessed on 5th April 2020.

NSSO (2010) *Migration in India 2007-08*, Ministry of Statistics and Programme Implementation, Govt. of India, New Delhi.

Press trust of India (2020a) Coronavirus: Haryana government provides over 800 buses to UP to ferry migrant workers to their villages. Deccan Herald, MAR 29 2020. Available at https://www.deccanherald.com/national/north-and-central/coronavirus-haryana-government-provides-over-800-buses-to-up-to-ferry-migrant-workers-to-their-villages-818917.html, accessed on 5th April 2020.

Press Trust of India (2020b) Covid-19: UP government arranges 1,000 buses to ferry stranded migrant labourers. Business Standard, 28th March, 2020. Available at https://www.business-standard.com/article/current-affairs/covid-19-up-govt-arranges-1-000-buses-to-ferry-stranded-migrant-labourers-120032800468_1.html, accessed on 5th April 2020.

Press trust of India (2020c) Coronavirus: MHA changes rules, State Disaster Relief Fund to be used to give food, shelter for migrant workers. Deccan Herald, 27th March 2020. Available at, https://www.deccanherald.com/national/coronavirus-mha-changes-rules-state-disaster-relief-fund-to-be-used-to-give-food-shelter-for-migrant-workers-818579.html, accessed on 5th April 2020.

Press trust of India (2020d) Coronavirus: Centre asks states to arrange food, shelter for migrant workers. Deccan Herald, 26th March 2020. Available at https://www.deccanherald.com/national/coronavirus-centre-asks-states-to-arrange-food-shelter-for-migrant-workers-817995.html, accessed on 5th April 2020.

Press Trust of India (2020e) Take actions for redressal of migrant labourers' grievances during lockdown: Health Secretary to states. Deccan Herald, 1st April 2020. Available at https://www.deccanherald.com/national/take-actions-for-redressal-of-migrant-laburers-grievances-during-lockdown-health-secretary-to-states-820164.html, accessed on 5th April 2020.

Rogovin, K, International Labor Rights Forum (2020) COVID-19 Impact on Migrant Workers in Thailand, 27th March, 2020, https://laborrights.org/blog/202003/covid-19-impact-migrant-workers-thailand.

Sirkeci, I., & Yucesahin, M. M. (2020). Coronavirus and Migration: Analysis of Human Mobility and the Spread of Covid-19. *Migration Letters*, 17(2), 379-398. https://doi.org/10.33182/ml.v17i2.935

Tharoor, I (2020) Migrants are the unsung heroes of the pandemic – https://www.wctrib.com/opinion/5030551-Ishaan-Tharoor-Migrants-are-the-unsung-heroes-of-the-pandemic

The Economic Times (2019) At 17.5 million, Indian diaspora largest in the world : UN report , 18th September 2019, Available at https://economictimes.indiatimes.com/nri/nris-in-news/at-17-5-million-indian-diaspora-largest-in-the-world-un-
report/articleshow/71179163.cms?utm_source=contentofinterest&utm_medium=text&utm_campaign=cppst

The Indian Express (2020) Coronavirus deepens struggles for migrant workers in Gulf countries, 14th April 2020, Available at: https://indianexpress.com/article/coronavirus/coronavirus-deepens-struggles-for-migrants-in-persian-gulf-6361636/

The Week (2020) www.theweek.in/news/world/2020/04/01/portugal-gives-migrants-full-citizenship-rights-to-avail-covid-19-treatment.html

United Nations, Department of Economic and Social Affairs, Population Division (2019) *International Migrant Stock 2019* (United Nations database, POP/DB/ MIG/stock/Rev2019).

World Bank (2020) *Covid 19 Crisis through a Migration Lens*, Migration and Development Brief 32, World Bank Group.

World Health Organization (2020): Refugee and migrant health in the COVID-19 response, The Lancet, Published online 31st March, 2020, https://doi.org/10.1016/S0140-6736(20)30791-1.

September 2020
Volume: 17, **No**: 5, pp. 719 – 731
ISSN: 1741-8984
e-ISSN: 1741-8992
www.migrationletters.com

MIGRATION
LETTERS

First Submitted: 25 May 2020 Accepted: 16 September 2020
DOI: https://doi.org/10.33182/ml.v17i5.1013

Reflections on Collective Insecurity and Virtual Resistance in the times of COVID-19 in Malaysia

Linda A. Lumayag[1], Teresita C. del Rosario[2] and Frances S. Sutton[3]

Abstract

Environments of human insecurity are a widespread problem in our globalised world, particularly for migrant workers, one of the most vulnerable groups in society today. These experiences of insecurity have been heightened in the context of the COVID-19 pandemic. In this article, we examine the collective experience of insecurity among migrant workers in Malaysia. In our analysis, we outline collective insecurity at two levels: the micro level of migrant workers' daily, subjective experiences of insecurity; and the macro level, in which insecurity is a consequence of structural forces, specifically the globalisation of labour. These two levels interact symbiotically, producing states of insecurity that are concretely experienced as anxiety and fear. Migrant workers in Malaysia also practice agency through small forms of resistance that they use to bolster one another and reduce their insecure experiences. Throughout the COVID-19 pandemic and subsequent Movement Control Order (MCO) in Malaysia, migrant workers have been further marginalised by the state, but they have also become connected to one another through acts of solidarity and resistance. However, the sustainability of these forms remains unclear.
Keywords: *collective insecurity; virtual resistance; Malaysia; COVID-19; migrant workers; migration*

Introduction

No one escapes insecurity today. Environments of insecurity created by conflict have become a basic human experience in our increasingly globalised world. Those who experience more conflict at the micro (individual), mezzo (household, community), and macro (state, nation) levels are subject to higher amounts of perceived insecurity (Sirkeci, 2009). This article is an attempt to interrogate the environment of human insecurity experienced by migrant workers in Malaysia, where the COVID-19 pandemic has forced the tension across the micro, mezzo, and macro levels of conflict to come to the fore. We argue that migrants experience collective insecurity, which has intensified in the context of the COVID-19 pandemic (Cohen, 2020). Further, we argue that Malaysian migrants have developed forms of resistance in response to their collective insecurity, which have also become more pronounced in the context of Coronavirus.

Previous studies on human insecurity have incorporated frameworks from early security studies, focusing on broad concepts such as nation-states, sovereignty, territoriality, and nationalism, following the principle of Westphalian sovereignty (Vietti & Scribner, 2013). In security studies, migration is often examined at the macro level of institutions, organisations, and

---

[1] Linda A. Lumayag, Program Coordinator and Senior Lecturer, Politics and Government, Faculty of Social Sciences & Humanities, Universiti Malaysia Sarawak, 94300 Kota Samarahan, Sarawak, Malaysia. E-mail: allinda@unimas.my.

[2] Teresita C. Del Rosario, Senior Research Associate, Asia Research Institute, National University of Singapore, 10 Kent Ridge Crescent, AS-8, Level 07-27, Singapore. E-mail: delrosatess@gmail.com.

[3] Frances S. Sutton, PhD Candidate, Department of Anthropology, College of Arts and Sciences, Ohio State University, 4034 Smith Laboratory, 174 W. 18th Avenue, Columbus, Ohio, United States. E-mail: sutton.373.osu.edu.

nation-states and thus, 'securitisation' bias becomes dominant. Within this framework, migration is defined as a security problem that needs to be addressed through institutional and organisational responses from the state.

This article defines insecurity outside the prism of security studies. Here, insecurity is an expression of fear, anxiety and uncertainty caused by a lack of social protection. We argue that although migrants in Malaysia have different backgrounds and personal experiences with insecurity, as migrants, they share common environments of insecurity, resulting in "collective insecurity," a term we outline in this paper. To understand migrant workers' experience of collective insecurity, we first look at how migrants experience environments of insecurity at the micro-level. We then connect these micro-level subjectivities to the macro-realities of state power and its apparatuses. Our investigation provides insights into the minute, taken-for-granted ruptures, tensions, fears, conflicts and uncertainties that migrant workers navigate while they attempt to negotiate with macro-level power structures for increased security. In times of crisis, these negotiations become direr as migrants respond to different experiences of insecurity, including hunger, unemployment, and deportation, brought on by emergency situations, such as the COVID-19 pandemic. This article also investigates the forms of resistance that are currently possible and whether they are sustainable within the context of challenging social, religious, and political milieus in Malaysia.

The observations in this study are based on our ongoing research and engagement with migrant workers workers in Malaysia from Indonesia and the Philippines, with a focus on workers in the domestic and service industries. Migrant insecurity in Malaysia has been the focus of our research and writing for several years prior to the COVID outbreak. Although environments of insecurity prevail in migration contexts, these insecurities have intensified during the COVID-19 pandemic. Our study shows how the collective insecurity of migrants in Malaysia pre-dates the COVID-19 pandemic and why this insecurity must continue to be interrogated in the post-pandemic era.

Framing Collective Insecurity and Collective Resistance

Our analysis is guided by a two-pronged understanding of insecurity as both a) a psychological/subjective emotional state and b) the absence of adequate protection through policy measures and state interventions. Although migrants experience these two factors of insecurity individually, they are also common to the migrant experience in Malaysia. The result is a "collective insecurity" experienced amongst migrant workers in Malaysia. In this section, we outline the ways in which insecurity can be a collective experience for a population. We also examine how the response to migrant workers' intensified insecurity during the pandemic has been a collective one. Through small, united actions, migrant workers and their surrounding communities in Malaysia have helped one another survive during the current COVID-19 crisis. We do not see these actions as a mere response to their environment of insecurity. Instead, we view these tiny, invisible acts as "resistance" because they enabled migrant workers to challenge, reframe, and renegotiate their insecure situations as the pandemic continued. Migrant workers were conscious of their vulnerable and insecure status in Malaysia before the onset of the pandemic. The global health crisis only made this consciousness of insecurity and vulnerability clear to everyone, including the Malaysian citizens, inducing both overt and covert organizing on behalf of migrant communities. Thus, the actions that migrant workers and others are taking to survive more closely resemble resistance than responses to insecurity.

Cohen (2020) argues that insecurity takes many forms and thus it should be modelled as a continuum that tracks time, space, and physicality. Examining time and space allows us to see the full context of how insecurity is created and how people make decisions in response to their situations, including the decision to migrate. Although insecurity springs from fear, anxiety and uncertainty, it is also a physical experience with embodied burdens. Further, Cohen (2020: 406) reminds us that experiences of security and insecurity are relative and as such, "insecurity is a way to represent the collapse of security through time and in response to the assumption of security that may (or may not) have existed, but that nevertheless become concrete and real through history." Although this paper focuses on migrant workers' insecurity in Malaysia, their experience of insecurity is not limited to their current situation. Migrant workers experience insecurity within their own households even before they decide to embark on a migration journey (Cohen and Sirkeci, 2011). Poverty, joblessness, and lack of opportunities for upward mobility are just a few examples of the various personal circumstances that push them to consider labour migration. Migration becomes a strategy to overcome these "push factors" or what Del Rosario and Rigg (2019) refer to as "conditions of precarity."

However, once migrant workers arrive in receiving countries, their experiences of insecurity do not disappear. Instead insecurity transforms in relation to migrant workers' life in their new home. Chung and Mau (2014) emphasise that both institutional and contextual factors are important for the achievement of security in material and non-material ways. Security has a large psychological component that is linked to feelings of safety in a particular environment, but security can also be defined by material factors such as economic achievement and political protection. Migrant workers experience the subjective state of insecurity individually and through the lens of their own personal experiences. However, by examining their common material environments of insecurity, we can understand how migrant workers in a receiving country also experience insecurity as a collective population.

Hacker (2006: 20) argues that "insecurity requires real risk that threatens real hardship." The widespread joblessness, job displacement, and unemployment caused by the COVID-19 offer a robust example of a material environment of insecurity which we can compare with migrant workers' pre-COVID experiences and conditions in their material environments. Economic insecurity, according to the United Nations Department of Economic and Social Affairs (2008: vi), arises from the "exposure of individuals, communities and countries to adverse events, and from their inability to cope with and recover from the costly consequences of those events." COVID-19 is not the only "adverse event" migrant workers experience in the context of their working lives. Thus the collective insecurity migrant workers experience cannot be reduced to "economic insecurity." In addition to intensifying workers' economic insecurity, the COVID-19 pandemic has highlighted the crux of migrant workers' insecurity in receiving countries: lack of material and non-material protections.

Migrant workers are easy targets for discriminatory practices because of how they are perceived in many receiving-societies. Bauman (2016) reveals that in Europe, for example, the 'migration crisis' has triggered a deluge of racism and xenophobia, thus creating divisions of "insiders/outsiders", "us/them", and "all the others." This phenomenon is consistent with earlier research on migration and discrimination, such as Hall's (1978) investigation into 'moral panic' and Michael Bakhtin's concept of 'cosmic fear' (in Bauman 1998). These terms describe cases in which migrants are depicted as taking away job opportunities intended for citizens, the "insiders," and "rightful" recipients of rights. Foucault's notion of "biopolitics" asks us to consider where these depictions come from and direct our attention to the state's role in enabling discrimination toward migrant workers. Although the state recognizes the need for migrant workers to perform low-wage labour, governments also use policy to assert their power over foreign workers by controlling where they are allowed to be, the types of labour they are allowed to perform, and whether they deserve to be treated the same way as citizens. Political policies, or lack thereof, create and reinforce societal divides between citizens and non-citizens. These divisions are powerful, as evidenced by the extensive cognitive dissonance people are willing to maintain in order to preserve the social order. For example, foreign workers are often viewed as "dirty," yet society allows them to work as domestic workers as well as serve in restaurants, eating stalls or big malls where cleanliness and hygiene are required.

The lack of protective policies for migrant workers exacerbates their insecurities in material and non-material ways and is achieved through several "modalities": poor employment conditions (Lumayag, 2018, 2020a, 2020b; Kassim, 2013); restrictions against the formation of labour unions (Piper, 2013, 2015; Piper et al., 2016); lack of social protection mechanisms (Piper and Uhlin, 2002); access/(or lack of) to legal redress (Piper and Uhlin, 2002; Sadiq, 2005); racism, moral panic, and xenophobia (Sadiq, 2005; Lyons, 2007); weak governance on bribery and corruption; and weak worker protections from labour-sending governments.

The tendency to leave migrant's rights unaddressed by global and national institutions is the result of institutional failures at all levels and a lack of political will to respond to the human costs involved in temporary contract migration (Chi, 2008, as cited in Piper et al., 2016). It is also indicative of the downward spiral in labour standards occurring globally (Munck, 2002, as cited in Piper et al., 2016). However, it is possible that the lack of government protections for migrants is not simply a matter of negligence. When we examine all the ways insecurity is institutionalised for migrant workers, we are forced to the ask the question: should we categorize injurious policies and lack of protection as "institutional failure" or is it more accurate to describe it as intentional harm being inflicted on behalf of capital?

Since the onset of COVID-19, the term "biopolitics" has taken on a new meaning for migrant workers in Malaysia as state control over peoples' bodies has increased. In addition to limiting peoples' mobility, the government has also been limiting who has access to aid and resources during pandemic. These new policies have had a severe impact on daily survival for migrant workers. In many ways, the pandemic has opened peoples' eyes to the extent of migrant workers' vulnerability and made their collective insecurity increasingly difficult to ignore or go unaddressed.

Migrant workers in Malaysia have engaged in resistance against the heightened environments of insecurity created by COVID-19 and the government's response. We argue that in these insecure settings, migrant resistance is a community-based form of active engagement that is expressed in micro-activities in response to threats to basic survival. The current crisis provides opportunities for new ways of understanding the small, invisible political actions of vulnerable groups.

Past research on resistance has focused on direct confrontations with power (Foucault, 1997; Constable, 1997; Parreñas, 2001). Seminal studies by Scott (1985, 1990), Ong (1987), Constable (1997), Chin (1998), and Lumayag (2018) demonstrate the range of forms that resistance can take among vulnerable groups. Scott's (1985, 1990) focus is on everyday resistance among peasants in rural Malaysia, while Constable (1997), Chin (1998), and Lumayag (2018) examine how the state uses its power to reduce the opportunities for marginalised groups to confront the state. In all these studies, marginalised, vulnerable minorities conduct their resistance in the open, employing a physical, spatial, and/or social 'presence,' such as direct confrontation with their powerful employers.

Since the introduction of the internet, however, marginalised groups have been able to engage in resistance through a new and different platform where a crucial form of activism is information sharing (see earlier studies by Anderson, 2013 on the Arab Spring; Costa, 2013 on Turkey; Miller et al., 2016). Altogether, the widespread use of the internet becomes collective action, rather than an activity conducted and carried out by individual workers. When migrant workers use common platforms to share their experiences of insecurity, the individual sharing of experiences motivates others to extend their assistance and understand their common situations of insecurity. Migrant workers, who are subordinated, oppressed, and socially excluded, find strength in their own numbers. Echoing Scott, this online presence becomes an instance of the deployment of "weapons of the weak," especially throughout the current pandemic in which migrant workers have felt isolated and marginalised.

Collective Insecurity Among Migrant Workers

In the Southeast Asian region, Malaysia, Singapore and Thailand are key destination countries for migrant labour. Migrant labour makes up a significant portion of the economy in Southeast Asia. Malaysia and Thailand are unique in that they are both labour-sending and labour-receiving countries. Growing from approximately 500,000 migrant workers at the turn of the millennium, today Malaysia has about five to six million migrant workers employed across various industries, primarily in the construction, manufacturing, and service sectors.

Malaysia is a particularly interesting case for an investigation of migrant insecurity because of the country's strong supply and demand for global migrant labour. Migrants have been entering Malaysia through legal and illegal channels for several decades. Filipinos and Indonesians make up the majority of migrants into Malaysia, even as Malaysians themselves constitute migrant labour in neighbouring Singapore, Hong Kong and Japan. Meanwhile in Malaysia, the economy has been dependent on immigrants and migrant workers since colonial rule (Kassim, 2013; Kaur 2014; Lumayag, 2018). For example, the Malaysian plantation industry relied on labour migrants from southern India during British colonial rule and continues to rely on migrant labour today from Indonesia and Bangladesh.

Despite its central position in Asian migration, Malaysia lacks a comprehensive migration policy, a contributing factor to insecurity among migrants within the country. The Malaysian government has yet to address several key workplace issues that migrants face, including poor working conditions and lack of social protections and welfare measures, not to mention migrants' civil and political rights.

Thus, migrant insecurity in Malaysia is epitomized by an ongoing tension surrounding job insecurity. This tension can be seen in the interactions between migrants and the state, including recruitment and employment processes, as well as the unclear pathways to the right to redress among others. We do not argue that migrant insecurity only takes this shape in Malaysia. In fact, Piper et al. (2016: 1096) note that, "conditions of precarity starts from migrants' home country…The fundamental problem is not only the insecurity and vulnerability associated with migrant labour, but the lack of opportunities, rights, security and protection at home that causes large segments of the labour force to resort to migration as a survival strategy or in pursuit of aspirations for social upward mobility."

Insecurities among migrant workers in Malaysia became more pronounced during the three-month-long partial lockdown, known as the MCO (Movement Control Order). After the Perikatan

Nasional (PN) government took over the national leadership (23 February 2020), the MCO was declared and implemented. Although the COVID-19 pandemic has impacted the lives of Malaysian citizens, non-Malaysians citizens - especially migrant workers - were impacted even more. Not only were migrants involved in the cluster event responsible for a large portion of COVID-19 infections, they were also excluded from the relief package administered by the PN government during the MCO.

The coronavirus infection in Malaysia spiked in March after 12,000 attendees of an Islamic religious movement called the Tabligh[4], including about 2000 Rohingya refugees, gathered in a Sri Petaling mosque in Kuala Lumpur on 27 February-01 March for their annual regional meeting. This cluster was partly responsible for the increase in COVID-19 cases in West Malaysia, Sabah, and Sarawak. The Malaysian government found it challenging to conduct contact tracing for such a large group, especially the undocumented Tabligh members. As of 24 May, there have been 115 recorded deaths in Malaysia and over 7000 cases of infection, with an estimated 50% of infected cases linked to the Sri Petaling cluster.

When the MCO was declared, the PN government put forward a massive relief package of RM250 billion (approximately $58 million US dollars) to cushion the negative economic impact of COVID-19 on the citizens of the country. The relief package was extended to people in the lowest economic category of B40[5] ("bottom 40%") up to the employers of small and business enterprises. However, non-citizens, including both documented and undocumented immigrants, migrants and refugees, were not eligible for aid from the relief package. As the MCO progressed, migrant workers requested food aid from Non-Government Organizations (NGOs) and friendship networks. As daily wage workers in various industries, most migrants were stuck in their flats without employment throughout the MCO and worked for some employers who did not offer to pay or feed them during the period they were without work.

Virtual resistance as a form of activism: MCO and COVID-19

Historically, migrant workers have been at the forefront while challenging their conditions of vulnerability and precarity. Across time and space, workers have always negotiated their positions, more so in the digital era. The internet and other digital technologies have enabled migrant workers to connect with broader networks of people to help them fight for better conditions. Here we reflect on what transpired among the migrant communities in Malaysia during the MCO as a result of the global COVID-19 pandemic. This section is organized around three themes of resistance action: 1) Resistance through aid wherein community leaders and NGOs worked together to provide resources to migrants and block the state's attempts to use the MCO to identify, arrest, and deport undocumented workers; 2) Resistance through networks in which friends, employers, other migrants helped migrants survive during the MCO; and 3) Resistance through redundancy in which migrant workers feigned ignorance about aid to get additional aid. These themes form part of the ongoing resistance acts of migrant workers, which may transform the landscape of collective insecurity.

---

4 Tabligh is a religious movement with vast numbers of followers from all over Asia, which makes it a major social force underpinned by religious belief.

5 B40 is a category of household whose mean income is RM2,537 and a median income of RM2,629

Resistance Through Aid

The first small form of resistance observed on behalf of migrant workers involved community leaders and NGO's working together to provide aid to migrants during the MCO and blocking the state's attempts to use the MCO to "potentially" identify, locate and deport undocumented workers. Two local-based migrant NGOs, Our Journey and AMMPO[6] (Asosasyon ng mga Manggagawang Pilipino Overseas Malaysia), started organising the distribution of food aid packages[7] to Filipino and Indonesian domestic workers around Kuala Lumpur, Petaling Jaya, and the suburbs within the immediate vicinity of Kuala Lumpur. Everyday both groups received requests that ranged from food to diapers, formula milk, and sanitary pads (see for example Figure 1). The Our Journey teams purchased and distributed relief packages; meanwhile, AMMPO screened through the aid list, with names, locations and mobile numbers of affected migrants. As the food aid continued during the period of the MCO, Our Journey negotiated and collaborated with foreign embassies, including the Indonesian and Bangladeshi embassies, to reach out to affected thousands of migrant workers.

Figure 1. An AMMPO member packing food essentials to be distributed around Kuala Lumpur

Source: Lumayag, 2020(a). Aliran, 12 April 2020.

---

[6] Association of Filipino Workers Overseas
[7] Food aid packages contained 5 kg of rice, 1 liter cooking oil, 5 cans sardines, 1 kg sugar, 1 pack of 3-in-1 coffee, 1 kg noodles, 5 packs instant noodles, 1 tray (30 pcs) eggs, onions and garlic

Because movement was severely restricted during the MCO period, the implementation of aid programs was strictly monitored and proved to be extremely difficult and challenging for the NGOs delivering aid packages. To pass through police roadblocks, the NGO teams needed to show a permit issued by a foreign embassy allowing resource distribution to their nationals. During the first week of the movement restriction, NGOs were required to send all donations to the government for distribution through the Department of Social Welfare. After less than a week, the PN government relented and withdrew the restriction due to widespread protests from NGOs who were especially worried about the safety of undocumented migrant workers.

During the MCO, the government promised a moratorium on arrests and detention for millions of undocumented workers. However, this moratorium did not occur. On 01 May, organised arrests and detention occurred in downtown Kuala Lumpur along Jalan Masjid India where Malaya Mansion and Selangor Mansion are located. This area is home to the cluster that was thought to have started the spike of coronavirus infection among migrant workers. Close to 3,300 foreign workers were tested and 586 of them were undocumented workers. Although none of the undocumented workers tested positive for coronavirus, they were all sent to the nearest immigration depot to be deported. This action against migrant workers triggered online protests coordinated by labour unions, migrant communities, and NGOs arguing that raids, detentions and deportations were counterproductive. The United Nations office in Kuala Lumpur condemned the arrests in a widely shared press statement and offered to find alternatives to detention.

The global network of migration groups engaged in advocacy, organised webinar discussions about human rights issues, and suggested potential strategies should the arrests continue during the MCO. The plan to centralise the distribution of food aid to citizens and non-citizens was vehemently resisted by local groups and civil society organisations. Those opposed to state intervention or "assistance" in relief efforts feared the government would attempt to control and dominate the relief operations as well as use the aid distribution to monitor the locations of undocumented workers.

When the Philippine Embassy urged the distribution teams of Our Journey and AMMPO to provide them with a list of recipients before the embassy would release its letter of consent allowing food distribution to Filipino nationals, both groups reacted strongly against this demand. Rather than work with embassies directly, undocumented workers preferred to rely on migrant groups who connected with the embassy that represented the sending country (e.g., Philippines, Indonesia, Bangladesh). Many undocumented workers preferred not even to be seen receiving food packs, but some relented since their masks largely preserved their anonymity.

In Sarawak, undocumented workers in massage and beauty salons, restaurants, and construction experienced a work stoppage, which made it extremely difficult for them to survive. Sarawak holds a relatively high number of undocumented foreign workers, estimated at around 300,000 in 2015 (The Malay Mail, 11 April 2015). During the MCO, the state government seemed to downplay the presence of undocumented population in Sarawak. Nonetheless, during the third week of the MCO, two community leaders received persistent calls allegedly from someone representing a formal institution inquiring whether the Philippine Embassy was planning on sending money to purchase food for its nationals working in Sarawak, and if the community leaders wanted the caller's assistance with the food deliveries. Before these suspicious phone calls, the plan was for the community leaders to distribute the deliveries on their own by visiting the recipients at home. After handing the goods to recipients, the recipients would have their photo taken, and the photo would be uploaded to Facebook for documentation and public sharing.

The calls from the allegedly friendly officers caused the Sarawak community leaders to revise their plans. Instead they made their distribution practice more low profile to protect the identities of recipients and avoid having their food distribution become controlled by the state as it had in Kuala Lumpur. In Kuala Lumpur, where there was strict adherence to movement protocols, a measure passed that stated uniformed personnel had to accompany local distribution teams to each and every location of beneficiaries, which put the security of all undocumented citizens at risk. Thus, in Sarawak, the call from the "friendly" personnel catalysed a shift in distribution practices to avoid further attention from the state. The community leaders negotiated with local grocers to deliver the food packs directly to undocumented workers. They also stopped taking photos and sharing them on Facebook, which is what the Kuala Lumpur teams had done. On Facebook, photo uploads featuring food recipients were swiftly deleted to protect privacy. Most online surveys regarding aid also stopped and people, especially those who were undocumented workers, were warned not to participate in any online surveys unless they had thoroughly vetted the source of the survey. The community leaders were informed again that a "friendly officer" received a call from the embassy informing him of plans to distribute food packs after the MCO. The officer demanded that the authorities be informed if and when further aid was sent to the area.

Although the state used the MCO to further marginalize the already-vulnerable migrant worker population in Malaysia, community leaders, NGOs, and migrant workers used covert online and on-the-ground organising to protect workers' identities and deliver much needed aid to migrant communities.

Resistance Through Networks

The second small form of resistance observed on behalf of migrant workers involved assistance from neighbourhoods, friends, employers, and other migrant workers. Undocumented Indonesian workers in the construction industry relied mostly on their local friends[8] to survive. The Indonesian Embassy facilitated the distribution of food aid packages across geographical locations from Kuala Lumpur to Shah Alam, Klang as well as the Selangor areas and states in Western Malaysia. The Indonesian Embassy must have realised that it was impossible to reach out to migrant workers without logistical assistance from civil society groups and migrant communities. One Indonesian group of domestic workers known as PERTIMIG (Persatuan Pekerja Rumah Tangga Indonesia Migran)[9] in Kuala Lumpur assisted by organising the list of recipients and following up on distribution by keeping the donors of food aid informed. Indonesians represent a higher percentage of undocumented workers because of the shared and porous borders between Indonesia, East Malaysia, and the West Malaysia.

Since non-citizens did not receive any form of assistance from the PN government, migrant workers relied on networks of new friends. Organised based on interests (e.g. sports, religion, regional associations), migrant workers are connected with other Kuala Lumpur-based migrant communities. These communities extended as much help as they could to one another, even if it meant receiving less for themselves. For example, domestic workers who lived with employers quietly sent rations to their other friends across the geographical locations without even leaving the house. These domestic workers used their established Grab or taxi contacts to ferry rations to friends who did not live in their employers' homes. Sometimes, those live-out friends collected the goods

---

[8] Contextually referring to documented Indonesian immigrants who have "better" social position as opposed to undocumented Indonesian immigrants or migrant workers.

[9] PERTIMIG is Association of Indonesian Migrant Domestic Workers

from live-in domestic workers, prepared or cooked them, and then packed the food to be sent to others in need. For example, they baked bread and distributed portions of it to friends.

Migrant workers connected with friends and services in important ways using social media platforms. Most migrant workers have Facebook accounts, but during the MCO, undocumented workers were less active on Facebook, preferring instead to lie low, in case their accounts were being surveilled. WhatsApp became a much more popular social app because it offered more privacy. Some Indonesian workers used their documented friends' names to link to NGOs like Our Journey, AMMPO and PERTIMIG and escaped perceived potential surveillance.

Although Malaysian citizens may have received cash assistance from the Federal and State governments, a number of undocumented internal migrant workers (for example, Sarawakians) who could not access the application via the government online system were left out in the process. Instead, these internal migrants relied on their friendships with other foreign workers. Thus, a small number of internal migrants benefitted from the generosity of fellow migrants, as observed in Sarawak, East Malaysia.

Migrant workers in Malaysia also received much needed assistance from well-meaning Malaysian citizens. In some cases, employers of live-in foreign domestic workers attempted to "adopt" a few migrant workers and their families, providing them with basic foodstuffs to survive through the MCO. Nonetheless, there were also complaints from employees whose employers did not provide food for their workers.

J (name withheld), a 32-year-old, undocumented worker worked in a restaurant for 11 months before the MCO. J considered the husband-wife owners of the restaurant to be good people. However, throughout the MCO, his employers never asked him whether he had food to eat. He has also not been paid since the partial lockdown. We later asked J if he still thought his employers were good people, to which he just kept silent. According to J, he did not want to sound too demanding by asking for anything, because he was afraid that after the MCO he would be fired, which was the case for many of his friends. J wanted to earn enough money to buy a plane ticket and pay the overstaying fee on his compound.

In another situation, M, a full-time domestic worker, was paid half of her monthly salary as part of the employer's negotiation to keep her employed. M confided that she would rather take half her salary than return to the Philippines to join thousands of overseas Filipino workers (OFWs) retrenched abroad due to COVID-19.

Another group of five wood furniture makers reported that they experienced hunger, despite the plentiful stocks of rice and piles of noodles in the warehouse owned by their employer. The employer had not offered them anything since the MCO began. When a local religious charity offered them food and RM200 (approximately $46 US dollars) cash per worker, they were overcome with emotion.

Resistance Through Redundancy

Finally, migrant workers resisted the state and fought off surveillance by looking for redundancies within the aid system. One way workers did this was by denying that they received any form of food assistance from aid organisations even if they had. One group knew that their request for more food assistance would likely be denied by the Philippine government. Yet, when the list reached a migrant advocacy group in Kuala Lumpur, the request was referred to the office of the Welfare Attaché for the Overseas Welfare Work Association (OWWA) and granted in less than three days. Seventeen families with children received a food pack worth RM40 (approx. $9 US) each per family. We did an online chat with one of the recipients who said, "We are just testing the waters. If the government gives, well and good; if it doesn't, at least we tried." Some workers even capitalise on several friendship networks to be able to receive as much food packages as they could (Figure 2).

Figure 2. A sample of food pack distributed during the first phase of MCO

Source: Lumayag (2020a), Aliran, 12 April 2020.

Conclusion: forging a new engagement through virtual activism?

Amidst abundant threats today, human insecurity is omnipresent. The onset of COVID-19 globally and the ensuing MCO lockdown in Malaysia brought the economy to its knees. Those who have been most affected are daily wage earners, who constitute 85% of migrant workers, working in small and medium industries, and the foreign domestic workers confined to private homes. Millions of migrant workers are located in non-essential services such as domestic work, beauty salons, hotels, and restaurants. At the lifting of the first phase of the MCO, after two months, some workers were already issued a travel exit pass, while other workers waited it out and reconsidered plans of returning home.

Could the new socio-political landscape as a result of the pandemic give way to a new mode of activist engagement that is more virtually visible? Workers who were able to wait out the crisis survived the critical two months under confinement because of engagement with other migrant communities and new alliances with advocacy groups (Hansen, 2019). Moving forward, can they sustain their virtual political engagement to mitigate insecurities and to improve their work conditions (Gurowitz, 2000; Basok, 2010; Piper et al., 2016)? Will this crisis lay the groundwork to push for more social protection? At the same time, has the pandemic created a deepened digital surveillance that risks civil liberties and rights, just as migrant workers have realised the importance of virtual resistance to achieve change? These questions raise possibilities for generating new knowledge that would help understand the new landscape for human action within the context of a global pandemic.

References

Anderson, C. W. (2013). Youth, the "Arab Spring and Social Movements. Review of Middle East Studies, 47 (2), 150-156.

Basok, T. (2010). Opening a dialogue on migrant (rights) activism. Studies in Social Justice, 4(2): 97.

Bauman, Z. (1998). In Search of Politics. UK: Polity Press.

Bauman, Z. (2016). Strangers at our Door. UK: Polity Press.

Chin, C. B. N. (1998). In service and servitude: Foreign female domestic workers and the Malaysian "modernity" project. New York: Columbia University Press.

Chung, H. and S. Mau (2014). Subjective insecurity and the role of institutions. Journal of European Social Policy, 24(4): 303-318.

Cohen, J. H. (2020). Editorial: Modeling Migration, Insecurity and COVID-19. Migration Letters, 17(3): 405-410.

Cohen, J. H. and I. Sirkeci (2011). Cultures of migration: the global nature of contemporary mobility. Austin: University of Texas Press.

Constable, N. (1997). Maid to order in Hong Kong: Stories of Filipina workers. Ithaca & London: Cornell University Press.

Costa, E. (2013). The Wider World: politics, the visible and invisible. Social Media in Southeast Turkey, 3(1): 128-162.

Del Rosario, T. C. and J. Rigg (2019). Introduction. "Special Issue on Precarity in Asia." Journal of Contemporary Asia, 49(4): 517-527. https://www.tandfonline.com/doi/full/10.1080/00472336.2019.1581832

Foucault, M. (1997). Society Must be Defended. New York City, NY, USA: Picador.

Gurowitz, A. (2000). Migrant rights and activism in Malaysia: Opportunities and constraints. The Journal of Asian Studies, 59(4): 863-888.

Hacker, J. S. (2006). The Great Risk Shift: The Assault on American Jobs, Families and Health Care, and Retirement and How you can Fight Back. New York: Oxford University Press.

Hall, S. (1978). Policing the Crisis: Mugging, the state and law 'n' order. London: Macmillan.

Hansen, C. (2019). Solidarity in Diversity: Activism as a Pathway of Migrant Emplacement in Melano. Doctoral Thesis, University of Malmo.

Kassim, A. (2013). Current trends in transnational population in Malaysia: Issues, policy and challenges. In: International Population Conference on Migration, Urbanisation & Development. Unpublished work, Faculty of Economics and Administration, University of Malaya.

Kaur, A. (2014). Managing labour migration in Malaysia: Guest worker programs and the regularisation of irregular labour migrants as a policy instrument. Asian Studies Review, 38(3), 345–366.

Lee, J. C. H. (2018). Women's Activism in Malaysia. Voices and Insights. Cham, Switzerland: Palgrave Pivot. https://doi.org/10.1007/978-3-319-78969-9

Lyons, L. (2007). Dignity Overdue: Women's Rights Activism in Support of Foreign Domestic Workers in Singapore. Women's Studies Quarterly 35(3): 106-122.

Lumayag, L.A. (2018). Contesting Disciplinary Power: Transnational Domestic Labour in the Global South. Asian Studies Review, 42(1): 161-177. DOI: 10.1080/10357823.2017.1413072

Lumayag, L. A. (2020a). Undocumented migrants: strangers, 'moral panics' and betrayal of trust. https://aliran.com/thinking- allowed-online/strangers-moral-panics-and-betrayal-of-trust/

Lumayag, L. A. (2020b). Fear, now hunger: undocumented in the time of coronavirus. https://aliran.com/thinking-allowed-online/fear-now-hunger-undocumented-in-the-time-of-coronavirus/

Miller, D. et al. (2016). How the World Changed Social Media. California: UCL Press. http://www.jstor.org/stable/j.ctt1g69z35.9

Ong, A. (1987). Spirits of resistance and capitalist discipline: Factory women in Malaysia. New York: State University of New York Press.

Ong, Aihwa (1999). Flexible Citizenship: The Cultural Logics of Transnationality. UK: Duke University Press.

Parreñas, R. (2001). Servants of globalisation: Women, migration and domestic work. Stanford: Stanford University Press.

Piper, N. (2013). 'Resisting Inequality: Global Migrant Rights Activism'. In T. Bastia (ed.) Migration and Inequality, pp. 45–64. New York: Routledge.

Piper, N. (2015). 'Democratising Migration from the Bottom Up: The Rise of the Global Migrant Rights Movement', Globalizations, 12(5): 788–802.

Piper, N. and S. Rother (2011). 'Transnational Inequalities, Transnational Responses: The Politicisation of Migrant Rights in Asia'. In B. Rehbein (ed.) Globalisation and Inequality in Emerging Societies, pp. 235–55. London: Palgrave Macmillan.

Piper, N. and A. Uhlin (2002). Transnational advocacy networks and the issue of female labour migration and trafficking in East and South East Asia: A gendered analysis of opportunities and obstacles. Asian and Pacific Migration Journal, 11(2): 171-196.

Piper, N. et al. (2016). Redefining a Rights-based approach in the context of temporary labour migration in Asia. UNRISD Working Papers 2016-11. http://www.unrisd.org/80256B3C005BCCF9/(httpAuxPages)/72E2E53E545B067BC 12580250043BA1D/$file/Piper%20et%20al.pdf

Sadiq, K. (2005). When states prefer non-citizens over citizens: Conflict over illegal immigration into Malaysia. International Studies Quarterly, 49(1), 101–122.

Scott, J. (1985). Weapons of the weak: Everyday forms of peasant resistance. New Haven & London: Yale University Press.

Scott, J. (1990). Domination and the arts of resistance – hidden transcripts. New Haven & London: Yale University Press.

Sirkeci, I. (2009). Transnational mobility and conflict. *Migration Letters*, 6(1), 3-14.

The Malay Mail. https://www.malaymail.com/news/malaysia/2015/04/11/illegal-immigrants-in-sarawak-a-huge-problem- deputy- home-minister-admits/876739

United Nations Department of Economic and Social Affairs (2008) 'World Economic and Social Survey 2008: Overcoming Economic Insecurity.' http://www.un.org/en/development/desa/policy/ wess/wess_archive/2008wess.pdf

Vietti, F. and T. Scribner (2013). Human Insecurity: Understanding International Migration from a Human Security Perspective. Journal on Migration and Human Security, 1: 17-31731731.

September 2020
Volume: 17, **No**: 5, pp. 733 – 746
ISSN: 1741-8984
e-ISSN: 1741-8992
www.migrationletters.com

MIGRATION
LETTERS

First Submitted: 17 February 2020 Accepted: 2 May 2020
DOI: https://doi.org/10.33182/ml.v17i5.925

CASE STUDY:

Foreign Workers in Malaysia

Sheikh Mohammad Maniruzzaman Al Masud[1], Rohana Binti Hamzah[2] and Hasan Ahmad[3]

Abstract

Malaysia has become a popular destination for many foreign workers since getting independence in 1957, owing to its rapidly growing economy and industrialisation. Most of the migrant workers in Malaysia are low-skilled or uneducated, and public debate is going on their outcome, whether it is substantial or not. The purpose of this study is to manifest the role and contribution of imported labour to the Malaysian economy. Evidence is collected from secondary sources- journal article, relevant books, and online databases. The review finds that the impact of migrant labour on Malaysian growth has not been studied holistically and sufficiently. Existing evidence shows that although it is somewhat positive, the public attitude is most adverse to illegal and irregular migrants. Therefore, more empirical research is required to determine the role of imported temporary workers on the economy of Malaysia, for its ongoing vision- to become a high-income nation.

Keywords: low-skilled foreign workers; economic growth; employment; productivity; development.

Introduction

Human migration, an age-old phenomenon, relates to economic, social, political and technological transformations that affect both the source and receiving countries, as well as transit countries. Almost 3.5% of the world's population were international migrants globally in 2019, which equates to around 272 million people out of a global population of 7.7 billion, or 1 in every 30 people (IOM, 2019). Among them, 164 million were migrant workers—nearly 60% of total international immigrants. Recently, international labour migration has been considered one of the key global issues that affect almost every nation's socio-economic development (ILO, 2010). The *World Migration Report 2020* mentions that Malaysia ranked 18th (3.4 million people) among the top 20 destination countries of international migrants in 2019 (IOM, 2019), at 10.7% of the total population on 1 July 2019 (UNDESA, 2019).

In the last three decades, Malaysia has witnessed a hasty upsurge of immigration, mainly due to its speedily expanding economy, increasing urbanisation (ILO, 2016), burgeoning industrial plans (Othman & Rohani, 2017), the relatively cheap cost of foreign labour (Ramlee, 2017), and acute labour shortages in the countryside owing to low levels of participation from local citizens

---

[1] Sheikh Mohammad Maniruzzaman Al Masud, PhD Student, Centre for Human Sciences, Universiti Malaysia PAHANG, Malaysia. E-mail: PBS17011@stdmail.ump.edu.my.
[2] Dr Rohana binti Hamzah, Senior Lecturer, Centre for Human Sciences, Universiti Malaysia PAHANG, Malaysia. E-mail: rohanahamzah@ump.edu.my.
[3] Dr Hasan Ahmad, Associate Professor, Centre for Human sciences, Universiti Malaysia PAHANG, Malaysia. E-mail: hasanahmad@ump.edu.my.

(Kassim, 2017). Immigration involves mainly low-skilled foreign workers, who are now responsible for roughly 20% to 30% of the total Malaysian workforce (ILO, 2016). Almost one-third of the workforce of the agricultural, manufacturing, and construction sectors in Malaysia are migrants (ILO, 2016). Based on job distribution, the manufacturing industry carries the highest percentage of migrant workers (36%), while the construction and plantation sectors have 19% and 15%, respectively (figure 1). Many of the rest are in the services (14%) agriculture (9%), and domestic maid (7%) sectors (Loh, Simler, Wei, & Yi, 2019). Malaysia is among the countries in East Asia and the Pacific with the highest ratio (figure 2) of migrants to the total population (UNDESA, 2019).

Figure 1. Sectoral distribution of foreign workers in Malaysia.

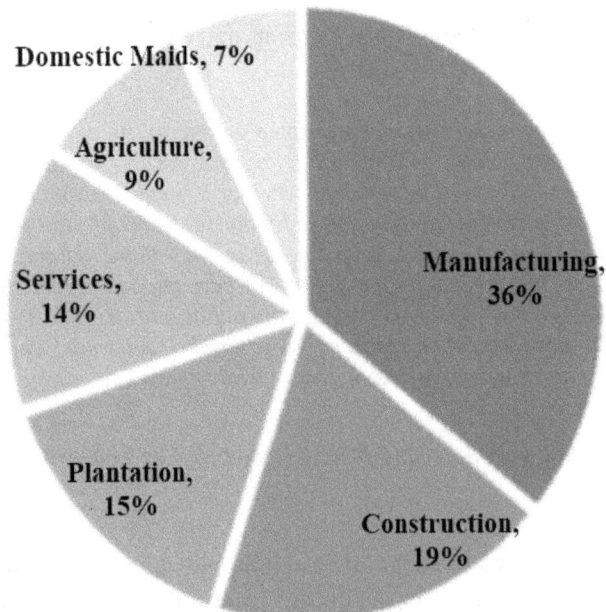

Source: Loh, W. S., Simler, K., Wei, K. T., & Yi, S. (2019), p.20

According to the Ministry of Home Affairs' records (2000–2015), the major source countries of labour are Indonesia, Nepal, Bangladesh, Myanmar, Thailand, Philippines, Pakistan, and India (Ramlee, 2017). The first four countries mentioned above are active source countries based on their supply pattern. Although the management of migrant workers in Malaysia is focused at the apex level of policymakers, the real number of temporary imported labour workers is extremely difficult to determine because different sources denote this in various ways. Following to government report, the number of total migrant labourers was 6.7 million in 2014, and this dropped to 3.8 million in 2016 (Hwok-Aun & Leng, 2018). According to the Malaysian Employers Federation (MEF), the total number of estimated foreign workers (both legal and illegal) is 6 million, whereas The Associated Chinese Chambers of Commerce and Industry of Malaysia (ACCCIM) suggests that 1:2 would be the ratio of legal and illegal foreign workers (Ramlee, 2017). The number of low-skilled migrant workers has now escalated to over 93% of foreigners in Malaysia, and most of them work in Peninsular Malaysia, where manufacturing takes the top position for its rapid industrialisation, while Sabah and Sarawak depend more on agriculture and plantations (Kassim, 2017).

Malaysia has a vision to become a high-income nation (WorldBank, 2015), and it needs both high- and low-skilled workers to achieve the target. However, excessive numbers of low-skilled labourers and irregular migrants create immense pressure on the economy of Malaysia, an issue which has been discussed frequently. Many scholars believe that Malaysia will remain a low-wage and low-skill destination due to a heavy reliance on low-skilled migrant workers, and economic transformation through automation will be less likely to be achieved. Malaysia's has become increasingly concerned about the vast number of immigrants, both legal and illegal (Kassim, 2017). Recent policy has mainly emphasised dealing with foreign labour to ensure Malaysia becomes a high-income nation by 2020 by facilitating growth and reducing the negative aftermath of the economy and society (Kanapathy, 2006). Malaysia would become a high-income country if its economy were to be globally competitive and resource-sustainable for future generations (Rafael, 2016).

Figure 2. Share of total migrants to population- regional peers of Malaysia.

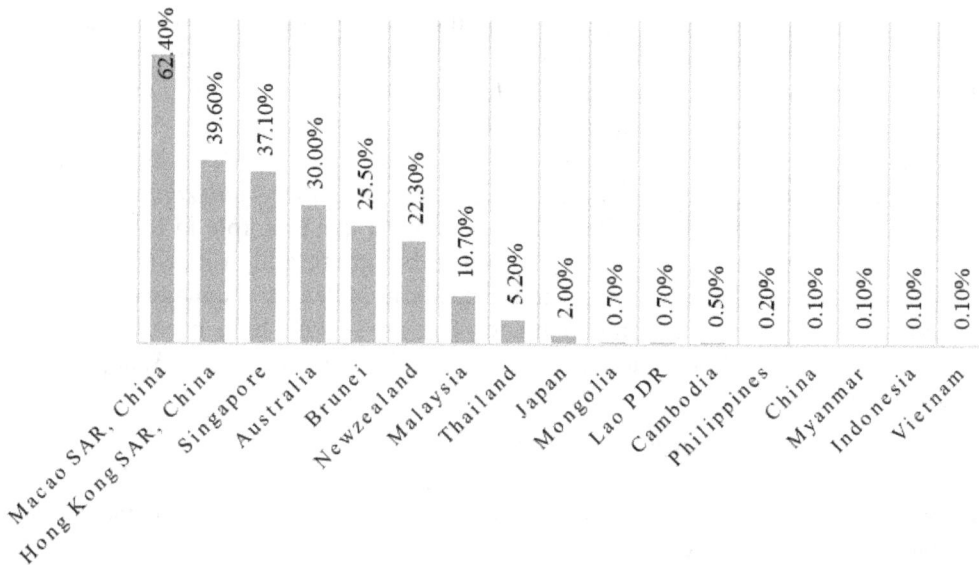

Source: UNDESA (2019), p.1

The core aim of this study is to explore, integrate, and evaluate the recent economic development and achievements of Malaysia in connection with international labour migration. Malaysia has tremendous experiences with foreign worker issues, as its economy has long benefited from a supportive immigration stance. This study has accumulated information on almost all recent development features, as well as challenges, and examines to what extent foreign workers in Malaysia are a boon or bane for its economy and development.

Method

In this study, secondary sources are the main method of data collection. These sources are relevant books and articles (on migrant labour in Malaysia) or official statistics and reports produced by the Malaysian government and international organisations such as ILO, IOM, UN DESA, and the World Bank. Some prominent Malaysian migration researchers are also covered. Pertinent information from newspaper/journal reports and articles are utilised. The content analysis method is used to obtain consistent findings and outcomes. This study did not follow any specific theoretical framework.

Results and Discussion

The International Labour Organisation clearly mentions that the impact of foreign workers on destination countries is not as well documented as that on origin countries (ILO, 2010). Though many researchers and academicians have attempted to address the issue of migrant labour in Peninsular Malaysia, the contribution of migrant labour to Malaysian development has not been assessed seriously (Ismail & Yuliyusman, 2014). The government of Malaysia always gives priority to national security and people's safety, when it creates policy around immigrant labourers, rather than concentrating on their immense involvement in the country's development (ILO, 2016). Empirical research on the contributions of low-skilled imported workers in Malaysia is scarce, and existing studies have tended to concentrate mostly on the manufacturing sector (Devadas, 2017).

Impact on the Economy

Migrants workers have played a crucial role in the Malaysian economy since their arrival in this region. The World Bank's senior economist, Rafael Munoz Moreno (2016), states that two remarkable achievements, one being the eradication of extreme poverty and the other the promotion of inclusive growth, have occurred in Malaysia over the previous few decades (Rafael, 2016). One of the major sources of the impact of foreign workers on the economic development of Malaysia has been the World Bank's report titled *Malaysia Economic Monitor: Immigrant Labour*, in which it was noted that both skilled and unskilled labour had had a dynamic role in Malaysia's growth, and both are needed to achieve the country's vision of becoming a high-income nation by 2020 (Cecilia, 2018). As education levels have risen drastically in Malaysia, the majority of Malaysians are now seeking higher-skilled jobs, and contracted foreign workers have been needed to fill the gaps in at the bottom of the labour market, mostly in low- to mid-skilled jobs (WorldBank, 2015). The findings of the report are presented in Table 1

Another World Bank assessment strongly supported migrant labour as an enabler for development and stated that migrant workers, "… generate jobs for Malaysians by reducing costs of production making Malaysian firms cheaper and more competitive in the global market, allowing them to expand and consequently increasing their demand for Malaysian workers." (WorldBank, 2013, p-11 cited in Kassim 2017). The report also highlights that, whilst expatriates (highly skilled) remains on the top and do not displace local workers, hence having a negligible influence on the wages and employment of Malay citizens whereas a mammoth number of low-skilled workforces stay at the bottom of the Malaysian job hierarchy (Kassim, 2017).

Some sectors are treated as pivotal to growth, for example, manufacturing, construction and palm oil; while remaining profitable and competitive, these sectors profoundly rely on unskilled foreign workers (Kanapathy, 2006). These so-called problematic low-skilled workers are also consumers who can play a positive role in the creation of demand for daily commodities such as food, clothing, housing, medical services, banking, and transportation services (Kassim, 2001).

Some studies specify the correlation between migrant workers and economic growth is positive, owing to the creation of jobs and capital accumulation, whereas many others believe that unskilled immigrants plummet economic growth (Ramlee, 2017). For instance, the Bank Negara Malaysia differs in its opinion on foreign labour productivity. It perceives that the productivity of industries negatively correlates (figure 7) with the share of foreigners (Wei, Murugasu, & Wei, 2018a).

Table 1. Findings of the World Bank's report.

Serial	Issues	Results
01	An influx of 10 new foreign workers in a given state or sector	Creates 5.2 new jobs for Malaysians (figure 3), 2 of them are female (WorldBank, 2015)
02	A 10% net increase of low-skilled foreign labour	May upsurge real gross domestic product (GDP) of Malaysia by 1.1% (Rafael, 2016)
		Slightly increases the wages of local people (Malaysian) by 0.14% (Melissa, 2015)
		Decreases wages of the least-educated Malaysians by 0.74% (figure 4), who represent 14% of the total labour force (Cecilia, 2018)
		Reduces significantly salaries of existing migrant workers (figure 5), who are already in Malaysia, by 3.9% (WorldBank, 2015)
03	Low-skilled immigrants in Malaysia	Fill workforce gaps, reduce production costs, increase investment and expand output and exports (Melissa, 2015)
04	Untrained migrant labourers	Create demand for skilled Malaysian employees and contribute to the country's economic growth (Melissa, 2015)
05	The fiscal impact of legal immigration	Is likely to be small (WorldBank, 2015)
06	Documented unskilled immigrant workers pay levies for work permits	Created 1.2% of the total national revenues of Malaysia in 2014 (WorldBank, 2015)
07	Legal low-skilled foreign labourers raise wages and employment	Which in turn contribute to public revenue (WorldBank, 2015)
08	Documented migrant workers (both high and low-skilled) have health insurance	This reduces the burden on the government of Malaysia (WorldBank, 2015)
09	Undocumented and illegal foreign workers in Malaysia	Create a fiscal burden for the government (Melissa, 2015)
10	The influx of foreign labor	Has a negative impact on the wages of some groups of Malaysians (Cecilia, 2018)
11	Firms with migrant workers	Value added (figure 6) per worker (Moreno et al., 2015)

Figure 3. An additional 10 new immigrants increase the employment of local citizens

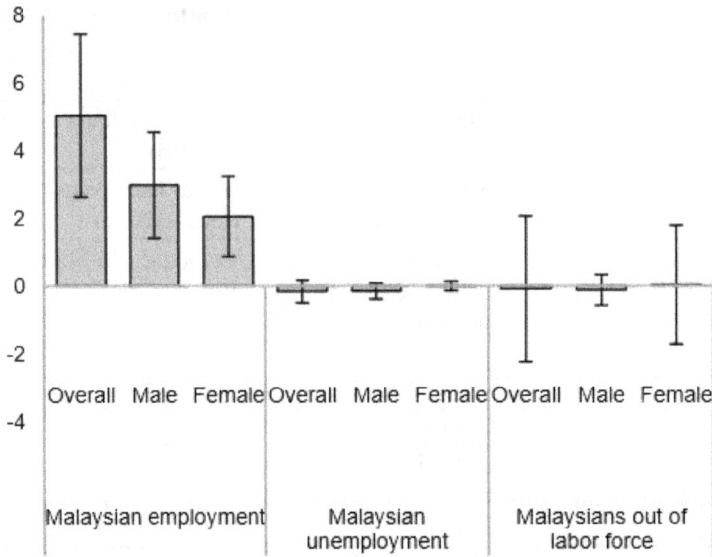

Source: WorldBank (2015), p.42.

Figure 4. The impact of immigration on the wages of Malaysians differs based on their educational background

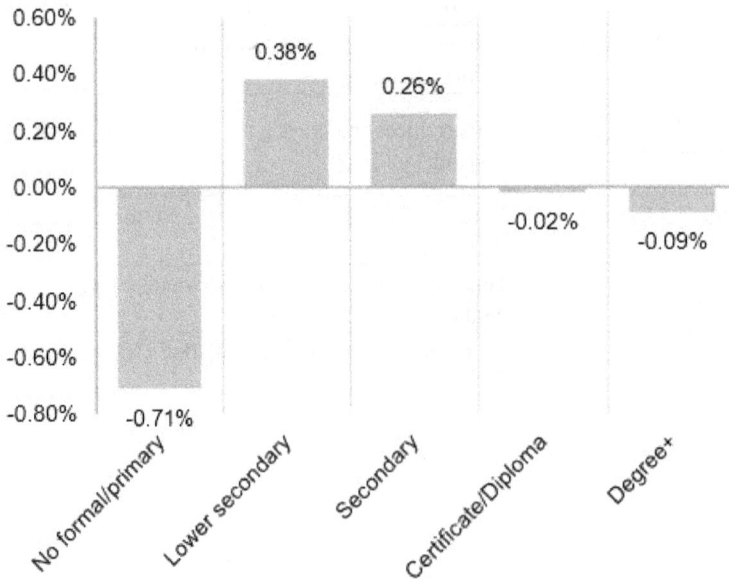

Source: Özden & Wagner (2014), p.43.

Figure 5. A 10% increase of foreign labourers causes a small upsurge in the wages of Malaysians, but reductions in immigrant workers' wages

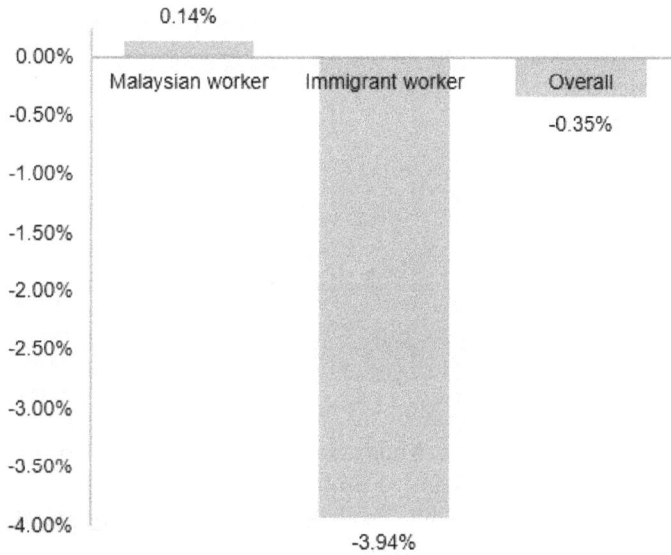

Source: Özden & Wagner (2014), p.43.

Figure 6. Firms with immigrant workers have higher value-added per worker

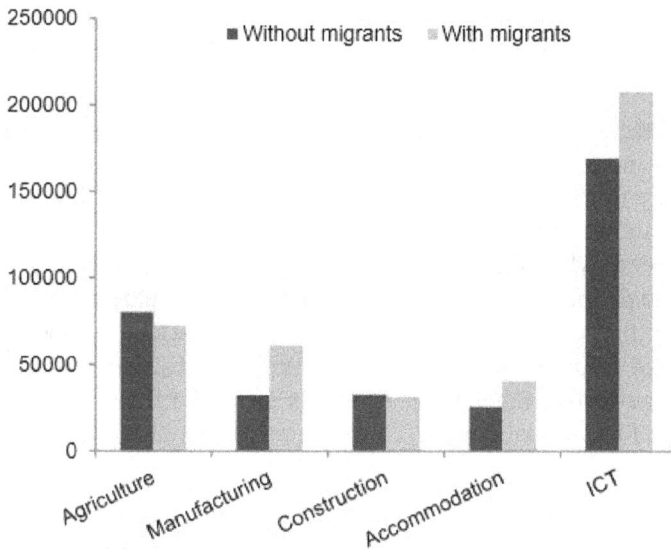

Source: Moreno et al. (2015), p.44.

Figure 7: Productivity and share of foreigners by industry

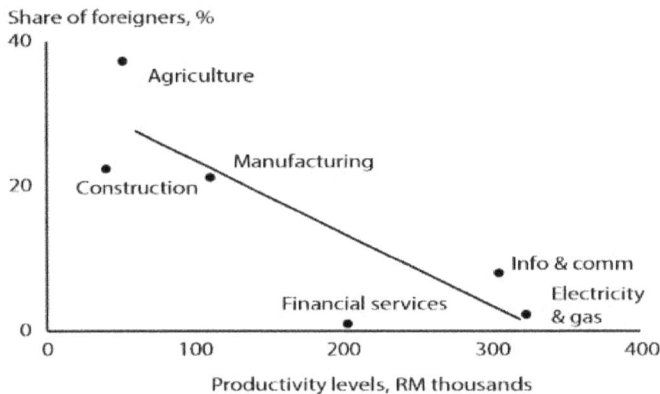

Source: Wei, Murugasu, & Wei (2018b), p.5.

Foreign workers have played a vital role in Malaysia's plantation sector from the very beginning when they entered this land. Malaysia has 1.4 million hectares of palm oil plantations, which largely rely on foreign workers (78%), with locals representing the remainder of the workforce (22%) (Ramlee, 2017, p-11). Indonesians primarily work in the plantation sector as harvesters. Palm fruits need to be processed within 24 hours after harvesting. The country has long suffered from a loss in the form of unharvested fruits because of the time at the mills being too long, due to insufficient labour (Ahmad, 2019). Without the migrant labour force, the plantation sector would be unable to function. Palm oil investors worry about this because as Indonesia expands its plantations, Malaysia will lose more harvesters (Ahmad, 2019). Low-skilled foreign workers commonly engage in so-called 3D jobs (dirty, dangerous, and demeaning), which locals shun. Nevertheless, these jobs form a critical element of the Malaysian economic jigsaw (Ahmad, 2019). He also mentions that the ongoing highway projects cannot proceed without workers from Bangladesh.

Nizam et al. (2017) studied the effect of the influx of low-skilled immigrants on Malaysian economic growth based on MRW model or Mankiw-Romer-Weil model (Nizam, Ahmad, & Aziz, 2017). Following this model, they found that the rate of human capital, stock of knowledge and skills, decreased for domestic labour from 0.6855 to 0.6661 (2010 to 2013) because of the participation rate of them is lessened, while the rate of human capital for foreign labour increased from 0.0745 to 0.1040 for the same period due to sharply swelling their involvement ratio. Whereas, it was also found from their study that physical capital accumulation per effective labour with the presence and the absence of foreign labour differs significantly. With the absence of foreign labour physical capital accumulation per effective labour was 3.5158 in 2013. On the other hand, it was 3.0756 in 2013 with the presence of foreign labour. So, employment of migrants reduces the rate of physical capital.

A study of the case of the impact of immigration on employment of Malaysia's native workers found that scale effects outweigh substitution effects (Özden & Wagner, 2014). Approximately one-third of the agricultural, manufacturing, and construction workforce is migrants; these are industries which collectively contributed MYR 297 billion (US$ 68 billion), or 35.7% of Malaysia's gross domestic product, in 2014 (ILO, 2016).

Table 2. Some studies related to the impact of foreign workers on the manufacturing sector.

Serial	Name	Topic	Findings
01	Zaleha Mohd Noor Noraini Isa Rusmawati Said and Suhaila Abd Jalil (Noor, Isa, Said, & Jalil, 2017)	The Impact of Foreign Workers on Labor Productivity in the Malaysian Manufacturing Sector	If there is a 1% increase in foreign labour, productivity will increase by 0.172%. Foreign labour neither complements nor substitutes for local labour.
02	Nasri Bachtiar, Rahmi Fahmy and Rahmah Ismail (Bachtiar, Fahmy, & Ismail, 2017)	The Demand for Foreign Workers in the Manufacturing Sector in Malaysia	Professionals and technical personnel have positive relationships with wages and production, but the relationship with the capital price and the local wage rate is negative.
03	Rahmah et.al. (2003) Cited in (Bachtiar et al., 2017)	The role of foreign labour on output growth, job opportunity and wage in the Malaysian manufacturing sector	Output growth is significantly influenced by professional immigrants. Moreover, local workers and professional migrants are complementary, whereas unskilled imported workers and local workers are substitutes.
04	Jajri Idris Ismail Rahmah (J. Idris & Rahmah, 2006)	The elasticity of substitution between foreign and local workers in the Malaysian manufacturing sector	At the production level, foreign labour is not a competitor for Malaysian workers. They are more of a substitute than complement.
05	Rahmah Ismail and Ferayuliani Yuliyusman (Ismail & Yuliyusman, 2014)	Foreign labour on Malaysian growth	Both foreign and local unskilled workers are negatively related to economic growth. There is a meaningful impact on skilled and semi-skilled workers in both the short and long term.
06	Jacob A. Jordaan (Jordaan, 2018)	Foreign workers and productivity in an emerging economy: The case of Malaysia	1. Foreign workers generate positive productivity effects, especially when the endogeneity of the industry share of foreign workers is controlled. 2. Positive productivity effects are linked to the presence of both highly-skilled and low-skilled foreign workers. 3. Industry heterogeneity is important.

Sharmila Devadas (2017) tried to find out the effect of immigration on labour productivity, which is quite varied across individual countries. For example, the proportion of positive total immigrant effects are notably lower for Malaysia (Figure 9a,b), but are higher for the United Kingdom and the United States (Devadas, 2017).

Bank Negara Malaysia clearly mentions that cheap migrant labour creates distortions in the economy (Wei, Murugasu, & Wei, 2018). This is because most Malaysian firms depend on low-skilled migrant workers, and have no interest in moving towards sophisticated technological advancement requiring a huge amount of investment. Bank Negara (National Bank) Malaysia strongly believes a high reliance on low-skilled foreign workers, which is the predominant feature of Malaysia's economy, is a key issue causing declining local wages, as well as delaying the country's expected progress towards becoming a high-productivity nation. In addition, it says high dependence on low-skilled foreign workers will also have an adverse effect by shaping Malaysia's reputation as a low-skilled, labour-intensive destination. The country remains in a low wage and low productivity trap that may benefit individual firms in the short term, but could lead to macroeconomic costs to the economy over the longer term (Cecilia, 2018).

Figure 8: Share of GDP and employment of migrants for key economic sectors 2005–2014 (%)

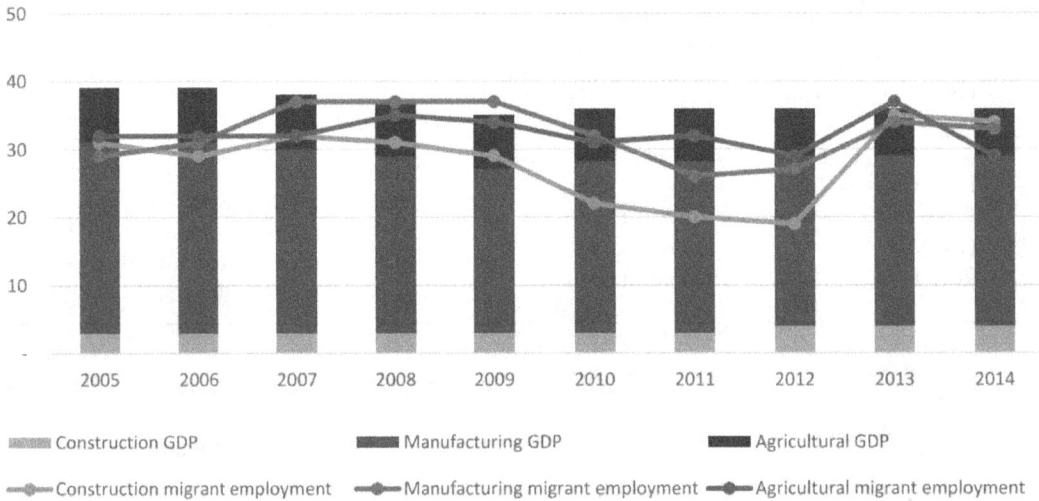

Source: ILO (2016), p.2.

Figure 9. Effects of total immigrants on labour productivity and its components.

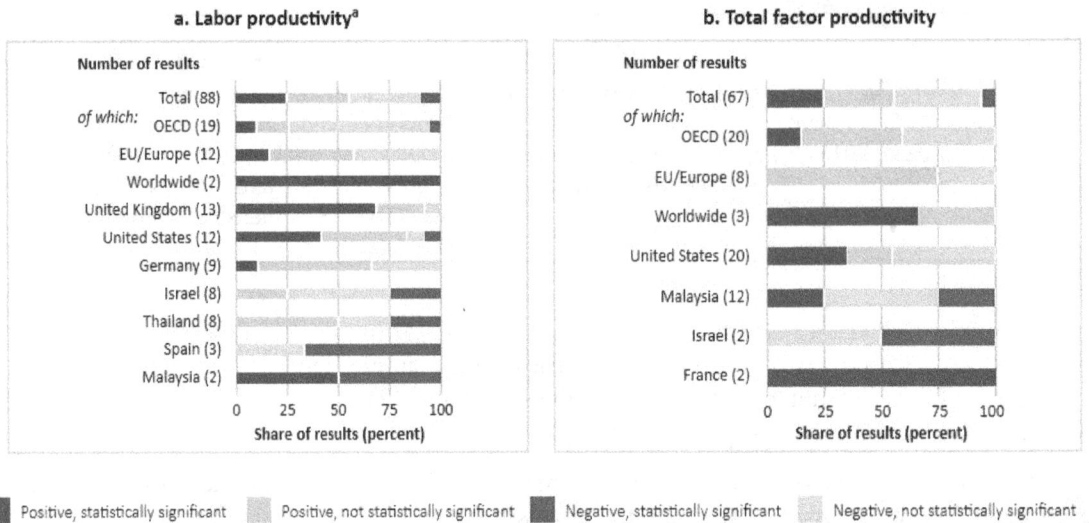

Source: Devadas (2017), p.3.

Economically, there are concerns that the dependence on migrant labour may cause a delay in upgrading technical skills, factory automation, and productivity improvement. There are many claims around how outward remittances (migrants usually repatriate a large share of their income) limit the spillover or multiplier effect on the domestic economy, despite the high cost of monitoring, control, detention, and deportation of illegal immigrants (Pillai, 1999; Tham & Liew, 2004). From 2011 to 2017, the share of low-skilled jobs in Malaysia increased significantly to 16%, compared with an increase of only 8% in the period of 2002 to 2010 (Cecilia, 2018). The trend in employment of low wage foreign workers that allows employers to keep salaries low (ILMIA, 2016).

Addressing the Challenges

Finding the appropriate formula for reducing the negative effects of foreign labour, as well as maximizing their benefits, is one of the prime challenges for Malaysia. Bank Negara (National Bank) Malaysia proposes a five-pronged approach to managing foreign workers in Malaysia (Cecilia, 2018). Firstly, the role of low-skilled migrant labour in the Malaysian economy should be clear and focused. Secondly, clear communication to the relevant industries should be developed regarding policy implementation and any changes. Thirdly, following the Malaysian economic objectives, existing labour management tools—for example, quotas, levies and dependency ceilings—might be reformed to be more market-driven. Fourthly, Malaysia should ensure a place for foreign workers in the Malaysian economy, and treat them better in terms of their rights and ensure agreed payments. Finally, robust and effective monitoring should be confirmed and enforcement for the proposed reform should take place while paying special attention to undocumented foreign workers.

The World Bank proposed six possible directions to strengthen the Malaysian immigration system (WorldBank, 2015):

- To identify labour market demand for immigrants
- To revise employment immigration policies focusing on new HRD
- To adopt a live-levy system for labour market needs
- To categorise immigrants by a broader set of criteria
- To promote productivity-enhancing technology
- To strengthen monitoring and enforcement efforts

Conclusions

In summary, the inadequate existing evidence does not provide distinct information on the impact of low-skilled migrant workers on the Malaysian economy and entire development. It has both positive and negative effects. Some evidence indicate that Malaysia has clearly benefitted from the presence of migrant labourers, so it is necessary to define an optimum number of foreign workers, in order to minimize the adverse effects on the economy. Malaysian labour migration policies have remained an "interim solution" or "ad hoc approach" to fill immediate labour shortages since it was introduced. The current policy has inbuilt weaknesses, owing to not successfully controlling illegal and irregular foreign workers.

Moreover, the present systems were formulated based on focusing public safety and security, rather than on labour administration and the long-term sustainable development of Malaysia (ILO, 2016, p-3). ILO found that these measures were taken when popular media raised their voices frequently against the foreign workers which shaped public attitudes and political decision, and subsequently, migrant workers are treated as a potential thread for social problems ranging from electoral fraud to street crimes. So, ongoing policy neither confirms economic transformation to a high-income nation nor reduces its heavy reliance on low-skilled imported workers. Though low-skilled migrant workers have both positive and negative effects on the Malaysian economy, the persistent influx of irregular migrants creates various adverse effects in the long term. To address the labour migration affairs more effectively, this study suggests the following recommendations:

- It is urgently required to define a place for migrant workers in the Malaysian economy. Unscrupulous individuals should not be able to exploit foreign labourers for their own financial gain. There needs to be a win-win policy that provides benefit to both parties.
- Management of foreign workers must evolve over time so that no loopholes are left unattended. A necessary structural adjustment may help the current situation.
- To become a high-income and high-productivity nation, Malaysia needs highly educated and skilled workers from abroad. Notwithstanding, to reduce the dependence on foreign labour, Malaysia must create a capable workforce that will fill positions successfully.

Overall, the contribution of low-skilled imported workers is not well researched yet. There are undoubted positive effects from these workers—a boon for the Malaysian economy; however, it is an undeniable truth that public attitudes are gradually souring towards migrant labour in Malaysia, and several factors have become widely considered a "bane" in the long run. Consequently, more independent research is urgently needed to find the evident-based impact of foreign workers on the Malaysian growth.

References

Ahmad, I. (2019). Place for migrant workers in our economy. The Star Online, 26 February 2019. Retrieved from https://www.thestar.com.my/opinion/letters/2019/02/26/place-for-migrant-workers-in-our-economy

Aziz, M. Z. A. (2011). Pendatang asing tanpa izin: Dasar dan pelaksanaannya. Paper presented at the Seminar Pekerja Asing dan Pendatang Asing Tanpa Izin di Malaysia, IKMAS, Universiti Kebangsaan Malaysia, 5 May 2011.

Bachtiar, N., Fahmy, R., & Ismail, R. (2017). The Demand for Foreign Workers in the Manufacturing Sector in Malaysia. Putrajaya: Ministry of Higher Education Retrieved from http://mycc.my/document/files/PDF%20Dokumen/Foreign%20Labour%20in%20Malaysia%20Selected%20Works.pdf.

Cecilia, K. (2018). Economist: Manage labour issues to achieve high-income economy. The Star Online, 31 March 2018. Retrieved from https://www.thestar.com.my/business/business-news/2018/03/31/economist-manage-labour-issues-to-achieve-highincome-economy

Devadas, S. (2017). Threat or Help?: The Effects of Unskilled Immigrant Workers on National Productivity Growth. https://papers.ssrn.com/sol3/papers.cfm?abstract_id=3249557

Dollah, R., Hassan, W. S. W., Peters, D., & Omar, M. A. (2003). Pendatang using Filipina di Sabah: Satu pemerhatian dari sudut keselamatan. JATI, Jabatan Asia Tenggara, Universiti Malaya

Hwok-Aun, L., & Leng, K. Y. (2018). Counting Migrant Workers in Malaysia: A Needlessly Persisting Conundrum. Retrieved from https://www.think-asia.org/handle/11540/8244

Idris, J., & Rahmah, I. (2006). Elasticity of substitution between foreign and local workers in the Malaysian manufacturing sector. Pertanika Journal of Social Science and Humanities, 14(1), 63-76.

Idris, N. A. (2005). Hubungan Malaysia Indonesia dan isu pendatang tanpa izin. In Politik Dan Keselamatan, ed. Siti Daud & Zarina Othman, pp. 146168. Bangi: Penerbit Universiti Kebangsaan Malays.

ILMIA. (2016). National Employment Returns Report 2016. Putrajaya: Institute of labour Market Information and Analysis Retrieved from https://www.ilmia.gov.my/ebook/research/NER-2016.html.

ILO. (2010). International labour migration: A rights-based approach. (9221191214). from International Labour Office https://www.ilo.org/global/publications/books/WCMS_125361/lang--en/index.htm

ILO. (2016). Review of labour migration policy in Malaysia. Tripartite Action to Enhance the Contribution of Labour Migration to Growth and Development in ASEAN (TRIANGLE II Project). Retrieved from https://www.ilo.org/wcmsp5/groups/public/---asia/---ro-bangkok/documents/publication/wcms_447687.pdf

ILO. (2016, p-3). Review of labour migration policy in Malaysia Tripartite Action to Enhance the Contribution of Labour Migration to Growth and Development in ASEAN (TRIANGLE II Project) Retrieved from https://www.ilo.org/wcmsp5/groups/public/---asia/---ro-bangkok/documents/publication/ wcms_ 447687.pdf

ILO. (2019, p-26). Public attitudes towards migrant workers in Japan, Malaysia, Singapore, and Thailand. Retrieved 26 February 2020, from International Labour Organization https://www.spotlightinitiative.org/sites/default/ files/publication/public_attitudes_online.pdf

IOM. (2019). World Migration Report 2020. from International Organization for Migration https://publications. iom.int/system/files/pdf/wmr_2020.pdf

Ismail, R., & Yuliyusman, F. (2014). Foreign Labour on Malaysian Growth. from JSTOR https://www.jstor.org /stable/43150573?seq=1

Jordaan, J. A. (2018). Foreign workers and productivity in an emerging economy: The case of Malaysia. Review of Development Economics, 22(4), 148-173.

Kanapathy, V. (2006). Migrant workers in Malaysia: an overview. Paper presented at the Country paper prepared for Workshop on East Asian Cooperation Framework for Migrant Labour, Kuala Lumpur. http://www. isis. org. my/files/pubs/papers/V K_MIGRATION-NEAT_6Dec06. pdf (Accessed 13 January 2007.) Amarjit Kaur.

Kassim, A. (1987). The unwelcome guests: Indonesian immi-grants and Malaysian public responses. Journal of Southeast Asian Studies 25(2): 265278.

Kassim, A. (2001). Integration of foreign workers and illegal employment in Malaysia: OECD.

Kassim, A. (2005). Security and social implications of cross national migration in Malaysia. In Pacifying the Pacific: Confronting the Challenges, ed. Mohamad Jawhar Hassan, pp. 259-288. Kuala Lumpur: Institute of Strategic and International Studies.

Kassim, A. (2011). Transnational migration and the contestation for urban space. In Malaysia at a Crossroads: Can We Make the Transition, ed. Abdul Rahman Embong & S.Y. Tham, pp. 86-117. Bangi: Penerbit Universiti Kebangsaan Malaysia.

Kassim, A. (2017). Recent Trends in Transnational Population inflows into Malaysia: Policy, Issues and Challenges. Putrajaya: Ministry of Higher Education Retrieved from http://mycc.my/document/files/PDF%20Dokumen/ Foreign%20Labour%20in%20Malaysia%20Selected%20Works.pdf.

Kassim, A., & Zin, R. H. M. (2011). Policy on irregular migrants in Malaysia: An evaluation of its implementation and effectiveness. Final report for research on Different Streams, Different Needs and Different Impacts: Managing International Migration in ASEAN. Submitted to the Philippines Institute of Development Studies, Manila.

Loh, W. S., Simler, K., Wei, K. T., & Yi, S. (2019). Malaysia: Estimating the Number of Foreign Workers. from The World Bank http://documents.worldbank.org/curated/pt/953091562223517841/pdf/Malaysia-Estimating-the-Number-of-Foreign-Workers-A-Report-from-the-Labor-Market-Data-for-Monetary-Policy-Task.pdf

Melissa, C. (2015). World Bank: Foreign workers help Malaysians, country scale economic ladder. Malay Mail, 18 December 2015. Retrieved from https://www.malaymail.com/news/malaysia/2015/12/18/world-bank-foreign-workers-help-malaysians-country-scale-economic-ladder/1025415

Moreno, R., Del Carpio, X., Testaverde, M., Moroz, H., Carmen, L., Smith, R., . . . Yoong, P. (2015). Malaysia Economic Monitor—Immigrant Labour. World Bank: Washington, DC, USA.

Nizam, S. S. A., Ahmad, R., & Aziz, N. A. B. (2017). The effect of the influx of foreign labour in Malaysia by augmented MRW Model. Putrajaya: Ministry of Higher Education Retrieved from http://mycc.my/document/files/PDF%20 Dokumen/Foreign%20Labour%20in%20Malaysia%20Selected%20Works.pdf.

Noor, Z. M., Isa, N., Said, R., & Jalil, S. A. (2017). The Impact of Foreign Workers on Labour Productivity in Malaysian Manufacturing Sector. Putrajaya: Minstry of Higher Education Retrieved from http://mycc.my/document/files /PDF%20Dokumen/Foreign%20Labour%20in%20Malaysia%20Selected%20Works.pdf.

Othman, S. A., & Rohani, A. R. (2017). Migrant Workers in Malaysia: Protection of Employers Putrajaya: Ministry of Higher Education Retrieved from http://mycc.my/document/files/PDF%20Dokumen/Foreign%20Labour %20in%20Malaysia%20Selected%20Works.pdf.

Özden, Ç., & Wagner, M. (2014). Immigrant versus natives? Displacement and job creation. Washinton DC: The World Bank.

Pillai, P. (1999). The Malaysian state's Response to Migration, Journal of Social Issues in Southeast Asia 14(1): 178-197. Journal of Social Issues in Southeast Asia 14(1): 178-197., 14(1), 178-197.

Rafael, M. M. (2016). Immigrant labor: Can it help Malaysia's economic development? . Retrieved from https://blogs.worldbank.org/eastasiapacific/immigrant-labor-can-it-help-malaysia-s-economic-development

Ramlee, A. R. (2017). Divulging Foreign Workers Issues in Malaysia. Putrajaya: Ministry of Higher Education Retrieved from http://mycc.my/document/files/PDF%20Dokumen/Foreign%20Labour%20in%20Malaysia%20Selected %20Works.pdf.

Ramlee, A. R. (2017). Divulging Foreign Workers Issues In Malaysia. Putrajaya, Malaysia: Ministry of Higher Education Retrieved from http://mycc.my/document/files/PDF%20Dokumen/Foreign%20 Labour%20in%20Malaysia %20Selected%20Works.pdf.

Sadiq, K. (2005). When states prefer non-citizens over citizens: Conflict over illegal immigration in Malaysia. International Studies Quarterly, 49(1), 14-18.

Tham, S. Y., & Liew, C. S. (2004). Foreign labour in Malaysian manufacturing: enhancing Malaysian competitiveness? In Globalisation, Culture and Inequalities, ed. Abdul Rahman Embong, pp. 253-274. Bangi: Penerbit Universiti Kebangsaan Malaysia.

UNDESA. (2019). International migrant stock 2019: Country Profile Malaysia. from Population Division, Department of Economic and Social Affairs, United Nations https://www.un.org/en/development/desa/population/migration/ data/estimates2/countryprofiles.asp

Wei, A. J., Murugasu, A., & Wei, C. Y. (2018). Low-Skilled Foreign Workers' Distortions to the Economy. Kuala Lumpur: Bank Negara Malaysia Retrieved from https://amlcft.bnm.gov.my/files/publication/ar/en/2017/ cp01001_box.pdf.

WorldBank. (2013). Foreign Workers in Malaysia: Assessment of their Economic Effects and Review of the Policy. https://www.knomad.org/sites/default/files/2017-06/KNOMAD-MALAYSIA-NEW.pdf

WorldBank. (2015). Malaysia Economic Monitor, December 2015 - Immigrant Labor

(Report). from World Bank https://www.worldbank.org/en/country/malaysia/publication/malaysia-economic-monitor-december-2015-immigrant-labour

Kassim, A. (2017). *Recent Trends in Transnational Population inflows into Malaysia: Policy, Issues and Challenges*. Putrajaya: Ministry of Higher Education Retrieved from http://mycc.my/document/files/PDF%20Dokumen/ Foreign%20Labour%20in%20Malaysia%20Selected%20Works.pdf.

Wei, A. J., Murugasu, A., & Wei, C. Y. (2018a). *Low-Skilled Foreign Workers' Distortions to the Economy*. Kuala Lumpur: Bank Negara Malaysia Retrieved from https://amlcft.bnm.gov.my/files/publication/ar/en/ 2017/cp01_001_box.pdf.

Wei, A. J., Murugasu, A., & Wei, C. Y. (2018b). Low-Skilled Foreign Workers' Distortions to the Economy. Retrieved from http://www.bnm.gov.my/files/publication/ar/en/2017/cp01_001_box.pdf

WorldBank. (2013). *Immigration in Malaysia: Assessment of its economic effects and a review of the policy and system*. Paper presented at the Manpower Issues in Key Sectors of the Malaysian Economy, Putrajaya. https://www.ilmia.gov.my/index.php/en/component/zoo/item/world-bank-study-immigration-in-malaysia -assessment-of-its-economic-effects-and-a-review-of-the-policy-and-system

September 2020
Volume: 17, **No**: 5, pp. 747 – 752
ISSN: 1741-8984
e-ISSN: 1741-8992
www.migrationletters.com

MIGRATION LETTERS

First Submitted: 5 February 2020 Accepted: 22 May 2020
DOI: https://doi.org/10.33182/ml.v17i5.922

REVIEW:

Migrant youth and politics: a workshop

Elizabeth Mavroudi[1] and Cintia Silva Huxter[2]

Abstract

On 9-10th September 2019 academics from universities around the UK met at Loughborough University to discuss working with children and young people, particularly those with a migrant/diasporic background. The workshop stemmed from the authors' research project on youth identity and politics in diaspora (www.youth-diaspora-politics.org) which has shown that young people in diaspora are, on the whole, politicised. All participants work/have worked with children and young people on themes of identity and politics and presented their work at the workshop. One of our main conclusions is that, despite the challenges, a stronger research focus is needed on young migrants and those in diaspora; their opinions, identities and experiences are important in their own right. After a short overview of each presentation, in the last section, we consider some methodological and ethical challenges we all shared and discussed, as well as some issues that need to be considered in the future.

Keywords: working with children; young people; identity; diaspora.

Introduction

In this review, we would like to use our research project and subsequent workshop to add to theoretical and methodological debates on the identity and politics of young migrants and young people in diaspora. Both the workshop and the project build on research which stresses the importance of listening to young migrants and young people in diaspora (Bak von Brömssen, 2010; Tyrell et al., 2013), their identities (Gardner, 2012; Reynolds and Zontini, 2016; Faas, 2015), politics (Fiddian-Qasmiyeh, 2013; Leurs, 2016; Müller-Funk, 2019; Baser, 2015) and the need to pay attention to their emotional, classed, ethnicised and gendered nature (Michail and Christou, 2016).

The research project

The research project (www.youth-diaspora-politics.org), funded by the Leverhulme Trust, explored how young Greeks, Palestinians and Jews in diaspora construct and articulate their identities and their views on politics and ways to be political in the UK. We spoke to young people aged 11-25, their parents and gatekeepers from each diasporic group. This was an exploratory study, in which we viewed the different groups alongside each other, in order to discover similarities and differences between them. The main findings reveal that young people are, on the whole, politicised, hold political views and often have a good understanding of what politics entails and how it impacts upon their own lives, their communities, countries and global relations. However, despite having

[1] Cintia Silva Huxter, University of Loughborough, United Kingdom. E-mail: c.silva-huxter@lboro.ac.uk
[2] Elizabeth Mavroudi, University of Loughborough, United Kingdom. E-mail: E.Mavroudi@lboro.ac.uk

strong opinions on issues such as climate change, young people felt that those in positions of power often did not listen to their views and frequently dismissed them because of their age. Overwhelmingly they did not trust politicians and wished that there were better ways to have their opinions taken seriously by those in positions of power.

The workshop

The research prompted us to devise a workshop which was generously funded by Loughborough University's Institute of Advanced Studies. The workshop took place on 9-10th September 2019. One of the main conclusions of the workshop was that a stronger research focus is needed on young migrants and those in diaspora; their opinions, identities and experiences are important in their own right.

The list of invited participants was as follows:

Professor Myria Georgiou, London School of Economics

Dr Daniel Faas, Trinity College Dublin

Dr Caitríona Ní Laoire, University College Cork

Dr Anastasia Christou, Middlesex University

Dr Bahar Baser, Coventry University

Dr A Erdi Öztürk, London Metropolitan University

Dr Elisabetta Zontini, The University of Nottingham

The discussions in the workshop centred around two main themes: valuing young people's voices, particularly the question of agency and the (new) spaces and networks that can potentially empower young people and help them to negotiate their identities and politics; and the complex interactions between the state and young people.

Valuing young people's voices, politics and the question of agency

Research has highlighted how children and young people are often silent and silenced (Spyrou, 2016) and that a critical discussion on how to better listen to them is needed. This is linked to the ongoing project of countering adult centrism in migration studies, which was an issue all participants felt was important. We also agreed that being a young migrant and/or in diaspora mattered when it came to identity and politics. The concept of 'transnational habitus', put forward by Zontini, highlights what sets children with a migrant background apart from children without migrant backgrounds – this has an impact on how young migrants understand the world around them and also on the role they can play in tackling global issues such as racism. As a result, as highlighted by Ní Laoire, it becomes crucial to explore how diasporic youth construct their own im/mobility trajectories and identities and understand the ways in which they engage selectively, and sometimes critically, with wider discourses of migration and mobility (Ní Laoire, 2020).

Despite the clear potential for young people to have a voice, to be heard and to be listened to, there are ongoing debates around young people's agency and participation (Gallagher, 2019; Holloway et al., 2019). During the workshop, participants outlined how agency and empowerment are certainly not a given, and that marginalisation and exclusion (still) need to be addressed. This was introduced by Christou who highlighted the ongoing realities of oppression and injustice that young people face and presented education as a platform for resistance to help carve out alternative futures. This stresses the need to pay more attention to localised and grounded realities which dismantle myths and stereotypes of young people adopted by politicians, the mass media, and others in positions of power. In this context, Christou also discussed how youth agency can manifest itself in the form of 'connected civics', as young people come together to build shared contexts, and argued that more attention needs to be paid to young people's 'affective habitus', or the ways in which young lifeworlds are shaped by feelings.

We need, therefore, to look beyond assumptions around what constitutes the political for young people (Elwood and Mitchell, 2012). While discussing her research, Baser mentioned how young people she spoke with added 'likes' on Facebook without necessarily engaging with the content any further: does this constitute a political act? Similarly, when they attended political events, it wasn't necessarily to be political but sometimes it was a way to find friends, a community or even a spouse. For Baser, it was clear that some young people were actively 'choosing' a diasporic identity as a career. This can be seen as a political act in itself, but also demonstrates that there are decisions to be made, which have ramifications for identity and politics, for example, in relation to how migrant or diasporic parents raise their children, and what they teach them about their homeland and politics.

Therefore, rather than being unengaged and not having opinions, research has increasingly pointed out that young people connect, interact, engage and participate in different ways (Chryssochoou and Barrett, 2017). This was clearly demonstrated by Georgiou's ongoing Horizon 2020 project on young refugees. Georgiou shared her expertise on media and communications, outlining the role that smartphones play in the lives of young refugees by enabling them to navigate transnational journeys and have a voice in their new environments. She added that smartphones can also lead to the creation of virtual spaces of belonging and connection, where young people are able to set their own boundaries. This small window of potential agency comes in the face of increasing surveillance and digital control, where even young migrants feel the need to perform the role of 'the good migrant' as they struggle to deal with loss of dignity and other obstacles. By focusing on young people's perspectives, we can potentially see what particular challenges they face and what role new technologies can play in helping them feel empowered.

Young people and the state

There are increasingly complex relations between young people and the state, and although research has stressed the need to view young people as political (Skelton, 2010), their views are often ignored by the state. Ní Laoire stressed the need for critical interpretations of government discourses of young e/migrants. Her research, focused on an Irish governmental campaign to lure Irish emigrants back to Ireland, highlighted the tendency to infantilise and romanticise young people, erasing, in this way, the complex differences between them. This link between the state and young migrants has also been the focus of Faas' work. His research focused on different types of schools in Ireland, and on how different schools teach and approach religion and education. Through interviews with 10-11 year olds in focus groups, Faas found that young people were unhappy with how religious teaching was being delivered. Although this research went on to change government policy, demonstrating the value and importance of listening to, and acting upon, young people's voices, both Ni Laoire's and Faas' projects show how governments make assumptions, or simply don't consider, the views of young people.

Öztürk's research on Turkish nationalism, and the ways in which it has attempted to influence young people in diaspora, also contributed to our discussions around young people and the state.

Öztürk stressed the need for critical interrogations of the state, how homeland state policies and discourses are played out on a local and individual level, and also how they spread across borders and attempt to influence diasporas in negative ways (Öztürk and Taş, 2020). Öztürk talked specifically about the Turkish context and the government's attempts to use what they call the 'golden generation', who are able to bridge 'here' and 'there', to control how they are represented, what is taught in diasporic schools, and by selectively financing certain cultural events/projects. This is a reminder of the negative role that states can play in young diasporic people's imaginations and politics (Wilmers and Chernobrov, 2019).

Zontini added to the discussion by exploring the ways in which the macropolitical is played out in young people's lives and identity constructions. In her project on EU children in Brexit Britain, Zontini demonstrated not only the importance of context, but also, of timing; young people are acutely aware of 'big' and potentially abstract issues such as Brexit and how they have an impact on their lives and identities. Zontini was keen to stress the need to be mindful of the differentiated impacts of transnational connections and the role of place. She has also found that since the Brexit vote, EU children in the UK feel like they have to 'pick' an identity, and that there is less space for mixed or hybrid identities. It may be that Brexit is creating more nuanced ways in which young people are negotiating and performing their identities in different spaces. In turn, this stresses the need to explore the geographies of how young people practice their identities and politics (Kallio and Häkli, 2011).

Reflections and future directions

Our discussions highlighted the need to define what is meant by politics and the political. We all agreed that politics is everywhere, but that more research is needed on how young people view politics and act politically. In doing so, we may then be able to unravel the complexities around how young people are actually doing politics their own way, informally.

This final part of the paper will consider some methodological and ethical challenges we all shared, as well as some issues that need to be considered in the future. One of the main methodological challenges that any researcher working with young people faces is defining and justifying the age range of their participants. There are different views here stemming from the various ways in which research is conducted and where it takes place. If one has control over the context (such as in a school), it may be easier to find specific groups to participate. If, however, one is researching hidden or marginalised groups which are harder to access, then in order to speak to as wide a cross-section as possible, it may be advisable to work with a wider age range, bearing in mind that different age groups are likely to hold different views and are positioned differently.

In discussing the value of comparative research, there was debate about whether the best course of action is to compare like with like in terms of age, or to use more ethnographic inspired methods such as multi-sited ethnographies, enabling us to look at groups alongside each other rather than directly comparing them. We are then able to identify parallels as well as paradoxes and contradictions. We all agreed on the need for robust methods and analysis and also on the need for innovative and creative methods which are more participatory and better enable the co-production of knowledge.

One of the main challenges for the future in terms of the realities of conducting research with young people is the more recent role of university ethics committees, and the ways in which they dictate what can and cannot be done. This has meant ever greater restrictions on how research is conducted and that increasing numbers of projects with young people fail to get the go-ahead or need to be changed. Whilst we recognise the need to safeguard academics and young participants, we fear that new researchers and PhD students will be discouraged from conducting research with young migrants.

Finally, we wish to re-iterate the value of conducting research with young migrants and those in diaspora, despite the challenges; as extreme nationalisms and right wing propaganda continue to rise, as academics we need to critically examine how politics can be used in negative ways, potentially creating hatred and division as we acknowledge that extremisms and prejudice continue to exist within and beyond diasporic and migrant communities. To help counter that, and following research by Mansouri and Mikola (2014) on the ways in which young migrants in Australia 'step out' as they contest and negotiate belonging and politics, one might argue that young migrants have a key role to play. They, like other young people, use new ways to engage on and offline politically and in positive articulations of difference in a globally connected world (Leurs and Georgiou, 2016). However, young people 'on the move' have the potential to use their migrant and diverse backgrounds, as well as their transnational connections, to disrupt conventional forms of belonging (Reynolds and Zontini, 2016). In this way, although diasporic and transnational identities can be hard to articulate and deal with, they can also potentially create positive changes in not only normalising but also celebrating difference and diversity.

References

Bak, M., and von Brömssen, K. (2010). Interrogating Childhood and Diaspora Through the Voices of Children in Sweden. *Childhood, 17* (1): 11-128.

Baser, B. (2015). *Diasporas and Homeland Conflicts: A Comparative Perspective.*

Chryssochoou, X. and Barrett, M. (2017). Civic and Political Engagement in Youth Findings and Prospects. *Zeitschrift für Psychologie, 225* (4): 291–301.

Elwood, S. and Mitchell, K. (2012). Mapping Children's politics: spatial stores, dialogic relations and political formation. *Geografiska Annaler: Series B, Human Geography, 94* (1): 1-15.

Faas, D. (2010. *Negotiating Political Identities Multiethnic Schools and Youth in Europe*. London: Ashgate.

Fiddian-Qasmiyeh, E. (2013). Transnational childhood and adolescence: mobilising Sahrawi identity and politics across time and space. *Ethnic and Racial Studies*, 36 (5): 875-895.

Gallagher, M. (2019). Rethinking children's agency: Power, assemblages, freedom and materiality. *Global Studies of Childhood, 9* (3): 188-199.

Gardner, K. (2012). Transnational Migration and the Study of Children: An Introduction. *Journal of Ethnic and Migration Studies*, 38 (6): 889-912.

Holloway, S. L., Holt, L., and Mills, S. (2019). Questions of agency: Capacity, subjectivity, spatiality and temporality. *Progress in Human Geography, 43* (3): 458-477.

Kallio, K. P., and Häkli, J. (2011). Tracing children's politics. *Political Geography* 30: 99-109.

Leurs, K. (2015). *Digital Passages: Migrant Youth 2.0 Diaspora, Gender and Youth Cultural Intersections*. Amsterdam: Amsterdam University Press.

Leurs, K. and Georgiou, M. (2016). Digital Makings of the Cosmopolitan City? Young People's Urban Imaginaries of London. *International Journal of Communication,* 10: 3689–3709.

London: Ashgate.

Mansouri, F. and Mikola, M. (2014). Crossing Boundaries: Acts of Citizenship among Migrant Youth in Melbourne. *Social Inclusion, 2* (2): 28-37.

Michail, D. and Christou, A. (2016). Diasporic youth identities of uncertainty and hope: second-generation Albanian experiences of transnational mobility in an era of economic crisis in Greece. *Journal of Youth Studies*, 19 (7): 957-972.

Müller-Funk, L. (2019). Fluid identities, diaspora youth activists and the (Post-) Arab Spring: how narratives of belonging can change over time. *Journal of Ethnic and Migration Studies*, 46 (6), 1112-1128.

Ní Laoire, C. Transnational mobility desires and discourses: Young people from return-migrant families negotiate intergenerationality, mobility capital, and place embeddedness. *Population, Space and Place*. 2020; e2310.

Öztürk A. E. and Taş, H. (2020). The Repertoire of Extraterritorial Repression: Diasporas and Home States. *Migration Letters*, 17 (1): 59-69.

Reynolds, T. and Zontini, E. (2016), Transnational and diasporic youth identities: exploring conceptual themes and future research agendas. *Identities*, 23 (4): 379-391.

Skelton, T. (2010), Taking young people as political actors seriously: opening the borders of political geography. *Area*, 42 (2): 145-151.

Spyrou, S. (2016). Researching children's silences: Exploring the fullness of voice in childhood research. *Childhood*, 23 (1): 7-21.

Tyrrell, N., White, A., Laoire, C. N., & Mendez, F. C. (2013). *Transnational migration and childhood*. London, Routledge.

Wilmers, L. and Chernobrov, D. (2020). Growing up with a long-awaited nation-state: personal struggles with the homeland among young diasporic Armenians. *Ethnicities*, 20 (3): 520-543.

www.ingramcontent.com/pod-product-compliance
Lightning Source LLC
Chambersburg PA
CBHW081739270326
41932CB00020B/3332